A MIDDLE EASTERN AFFAIR

A MIDDLE EASTERN AFFAIR

ELLIS DOUEK

PETER HALBAN
LONDON

First published in Great Britain by
Peter Halban Publishers Ltd
22 Golden Square
London W1F 9JW
2004

www.halbanpublishers.com

A CIP catalogue record for this book is available from the British Library.

ISBN 1870015 87 8

Typeset by Computape Typesetting, Scarborough, North Yorkshire
Printed in Great Britain by
MPG Books Ltd, Bodmin, Cornwall

Contents

Acknowledgements

Writing a memoir was not easy. Like trying to catch wisps of cobweb, some images were elusive, to the point that I did not feel sure they were there at all, while others, sticky but inappropriate, were difficult to brush aside as they re-emerged, again and again, for reasons that remained mysterious. In such circumstances I needed encouragement.

My old friend Martin Frishman was the first to point out that I did have a story to tell and that what I had seen mattered in the context of our time. Peter and Martine Halban are the gentlest and most encouraging of publishers and without Martine's help I may never have put it all together, while their editor Judy Gough, too, showed the kind persistence that made me feel protected. I am grateful to Claudia Roden, always a loyal and supportive sister, who has also been my life-long friend. Jackie Barnes, my secretary of so many years, typed and re-typed my earliest efforts with good humour.

My wife Gill, who picked up the pieces, provided the warmth and friendship which gave me the courage to look back at my world as the years have gone by.

To Danny and Joel
In memory of their grandparents
Cesar and Nelly

"He who has lost sight of his past has lost himself."

Arabic Proverb

I

Interweaving Strands

When I was a little boy my father told me of a time, near the end of the First World War, when he was standing in line at a bank in Cairo. An Arab, fully robed, an 'egal crowning his head in the style of the bedouins, walked in with a confidence then unknown in Egypt. After all, Arabs, as the Egyptians called them when they wanted to distinguish themselves from such desert people, were very different from the oil-rich princes of today and none had ever been seen in a bank as far as my father knew.

There was consternation therefore as the man pushed ahead of the queue and when, instead of being ushered out peremptorily, the fawning manager had come forward to greet him, my father had cried out: "Who is that?"

"Lawrence!" came the electrifying reply from those who realised who it was. As the man briefly turned towards him, my father caught the searing look from his pale eyes.

"You are confusing the boy," my mother interrupted him. He had been trying to explain who we were and our connection to the British and their Empire. It was something to cherish, to be proud of and yet how does one explain such subtle relationships to a child? How does one clarify being Jewish and Egyptian, British and French all at the same time?

And yet I was not at all confused. I had parents and grandparents and a nanny who loved me. I had a little sister and a baby brother and around them many aunts and uncles and countless cousins who enclosed us in a protective circle. And, after all I knew perfectly well that I was myself so that labels of that sort were neither here nor there.

The memory of his brief encounter with Lawrence of Arabia must have crept into my father's mind inspired by feelings he was trying to put into words and now I too find that my own memories emerge spontaneously, often apparently at random, images of events which, almost like dreams, I am left to interpret.

Perhaps these reinterpretations, honed time and again in the light of later experience or even of further knowledge as well as ordinary forgetfulness, explain why they can sometimes differ from the recollection of others who were also there at the time. Perhaps, on the other hand, the impact they had made in the first place was differently understood as inevitably we see things in diverse ways.

My story is not an autobiography, nor is it a history of my family, of Egypt or of the Middle East. It consists of strands of memory which, interwoven with other elements acquired here and there, I must not check too finically as in doing so, whatever they might gain in accuracy, they would lose in other ways. My story is not based on research or documentary evidence but only on how things appeared to me at the time and on what I can still remember.

My parents had landed at Heathrow in 1958. My father had looked tanned and happy, my mother beamed. She had been buying clothes as they had stopped off in Milan on the way from Khartoum in the Sudan. They were overjoyed to see my sister, brother and me. We had brought them a bunch of flowers. "Thank God for Nasser," my father said as he embraced me. "If it wasn't for him we might never have left the Mddle East."

Their arrival certainly marked the end of my family's long affair with the Middle East, though the real turning point, the one which had set the course of our history along a new path, had occurred two years before in 1956 when the British, the French and the Israelis invaded Egypt ostensibly to secure the Suez Canal.

*

At the end of the Second World War 80,000 Jews were living in Egypt. We were only one of the many minorities that had settled in the old Ottoman Empire and with the Armenians, Maronites, Greeks, and other Europeans, to a large extent sustained its commerce and industry. When the Empire had finally fallen apart, Egypt, a fragment which had already tended to go its own way, fell entirely under British domination during which period it had thrived, to many people's embarrassment. The last Khedive of Egypt Abbas II, had sided with the Turks who in turn had mistakenly backed the Germans in 1914. That, my father had said, was how the Ottoman Empire had ended, and how it was the British who were now protecting Egypt instead of the Turks, though he did not say what they were being protected from.

I did not ask as it was obvious that everyone benefited from protection, and those were details which did not concern me as all I needed to know, my mother insisted, was that we were Jews as that was our religion. We had British passports which ensured our ascendancy and we spoke French, it went without saying, because that was the best language.

By 1945 the Egyptians, like so many other people, had begun to seek another identity, one which required more than independence as that was there for the asking. They sensed the need for a victorious struggle otherwise they would not be rid of a sense of inferiority or a feeling of humiliation that had resulted from thousands of years of uninterrupted foreign domination. This expressed itself as hostility, often violent, towards those whose presence would contaminate their new homogenous society, reminding them of their past subservience. Foreigners were made to feel in danger and began to leave, and those most easily targeted were the Jews.

My parents had sent us to Europe and they themselves had moved to the Sudan in 1954 as my father was able to transfer his cotton business to Khartoum, a city suddenly invaded by merchants like himself as well as by the array of foreign embassies and consulates that an emergent country attracted. There was a shortage of accommodation and, together with all the other new-comers, my parents settled into the Grand Hotel on the banks of the river not far from Omdurman, where the White Nile joined the Blue.

It was a worrying time for me, then a student so far away, as I could see that our gentle way of life was ending and that our large family, extended to the point where we did not know who was related and who was just a friend, was now disintegrating, scattered among the nations. From Paris and then London I would hear that cousins had gone to São Paulo while others had found refuge in Tel Aviv, jobs in Milan or registered at the Sorbonne, and some were on their way to Australia. Each piece of news was a rent in the texture of our lives which I felt was being torn up like an out-of-date newspaper and the Suez War of 1956 was the culmination of this decade of uncertainty.

For the Europeans who lived in Egypt it was certainly a turning point in their lives as in due course, whether suddenly or in dribs and drabs, they virtually all had to go. Those who held British or French passports, and those who were Jewish were simply expelled with little notice in what has since become known as ethnic cleansing. For those who are interested in the history of cultures, the Suez War also marked something that was less easy to define and perhaps, in the general scheme of things, it was not very important. It was the end of the city of Cavafy, the Greek poet of Alexandria, and of the purple world of Lawrence Durrell. Olivia Manning's characters, too, have departed as have those of the French writer Robert Solé, without leaving descendants or successors. Those who have managed to stay have done so in the capacity of guardians of churches and synagogues and tenders of cemeteries, too old, too poor or too frightened to budge unless forcibly removed.

With foreign armies still hovering over Egypt this mass departure had been orderly in the sense that no one was killed. Though loss of property and employment were only a part of the disaster which struck these tens of thousands of people, the relative success of the refugees in their new lives was to mitigate any bitterness they felt towards the Egyptians.

The fact that the Egyptians did not further persecute or even massacre the refugees meant that some goodwill was retained by both sides. Isolated from contamination by western ideas, Egypt did not prosper as had been hoped, though the increasing poverty and military failure of the next twenty years was counterbalanced by an exultation and a psychological sense that something had been achieved, that after thousands of years of foreign rule the country had been given a new direction. For a long time, perhaps even now, the Egyptians remained convinced that they had triumphed and regained their dignity, while this difference in perception allowed those who had been expelled to view the country as they had always done, with nostalgia and affection.

This enforced departure was, of course, not without anxiety as none of those who had to leave could know how favourable the final outcome would be. They could sell only little and at ridiculous prices as there was no one to buy their property in the turmoil, and as the country's monetary reserves were non-existent there was no foreign currency for them to take. They were allowed, instead, to take whatever they could carry with them so many bought gold bangles and, in fear of the cold winters to come, rushed for the furriers, most of whom were leaving too and selling off their stock as best they could which occasionally led to some bizarre situations. Frightened refugees were greeted on landing by well-meaning people who had collected used clothing which they were ready to distribute in bundles, and found the would-be recipients wearing gold bracelets up to the elbows as they carried their minks on their arms. They may not have had much else but they did have clothes.

*

We, of course, had not left in such a dramatic manner as my mother had been particularly dismissive of our future in Egypt, though not because she feared physical destruction. She never explained her reasons as she always preferred assertion, implying that her statements were self-evident truths when she had convinced my father to send us to schools in England and in France and that they themselves should leave for the Sudan.

Indeed, there had always been a certain mystery as to her reasoning and intentions. At the age of nine, for instance, she had made me do *petit point* embroidery and I still have an example of my work. I had resisted at first on the grounds that it was for girls but she would not even consider that excuse.

"Nonsense!" she had said. "Suppose you decide you want to be a surgeon when you grow up? You have to start practising now."

Such a prospect had never entered my mind since at the time I was torn between wanting to become an inventor as I had just seen the film *The Boy Edison* and the wish to please my father by joining him in his textile business. As it turned out I did become a surgeon but it was only when I sat, half asleep at a meeting on the health services in London in the 1980s that my attention was awakened by a suggestion that the Department of Health had a hidden agenda. Suddenly I wondered whether my mother too had had such an agenda for her family and if so how much had she manipulated our hopes and ambitions from birth, and whether she had marked out a path which we were still unsuspectingly following? Mothers soon learn to persuade their children to do, or more probably not to do, this or that without disclosing their reasons as these may be incomprehensible to the child. The more I thought about it – while ignoring the Department of Health's problems – the more snippets of evidence came to my mind and suddenly I felt the need to find out what her plan was as she was now very old and not too well. The urge to do this at once was so strong that I excused myself from the meeting in a manner that only surgeons can contemplate and drove straight to my parents' house in north-west London.

I was careful not to confront her and I took advantage of her surprise and pleasure at my unexpected visit to hark back to the past in an attempt to trap her into revealing her intentions of the time. She soon became somewhat defensive and I felt I had struck something but it led nowhere and I began to wonder whether, if there had been a plan, a grand design which had directed our lives, she had now forgotten what it was. This left me anxious, rudderless for a while, with the fear that I might not know what I was supposed to do if she was gone from behind the scenes.

Perhaps she herself had never known the secret plan and she was only following an impulse which had come from way back, from grandparents and great-grandparents, passed on unwittingly through the generations and, if so, perhaps I am only such a vehicle myself.

We have all learned, if only from television documentaries, that life itself is swivelled around a double helix, a structure that we are shown in colour, magnified, rotating to music like a dance, transformed by our imagination into shapes we can understand. I wonder if this structure includes hidden agendas that guide us along the paths we take as we twist and turn in our colourful differences which make us what we are.

Ours was a group of families who came to Egypt where, during half a century they transformed themselves from Orientals to Europeans and then left under exceptional circumstances always conscious of a parallel with Jacob's children who had had a longer stay in Egypt but then left also under strange circumstances. Although particular to themselves, their story is also part of the general one of all migrating families be they Irish or Italian, Bangladeshi or Vietnamese and also of the vast exchanges of populations that took place in the twentieth century.

My parents who had slipped quietly out of Egypt in 1954 making their way to Khartoum where my father's cotton business continued to thrive under British protection, were present when the Union Jack was lowered for the last time two years later and the Islamic flag of the new Sudan was raised. They got on well with the Sudanese and I do not think that my mother had ever been as happy as during the two years she lived there.

She had my father to herself and spent all day helping out in his office. There were few suitable staff available so she also gave a hand at the British Embassy next door as they knew Mr Chapman Andrews, the ambassador, from Cairo. Her enjoyment of gossip and grasp of events meant that she quickly became a mine of information, passing it on wherever she felt it would be put to good use. She insisted on weekly letters from us as it was not possible to telephone and assiduously replied with stories that got more and more surreal.

"The new Egyptian Ambassador has just moved into the hotel," she wrote. "He seems very nice but when they searched our bedroom they put things back in the wrong place! Can you imagine such spies? I complained to Mr Spitzer the manager. I told him that our room has been searched every time a new ambassador moved in and everything was always done so discreetly that I have never minded. The Hungarians and Czechs have been the most meticulous at replacing things as they had found them, but this is unacceptable. Mr Spitzer apologised but said that there was nothing he could do. He said he thought it was the ambassador's wife who was responsible and she may not have been very experienced. Perhaps they are saving on trained staff."

Then suddenly an order giving them twenty-four hours to leave the country was presented. My father went to see the Foreign Minister, a very nice man he could call a friend. The Minister took the order and placed it in his drawer.

"There is no hurry," he said. "You can leave whenever it suits you but remember, this is a request from Gamal Abdel Nasser and we are not going to war with Egypt on your behalf."

Many years later, when he came to see me as a patient in

London, he told me how much he had regretted seeing my parents go. He had felt it was the end of his own era too. "Yours are a vanguard people," he had said. "When you leave it is an indication that everyone else who has something to offer will have to leave in their turn."

2

1934 Was Not a Good Year

In 1994 I was given as a birthday present a Pathé News video entitled "A Year to Remember". It was made up of film clips of events from the year of my birth and on the cover was the familiar black and white picture of the cock crowing. At least it was familiar to me.

I put the video aside at first as I felt that I should compose myself before looking at it as it seemed somehow private, not to be shown to my guests as though it was a collection of family photographs where everyone would laugh when they saw themselves or recognised someone from long ago. Of course there were no personal revelations on the video, but perhaps I was right to have been slightly apprehensive as more enters the mind than appears on the screen.

1934 started with Hitler meeting Mussolini in Venice. He had just proclaimed himself the Führer and acquired exceptional powers. He announced that his Reich, free of Jews, would last a thousand years. Persecution began and Himmler announced that the concentration camps would be made more efficient.

There were many other unpleasant events in that "Year to Remember" such as the assassination of Dollfuss, the Austrian chancellor, and of King Alexander I of Yugoslavia. The cameras must have got very close as you could see the dead King's face, his spectacles still on his nose, looking bemused. The assassin was cut down with a sabre and then torn apart by the crowd.

I watched the general strike in France with increasing gloom though the commentator's clipped, confident tone suggested that the depression would soon come to an end with the replacement of Waterloo Bridge and the opening of the Mersey Tunnel. Fred Perry won the tennis and England beat Australia. The little cheer at the end as things ought never to be that bad, according to Pathé News.

As always on my birthday I had gone to see my parents in their north London house and as usual I found them enveloped in heavy winter dressing-gowns even though it was the end of April. They had never got used to the climate and theirs had been the first house in Golders Green to install oil-fired central heating well before North Sea gas became available. My father who was holding a copy of *The Times* raised his head as I came in.

"It says here that since the war three million immigrants have come to this country. Can you imagine such a huge number? But when did they all come?"

"Papa," I replied, "when you came they came. We are part of that number. When they collected those statistics they included us."

He looked dubious. He had felt it was natural to be in England even when he had just arrived. He had never thought of himself as an immigrant no matter where he was living, certainly not an exile. Wherever he was was where he was expected to be.

My mother remembered my birth with nostalgia but now she veered towards pessimism and could see the future only darkly.

"It is not for your father and me that I worry," she insisted. "No, no, we don't matter. We are so old that what happens to us does not matter any more. No, it is for the grandchildren that I am sorry. The world is now such an awful place to be alive in. I think of them, of Simon and Nadia, of Danny and Anna and Joel, of Natalia and Isabelle, what a dreadful time it is for them!"

I noticed that she had listed them in order of seniority as that was fairer than to arrange them by gender or group them by family. I noticed also that she had not mentioned us, my sister, my brother or myself in any order at all. Did she mean that our lives too had been lived and did not matter?

"Simon and Nadia are in New York," I said somewhat irritated. "Anna is skiing in Switzerland, Danny is touring India. Joel phoned from Greece. He said he saw Natalia and a whole group of girls from South Hampstead getting off a ferry from Mykonos. The Greek Islands are awash with partying young people."

"Never," I added after a pause, raising my voice, "never, in the whole history of the world have young people ever had such a wonderful time."

She fell silent.

"You see," she explained after a while, "when you three were children, your father and I, we were having such a good time. The sun shone, it seems like it was a golden age."

But I could not let it go, as one cannot with one's parents. There is always the need to set the record straight even if it has ceased to be of consequence.

"It was during your golden age," I said, "that tens of millions of people were being tortured and murdered. While you were having picnics behind the Pyramids, six million Jews were herded into cattle trucks to concentration camps, starving Russia was plundered and bombs were ... "

But my father had raised his hand to change the subject. "We were young, Nelly, we were young. That is why it feels so good when we recall the time." He paused. "We can bring back the feeling for a moment."

Then he turned to me. "I was so proud when you were born. A boy!"

He had told me the story many times, every birthday that I could remember. He smiled before he started to speak, bringing back the memory. A rather sly smile as he recalled the telephone conversations he had had with his relatives and which he could remember word perfect, as the memory had given him satisfaction over the years. He had, he said, crafted the conversation carefully by giving no indication as to the sex of the newly-born child.

"Good news. Yes, early this morning. The baby is absolutely fine and Nelly, fine, fine."

"You see," he would explain to me as my mother could at last smile faintly, "by not mentioning if it was a boy or a girl they would assume it was a girl and that I could not bring myself to say it!"

He would chuckle at that point and my mother would laugh appreciatively. He would tell us how his aunts and sisters had tried to get round it by asking the name of the child ("not decided yet"). It was only when they could not bear the courtesies any longer and blurted out the question that his great moment had come.

"What?" he had feigned astonishment to prolong their agony. "What do you mean? But a boy, of course! What else could it be?"

He always repeated that final phrase several times, stressing different syllables so that we could savour the exact tone his voice had taken at the moment of his greatest triumph. "They don't understand, these days," he would say, "what a first-born son meant then."

Not all his aunts and older sisters were overjoyed. Some had disapproved of my mother whom they referred to as the "*franjiyah*" or Frankish woman as she spoke only French. They claimed that she despised the Syrian dialect of Arabic the older relatives still relied on. She also talked too much they added, and they would point out that she had insisted on living in town, in the new centre of Cairo with the more fashionable Europeans rather than in Sakakini where the immigrants from Aleppo had first settled and had remained.

"Too old fashioned, she says!" they had railed, "Just because she is *Mademoiselle* Sassoon she thinks herself superior! And she does not keep kosher either, apparently she is too *advanced* for that."

My mother's triumph in having produced a healthy son, however, was very difficult to dismiss, although one aunt had suggested that it was improper of my father to have informed them of the birth by telephone.

"A telephone is not a proper way of informing. He should know. When we were having our babies and he was still a boy mother sent him running round to all the houses. I remember him calling from the street 'Camille has gone into labour' or whatever."

But the friendlier aunts would not have it. "That was to call when we started labour, not for the announcement. Anyway we didn't have telephones in those days."

"It is perfectly proper," a senior aunt had finally pronounced, "as we must move with the times and the telephones are here to stay even if you cannot hear very well with them. No doubt they will improve."

As they had feared my mother did turn out to be the harbinger of new things. New fashions from Paris and a European nanny! The extravagance of that was never forgiven. And, as though living in town itself had not been enough, she had insisted on moving yet again, to Zamalek this time, on Gezira Island near the Sporting Club and near, it should be stressed, where her own parents lived.

But that was yet to come and although some aunts had felt threatened others were excited by what the modern new member of the family would bring. After the flat in town and the fancy nanny who had been engaged a whole month before I was due, if you please, so that she and my mother could get used to each other, it was announced that the birth would take place in a maternity hospital with a doctor instead of at home with a midwife like everyone else. The new hospital with all its modern facilities was run by Swiss deaconesses. And after all that flouting of tradition, to deliver a boy was definitely triumphalism carried to excess.

I was not the only boy born that day, however, as only minutes before, a German woman had been delivered of a dark, swarthy child. His father worked for a German bank in Egypt and even before Hitler had come to power in Berlin, the couple had been founder members of the Cairo chapter of the Nazi Party. Dr Hegi, a Swiss obstetrician, did not hold with racial theories and, overjoyed with the paradox, had not been able to resist picking me up as soon as my thin fair reddish hair had been wiped clean. Laughing out loud he had taken the two neonates, one in each arm all round the hospital.

"Tell me!" he called out to everyone he could find, nurses and midwives, patients and their relatives, "tell me! Guess! Go on, try! Which one is the Aryan and which is the Semite?"

That was another family story that was repeated many times, especially during the Second World War, as a further example of the folly of the racists, but for many years it left me uneasy. What if there had been a mistake of the sort that happens in maternity wards from time to time and I really was the Nazi baby? Or possibly even that the jovial Dr Hegi had wanted to play a trick on the Nazis by handing them the Jewish child? Uncertain, I craved the reassurance of being told that I looked exactly like this great-grandfather or that, but the photographs I was shown of old men with beards were hardly convincing. It was only as age has crept up on me that the distinctive features of my relatives have become obvious in my own appearance.

There is a mirror in my house placed at an angle. It is in such a position that I can just glimpse an image unexpectedly as I pass by. It is of a man of a certain age who for a moment I recognise as an uncle and a feeling of warmth and security urges me to hold out my arms expecting to be picked up. The moment is too brief to recognise which uncle it is as but as it passes I see that it is only my own reflection.

3

Feloukas on the Nile

Very early memories are only glimpses that come to us in a haphazard manner but they can do so repeatedly, triggered by outside events and perhaps more frequently as we get older. It is as though the doors that we have used to keep them out of sight in favour of more immediate and important events have weakened, their hinges becoming flimsier, so that we cease to be able to shut out these fragmented images. They intrude, out of sequence and disconnected from what lies around them, emerging unexpectedly here and there from among our thoughts, often leading us to talk about them at inappropriate moments.

According to my mother I could not have been quite three when we left for South America. I have few memories from that time but they are persistent. The first memory appears like a stage set; a dimly lit room with table lights illuminating only the areas that surround them. I recall an intense need to see more clearly what lies in the shadows, a feeling that I recognise now to be anxiety as I run from my parents, who are talking incomprehensibly on a settee, to Maria, my nanny, who is engrossed by her sewing. I realise that I cannot express myself but I am absolutely certain that there is something menacing lurking in the darkest corner.

I have often thought about this menace which has no form, and I cannot imagine what it will do to me, but I am drawn to the dark corner until the tension gets so great that I want to throw myself into it and cry out, "Eat me but just get it over with!"

This memory has never faded and must mean something,

perhaps indicating the pattern of my future behaviour when handling uncertainty or anxiety.

I also remember waking up in the morning, calling out, wanting to play, and my nanny hushing me. It is dawn, too early to wake Claudia, my baby sister, and the whole household. Maria picks me up, whispering soothingly, and places me in the arms of a very old woman. She wears a *mandil*, a black shawl over her head like a Spanish *mantilla*, from which it must be derived or *vice versa*. I wonder at the countless tiny fissures that line her face and I pass my fingers over them exploring their texture. I am not frightened by her age as her eyes, though dark and sunken, are comforting and full of love.

"*Ya rohi, ya albi!*" she murmurs in Arabic as she draws me to her breast "O my soul, my heart!"

But I am used to this as everybody I have ever met picks me up and loves me. It is all I know except for the formless menace which hides in the dark corner. Could that fear of being eaten be the deepest part of my being after all, the one to which, like all other creatures, I owe my survival?

I know that the old woman is my father's mother, Sara, and I am taken to her every morning. She too rises at dawn and has her own quarters. She also has her personal servant, a woman, equally old, called Miriam, who sleeps on a thin mattress stretched out across the door of my grandmother's bedroom in the old style, to protect the mistress from an intruder. Miriam was herself Jewish and as my mother, the chattering *franjiyah* or Frenchwoman, could not be entirely trusted to cater for her mother-in-law's kosher dietary requirements Miriam also prepared her food.

My mother would recall those times with some annoyance. "Those Jewish servants were impertinent," she would say. "They thought themselves the equals of their employers and they would even try on their dresses!"

I would climb on to Sara's lap as she sat on her balcony. I could see the haze rising so densely from the river that I could not tell which was water and which was land. Even the horizon was only an amalgam of grey shadows, more distinct at the front and barely perceptible further back where the palms, taller than the tallest buildings, and the fronds of the jacaranda trees could only just be distinguished from the mist itself. Behind it all I could see the dull yellow hue which, in time, would turn into the sun. It would burn up the whole vision which, as it disappeared, left the crisp, crawling image of the waking city.

But before that metamorphosis, as I peered into the dawn mist, the bridges over the Nile would be raised by their strangely soundless mechanism and a line of *feloukas* would glide swiftly along the river, their sails surprisingly still as they moved silently like a convoy of ghosts.

Miriam would make a thick, sweetly spiced Turkish coffee for my grandmother who would pour a drop on to the saucer so that I could lick it up as she smoked her flat fragrant cigarettes. I still seek comfort in the blended aroma of the coffee, enshrined by cardamon and cinnamon with its trace of nutmeg and a glass of iced water, barely scented by the essence of orange blossom. Miriam, using a pick, hacked a sliver from the huge block of ice delivered twice a day. The ice-man struggled up the stairs carrying the block wrapped in rough jute cloth on his shoulder, and placed it into the zinc-lined cupboard.

Sometimes a muffled rhythmical thumping sound would come up from below and my grandmother would raise me up above the balustrade so that I could see.

"Look!" she would say, pointing down to the street, "look at the camels!"

And I would watch the camel train, laden with goods, as the animals seemingly marching in step, crossed the city much as they had done for a thousand years but now permitted only at dawn so as not to interfere with the nascent motor traffic.

I have only one other memory from those early days and from the balcony. It is a cheerful one – of a funeral.

4

The Funeral

It is already broad daylight and the balcony is full of people. There is noise and activity with the perfumed scent of excited young women who pick me up and kiss me when I want to be held high to see what is going on. They tell me they are aunts, Aunt this and Aunt that and I understand that in some way I belong to all of them, or maybe it is they who belong to me; I am not yet clear about this nor about exactly who they all are. They are happy and some of them are clapping as there is a festive atmosphere so I ask whose birthday it is?

"Questions, questions, doesn't he talk well?" they laugh. "It is not a birthday, it is the funeral of King Fouad!"

I am still puzzled, I want to know what a funeral is but my questions make them laugh and I think some of them are teasing me though I don't understand how. There are lots of uncles too, young men who smell of tobacco. They don't kiss me as much but they seem to take my questions more seriously and answer patiently though I still don't understand their explanations. Naturally I keep on asking, trying to clarify what is going on until they tell me to stop and I know that they have had enough. But there is movement now, things to see as the coffin appears mounted on a gun carriage. It is pulled by horses covered in black capes, their heads crowned by black feathers, as drums beat a slow rhythm. Holding the bridles are men in baggy trousers, but what attracts my attention is that they are barefoot, trotting alongside the procession as though animals themselves, the soles of their feet stained by the ochre sand that has been strewn along the path of honour as a sort of red carpet.

"Ridiculous," says a grumpy great uncle. "The sand gets into the tramlines and it takes days to clear it up."

I want to know who the barefoot men with the red feet are.

"Albanians," they say. "The Royal dynasty is Albanian."

Musical sounds, the beat of the drums, high-pitched trumpets, melodies retained in my mind which I will one day learn are that curious blend of Turkish strains and European instruments which formed late Ottoman music. As the cymbals clash the young women who are holding me up so that I can see point out the new young King Farouk with the enthusiasm that youth offers one to another.

"It is a new reign and the new King is so good looking. It is a sign of wonderful things to come."

My eye catches one man as he walks in the procession behind the catafalque. He is tall, dressed in loose white robes with a hood covering his head.

"I think it is Abd-el-Krim" my mother says in answer to my question.

Many years later, in 1962, when I had decided to spend the gratuity from my national service in Morocco it was not the inviting country it has since become. Independence had been granted and the Sultan had been promoted to King with the name of Mohamed V, but an unexplained tension still reigned. Sitting in a dark and cavernous coffee house in Tangier I attracted some attention, perhaps suspicion, as I was the only foreigner there. Those at my table were curious as to why I had come and in turn I questioned the unease around us.

"It is the trouble in the Rif mountains," they said. "The followers of Abd-el-Krim have not accepted the rule of Mohamed V."

The memory came back and I told them that I had once seen Abd-el-Krim and that I had not forgotten. My news spread and men from other tables came to shake my hand. Others offered me cigarettes.

"For a friend of Abd-el-Krim," they said as they pressed their gifts on me, but when they brought *keif*, the name they give to hashish, I refused politely.

"You are wise," said an old man, "you are right to refuse. Tobacco is very good for the health, it helps you cough and clears the chest. And *keif* is also good as it helps the spirit to settle down. But both together is not so good."

"True," I replied. "We too have a saying that you must not mix your drinks."

"True," he repeated and we both nodded thoughtfully, he in old age and me in youth, at the unsuitability of mixing things, a common truth.

Then the police came and shut down the café as word had reached them that strangers, agents of Abd-el-Krim, were about.

State funerals offer an opportunity for national cohesion and Churchill's funeral with the choreographed symbolism of the tall cranes bowing in mourning as the barge sailed past the docks along the Thames, the heads of state following the catafalque represented not only Britain, but the whole Free World and on that occasion even I had a small role.

Winston Churchill did not die suddenly. He suffered a severe stroke, falling into a deep coma from which he never recovered, remaining in that state for many days. Although he had not been very active for a long time, there was a general acceptance that his death represented a final closure of momentous times and most countries wished to participate, each for its own reasons.

French television provided a medical bulletin for every news broadcast but their viewers did not find it sufficient. It was not enough, considering the importance of Churchill's life, simply to say that he remained unchanged and unconscious. They decided to interview someone who could speak French, ask him about the nature of a stroke and the way it evolved, and that was how I, too, found a place.

Day after day until the funeral, when a proper reporter described the scene, I appeared on *RTF* (La Radiodiffusion – Télévision Française) in front of a huge portrait of Winston Churchill explaining the way arteries narrow down and how clots form, or alternatively contrasting haemorrhage with thrombosis and the manner in which blood spurts out from a brittle vessel, ploughing up the tissues of the brain.

I was taken to supper each night at Simpson's in the Strand as it was not far from the studios in Bush House, while my relatives in Paris where they had sought refuge from Nasser's Egyptian revolution, assiduously watched the news as exiles tend to do. Indeed, *Oncle* Jacques, my great uncle, was allowed the best seat in front of the television at his club in the Rue du Faubourg St Honoré, just in case his nephew might appear again on the screen.

"Isn't it wonderful?" my relatives were heard to say. "So young and already Churchill's doctor!"

5

Mostly Hearsay

Across from our house on Rue Fouad I in Cairo there was an old palace with high walls and two Albanian guards who stood at the elaborate wrought iron gates and who often allowed us to peep though the grille.

We were told that it had belonged to a princess, but no one seemed to know who lived there now. I was fascinated with this decrepit old building as, at that time, I was being read stories from *The Arabian Nights* and in my mind I had somehow placed those beautiful fictional *houris* in palaces whose oriental architecture I thought must be similar to this one. My parents had pointed out the building which could be seen in its faded splendour from Bulak, across the Nile, where it seemed far away and indistinct presenting only a picture of its grand terrace on the banks of the river. My imagination, on the other hand, was fired by the glimpses I caught through the railings where I was able to perceive only a small portion at a time and where the patches of rust on the intricate iron work, the peeling paint and rotting window frames added an air of mystery. I had, of course, no idea then that the palace of the princess could have any connection with my family's coming to Egypt near the end of the nineteenth century, but even though the association is remote, they are tied up together, initiated by the same event.

When Ismail Pasha, Khedive of Egypt and Viceroy of the Ottoman Sultan, opened the Suez Canal in 1869, he made it a great festive occasion even building an opera house and commissioning Verdi to produce *Aida* to mark the occasion. He invited many dignitaries and the Empress Eugénie of France opened the celebrations marking the inauguration. Ismail Pasha built the Gezira Palace for her – this was the one we spied on each day. Ten years later he had had to sell the Palace because of mounting debts and it ended up in the hands of Prince Michel Lutfallah who turned it into a private residence.

Remotely connected or not, another outcome of the opening of the Suez Canal had been my father's family's move from Syria to Egypt. Grandparents and great-uncles and aunts told us stories of the different places in the vast empire of the Ottoman Turks from which they had come. One thing that is certain is that they had not come to Egypt, itself still only a part of that empire, as refugees. Their stories of grand houses built around beautiful courtyards, of shady trees surrounding pools and fountains, together with their accounts of friendships with the local Pasha or the Wali, in Istanbul, Antioch or Aleppo may have suggested some exaggeration and I wondered why they had left if things had been so good.

When I was old enough to ask and they had not yet declined into forgetfulness I had a brief opportunity to question them, though their answers were unclear and it seemed as though they were talking about a different world altogether. They spoke of the Ottoman Empire with wistful affection, as though referring to an elderly relative for whom admiration has turned into embarrassment as the mind crumbles and the faculties begin to fail. They remembered the past as a good time though everyone now insisted that it had left a lot to be desired in modern social terms.

"But it wasn't so bad, you know!" one elderly relative had insisted. "It was just old-fashioned, that is why Mustafa Kemal [Atatürk] changed the Arabic script to a Latin one as he thought that being old fashioned was what had brought down the Ottoman Empire. The Turks can now read French books and they will know all the modern things."

The merchant families of the Empire, like mine, had always been among those who craved stability and took advantage of ordered society. For at least four hundred years they had travelled with their wares from Basra in the Gulf to Baghdad and Aleppo, joining the caravans at dawn, their camels laden with goods as well as with the food and water necessary for the many days of the journey to the next post, sticking together as those were troubled times. But then are not all times troubled, and had not the great-grandfathers of the thieves of today also formed into bands ready to waylay the merchants?

Those caravans were huge. Hundreds combined under a captain with armed guards hired for security as their goods represented the wealth of Asia and Africa on its way to the rest of the Ottoman Empire, as well as to Europe. Indeed, these caravans would split up when they reached Aleppo, travelling on to Istanbul or turning west towards Egypt and the Mediterranean to be taken back on board ships.

Though no one could remember those times themselves they had been told the stories of those onerous journeys by their own grandparents and that was what they had passed on to me. The time on the road, walking or riding camels, always seems to have lasted forty days but I cannot tell whether that figure is true or simply symbolic. The call that would signal the start of the journey, they had been told, was sounded even before the sun emerged above the horizon.

"Ha!" the camel drivers shouted as they tapped their beasts with short whips, and then as the animals rose, slowly unfolding their complicated legs, the gruff men would click the side of their tongues against their teeth.

"K-K-K!" was the onomatopoeic signal from man to animal which had urged them forwards from time immemorial, and they would march slowly but without interruption in the hope of reaching the safety of the next caravanserai before sunset. The ruins of these places can still be seen and when I have visited them in the south of Anatolia or what was once Mesopotamia and Palestine, I have tried to imagine the spectacle as the animals were led into the large courtyard surrounded by stables and straw while the people climbed on to the upper floors, no doubt bedding down according to the degree of comfort and privacy that their purse could afford. The solid gates were then closed for the night and lookouts stationed on the turrets. When I once described the scene, a fanciful rhapsody, to my young brother Zaki he said thoughtfully that he supposed the caravanserai must have been a motel for camels.

When the railways were introduced in the second half of the nineteenth century, the caravanserais became hotels, the stopping places stations, and the rails were laid along the same old routes. Although trains had replaced the camels the trading network thrived, especially the primacy of Aleppo as its hub, and that was where my father's family continued to live.

When the Suez Canal came, however, severing the fragile isthmus which had held Africa to Asia, everything changed and as ships now took their cargos from the Indian Ocean and the Red Sea straight through to the Mediterranean they simply bypassed the Asiatic part of the Middle East altogether. As Aleppo gradually faded into anonymity, the merchants sent out their sons to create new commercial links. They settled in Didsbury in the great cotton manufacturing city of Manchester; they travelled to Flatbush and Atlantic Avenue in Brooklyn which, for the pedlars, had become the gateway to a whole continent; and they went to South America, but many settled in the new fulcrum of the encroaching British Empire, Egypt, the location of the fateful Canal itself.

My father was born in Cairo in 1898, his family having settled there ten years before together with many relatives and friends from Aleppo, Damascus and Antioch who had established businesses in Egypt. The new migrants had taken a leap of faith not just in relocating themselves, but in understanding that the move, in order to succeed, had to involve taking up a new culture. That was why my father was brought up to speak French and called Cesar, rather than Ezra after his grandfather, so as to identify with the Europeans. At around the same time my mother's family, the Sassoons, had established extensive outposts in places as far away as Shanghai and Bombay on one side of the world to Manchester on the other and my grandfather Isaac Sassoon and his brother Moise, brandishing their British passports, had set up in Cairo and Alexandria where the new trade routes crossed, bolstered by the valuable long fibres of the Egyptian cotton crop.

My father had met *Mademoiselle* Nelly Sassoon at a party where she claims to have thought that he looked American. Maybe she meant that he seemed modern, advanced in some way, and that he would take her further along the path her grandparents had initiated in moving that family from east to west.

When they described their courtship, it seemed to have been an easy matter since they had the advantage of having fallen intensely and instantly in love while their families were entirely compatible. But they followed their traditions and my great-uncle, Musa Douek, formally asked Isaac Sassoon, whom he knew well, for permission for his nephew to entertain his daughter.

My grandparents, broaching the subject tentatively, asked Nelly if she was interested in meeting this young man as they were well aware that good family connections held little sway in the minds of the young girls of those "modern" days. As sensible parents they were tactful in order to avoid trouble and hysterics, but they were surprised at the alacrity with which she had not only accepted but insisted on the formal introductions taking place forthwith, as it appeared she had met him already. Times were moving fast and it was hardly possible to keep control of young women any longer so they simply counted themselves lucky and it was arranged that Nelly and her parents would be at Groppi's the following day for the *thé dansant* and that the suitor would join them.

Isaac and Eugénie Sassoon sat watching over their daughter who seemed so lacking in decorum. The young couple refused to leave the dance floor until they were forced to do so as dinner was being served. Cesar and Nelly were totally bound up in each other and they remained so for sixty years, almost oblivious of others including their own children, until they simply died of extreme old age one soon following the other, with their faculties and their memories intact.

The wedding had taken place right away as there was nothing more to be said, at the modern synagogue known as *Le Grand Temple* in the Rue Adly Pasha. Although none of their older relatives spoke much English, technically the wedding was a very British affair. There was no doubt regarding the Britishness of the Sassoons and as my grandfather felt that his association with the Protecting Power was worth cultivating, he insisted on hiring the ceremonial guards or *kawass*, from the British Embassy for his daughter's wedding. Two *kawass* dressed in the uniforms which Mohamed Ali the Great, the ancestor of King Farouk, had brought from his native Albania when he became ruler of Egypt, stood at the doors of the synagogue greeting the guests.

The Doueks too, were British, though how they had acquired that nationality was still obscure at the time. In fact they tried not to make too big a deal of that connection and to keep their heads down, but on this occasion Isaac Sassoon was entitled to have his way at his own daughter's wedding. The cause of their reticence only became clear much later.

I was told by my Sassoon grandfather, that the first Sassoon, the founder of his family so to speak, had arrived as a boy in Mesopotamia at the time of the French revolution, a captive of Arab slave traders. He had said that he was Jewish, that he had been taken from the city of Hamazan in Persia and that his name was Raphael. The local Jews, as was the custom, bought him his freedom with a special fund which they kept specifically for the purpose and the boy was so happy that they gave him the name

"Sasson" which means "joy" in Hebrew. The British connection came later, of course, and the family were rather vague about it, saying "from India" when I asked.

My Aunt Rachel, my father's eldest sister, was the most informative about her own family's arrival in Egypt. She seemed quite old to me though childhood gives a different perception of age, and she still lived in the part of Cairo where they had originally settled but which was now abandoned by the younger members of our community.

Rachel told me that they had left Aleppo, *"Om el bilad"* she had called it, or the mother of all cities, by train to Beirut where they had boarded the ship of the Khedivial Line to Port Said as sea travel was safer and cheaper than other means of transport as well as more comfortable. She said that my grandfather Eliahu, whom I never knew as he had died before my parent's marriage, was tall and imposing with clear blue eyes and a large upturned moustache. A crimson tarboosh with a black tassel added to his height and everyone addressed him as *effendi* or *bey* out of respect as he stood surrounded by his wife and seven children as well as a couple of sisters who were travelling with him hoping to make a suitable match in Egypt. Rachel's eyes brightened as she remembered the scene on deck when the steamship, too big to dock at Port Said waited for sailing boats or caiques to collect the passengers.

My grandfather, who was responsible for the large group, had telegraphed in advance to book a caique whose captain had been highly recommended, to meet them.

"When we saw the sailing boat we all shouted: 'Osmanli! Osmanli' as that was the name of the captain, 'Osmanli! *La famille Douek!*'"

My grandfather had handed his passport, which consisted of a large sheet of paper, to the captain who was, according to Rachel, a powerful man who also had a large moustache though its tips were turned down rather than up. He leaned against the mast as the caique sailed slowly past the Turkish customs posts – for Egypt was still part of the Ottoman Empire and its ruler, the Khedive, was a vassal of the Sultan. British protection was very discreet.

"The Turkish officers were posted on both sides of the channel with their tarbooshes straight up on their heads," Rachel had remembered, "and Osmanli unfolded the passport holding it high up so that everyone could see, and he called out loudly: 'Ingliz! Ingliz!' so they stood to attention and saluted. We were all so proud!"

Rachel's husband, *hawaga* (Monsieur) Salomon, was definitely very old and had long ceased to work, whatever it was that he had done. He had never had much contact with French or English so there was not much to be said when I was brought in to his room. He always placed a hand on my head and mumbled a perfunctory blessing when it had been explained who I was, and returned to his reading of the Holy Book. It is from that time that I formed the belief that it was only old people who read holy books. I also remember that he smelled fresh, of expensive eau de Cologne, for which my mother credited Aunt Rachel whom she also admired for her constant good humour.

Salomon did not seem to die, though at the age of ninety he decided that he would take his leave of this world from the Holy Land. Rachel, attached to her children, grandchildren and great-grandchildren refused to go with him so, to his family's considerable annoyance, he had himself admitted to an old people's home in Jerusalem. He returned to Cairo six years later to everyone's amusement.

"You see," they mocked, "you did not like it. We told you so!"

"It is not my fault that I did not die," he replied.

In the turbulent events of the Levant, the revolutions and the wars, his demise may have been overlooked – it is unlikely that he is still around somewhere, unnoticed, reading the Holy Book.

There was another side to my family and it came through my maternal grandmother Eugénie. I always sensed the rather sceptical, even superior attitude that she showed towards those around her and, as a small child, I had been shocked when she told me that persons of her level of education did not believe in God. This was attributed by everybody to the fact that she had studied at the *École Normale* in Paris and had, for a while, become a teacher.

Atheism was confusing as no one would discuss it with me. My nanny Maria was a very devout Roman Catholic. She went to church all the time and was friendly with the local priests and nuns. The Muslim servants had their prayer mats and regularly prostrated themselves towards Mecca at the call of the muezzin, though not all of them prayed the prescribed five times a day. Every one I knew believed in God and then the sudden revelation that Eugénie Sassoon, my own grandmother, did not do so because she was much too highly educated was difficult for me to understand.

Her brother, *Oncle* Victor, was also not expected to believe in God as he too was highly educated. He always wore a spotless, white, linen suit and panama hat and carried a white horsetail fly swatter with which he would relentlessly attack those ubiquitous insects. He was a lawyer accredited to the *Tribunaux Mixtes*, a peculiar institution of Law Courts that had been established to try foreign residents by foreign judges, their cases pleaded by foreign lawyers. Its origin in the Ottoman Empire lay in the unwillingness of the Turks to get involved in foreign disputes. Each consulate was encouraged to try its own citizens and to come to some arrangement among themselves in civil cases. This had led, in Egypt, to a parallel legal system for foreigners which, in time, infuriated the Egyptian nationalists who saw the Europeans as holding themselves beyond the law of the land.

Oncle Victor's atheism was of an active kind, as from time to time he would write articles in magazines proving the absence of God or disproving His presence, depending on which approach seemed more suitable. He was a kind man and I was very fond of him despite the fact that he had a quick and disputatious temper. When I was a teenager I was told that he had been appointed a judge at the Beth Din, the Jewish religious court, and I questioned how an atheist could be given such a job. He took offence, saying that the existence of a deity had nothing to do with it. His knowledge of the Law, all laws in fact, was respected and he was fully capable of applying it.

Some years ago I was walking past a shop in Chiltern Street in London and saw an outfit in the window. I usually find it quite difficult to buy clothes for myself but I felt inexplicably drawn to these. Even though the jacket was perhaps a size too large, I could not resist and I bought the whole arrangement just as it was. I wore it at my elder son's wedding in the hot summer of up-state New York in 1998 but it was only later, when putting the photographs together, that I realised that in the white suit and panama hat I looked exactly like *Oncle* Victor.

Eugénie and Victor's father, Joseph Alphandary, had also been highly educated though he was careful to keep to himself whether he believed in God or not. He was a school teacher from Istanbul and worked for the *Alliance Israélite Universelle*, an organisation set up by French Jews to offer an education to Jewish children, both boys and girls, with the aim of rescuing them from the lack of modernity in the Islamic world and opening their minds through a French education to the enlightenment of the West. It was essentially a secular education but he could not risk offending the sensibilities of those he hoped to attract. As a young man he had taught in Haifa where he lodged with the Goldzweig family who had come from Odessa in the Ukraine following the pogroms. He had married the daughter of the house who had blonde tresses and was called Fanny. He became a headmaster in Safed in Palestine and later founded the school in Egypt.

He was a gifted painter though he never joined the Impressionists stylistically. The walls in my grandparents' house were covered with his pictures and I inspected them carefully every time I was there so that I can still remember some of them now. They were sold as a job lot by an aunt during her hasty departure at the time of the Suez war. He himself became ill of an undiagnosed disease and all the doctors could suggest was a Mediterranean cruise. He died as they sailed in the Aegean. A burial at sea was suggested but Fanny was distraught at the idea. She could not bear the thought of returning to her children and telling them that their father had simply been thrown into the sea. The captain agreed to drop her with her dead husband at the nearest island where there happened to be a Jewish community. Joseph was duly buried. From the island Fanny could see the lights of a city across the sea at night and was comforted when she was told it was Smyrna in Turkey as she had relatives there.

When she had got home Fanny had forgotten the name of the island where she had buried Joseph. She told my grandmother that all she could remember was that mastic trees grew there.

It was a chance visit in the 1970s that took me to the island of Chios off the coast of Turkey. The hotel porter had thrown open the doors of the balcony to let in the evening breeze and I could see the flickering lights of a city in the distance. He said it was Izmir.

"Smyrna?" I asked.

"You know the old name?"

"Can you tell me if there are mastic trees here?" I asked.

"Of course," he replied "all the mastic comes from here."

I looked for the Jewish cemetery but it had gone. It was the Germans, they explained. When they had come to take away the handful of Jews who for one reason or another had not escaped, they also took the trouble of destroying the cemetery. No one knew why it had mattered so much to the Germans to smash as many of the gravestones as they could before they left. Some suggested that it had a great symbolic importance but others said they were bored and the officer had to find something for them to do. The islanders of Chios later picked up all the pieces they could

find and I was shown where they were stacked against a wall
behind the museum.

As soon as she had finished her training in Paris the *Alliance* had
sent Joseph's daughter, Eugénie, back to Istanbul to teach. She was
very beautiful with a thick mane of red hair and she soon attracted
the attention of a young man who seemed to be waiting for her
every day as she walked along the old market in Kadiköy across
the road from the ferry landing to Galata Bridge. She was flattered
and the regular presence of the young man caused much amusement to the other young teachers and the girls in her care until it
came to the attention of the headmaster who had her followed.

"My poor child," he had said, according to my grandmother.
"You must leave immediately. The young man is the son of a
Pasha and if he takes a liking to you, he may never let you go!"

She was dispatched at once to Egypt to teach in her own father's
school although that was not the usual policy of the *Alliance*. That
was her story of how she arrived in Egypt where she soon met her
husband, Isaac Sassoon.

So my family came to Egypt near the end of the nineteenth
century, and within a little more than fifty years we had all left
again. They had been happy years for them and an idyllic childhood for me but when, without too much advance notice, we
were asked to leave so that the Egyptians could at last have a fresh
start by themselves quite free of foreigners, we were not entirely
sorry to go. We like to be where the action is and we could see
that it was further west. We left the tombstones of our grandparents in the cemetery by the Citadel just as their grandparents'
graves had remained in Aleppo or in Istanbul, names carved in
stone which may one day present an archaeological curiosity.

Eugénie survived to end her days in an old people's home in
Vevey, overlooking Lake Geneva and my last memory is of her
sitting, impeccably dressed and made up under a walnut tree. Her
brother Victor Alphandary and his descendants settled in São

Paolo, in Brazil and he was over a hundred years old when I was informed of his death.

When I went back to Cairo many decades later, I went to look for the old palace of the princess as I wanted to show my wife that romantic overgrown garden through the gap in the wrought-iron gates and, perhaps, let her too catch a glimpse of the mystery inside, but we found the gates had been polished and were held wide open while this time the doorman ushered us right in. It had become the Marriott Hotel and we sat in the garden, now hardly mysterious, as we took tea among the crowds and my memories.

6

South America

There was an interlude in our life in Egypt when we went to South America and then returned to Egypt three years later, in 1940, at a time when thousands of people were fleeing Europe. There were no long-range commercial aircraft at that time so it was ships that carried them. The first to leave Europe in the 1930s were the Jews who sought refuge from Nazi Germany. For many it had been difficult enough to get out at all, and they had left without permits allowing them sanctuary in any other country. Ships crowded with refugees went from port to port along the coast of South America, only to be turned away more often than not. Refugees began to leave Holland, Belgium and then France. Some managed to get to Spain or Portugal where they waited for visas to take them to the United States.

By 1940 the bombing of England with the piecemeal destruction of its cities had already begun and shiploads of refugees, many of them children, were organised into convoys also taking them across the Atlantic. The German Navy was not inactive, and groups of U-boats, submarines hunting together in the manner of wolf packs, roamed below the surface. Although their main targets must have been the convoys carrying food, oil and war materials they did not hesitate to sink any other ship which came their way, with enormous loss of life. Those who faced the ocean in 1940 did so with as much trepidation as those who sailed it at the time of Columbus and perhaps they were in even greater danger.

When everybody was running from Europe, some for their

lives, and attempting to get to America, my parents decided to travel in the opposite direction. My mother was in her seventh month of pregnancy when we set off from Colombia together with my sister and our nanny Maria who was delighted with the hope of seeing her family in Italy.

I was six so I remember the return journey well enough but when I later questioned my parents about what I had come to regard as irresponsibility on their part I hardly got an answer. I suspected my mother as she tended to make decisions on the spur of the moment and tried to put them into practice at once, but she claimed that she could not see the point of my enquiries. We had done well so what had been wrong with their decision? When I insisted that it could easily have gone the other way all she would say was that it had not. My father did not have much more to add other than that he had found that Baranquilla in Columbia was a hell-hole and that my mother had been unhappy there.

I was barely three when we went to South America so I remember nothing of the journey there and I had obviously not been consulted nor informed of their hopes or dreams in going in the first place. Again my mother had little to say other than that they had gone for the best of reasons and they were just as right to return, war or no war. Everything had gone well and their decisions had invariably been right. My father talked about it a little only when he was near the end of his life.

Ultimately it had to do with my Aunt Yvette, my mother's eldest sister. She had married very young and had left Egypt at once with her husband for the Republic of Colombia in South America, stopping only in Paris to buy the clothes which were needed to complement the trousseau which she had felt was hopelessly inadequate. Shamefully so, she still insisted bitterly seventy years later, for a person of her background and position. They settled in Baranquilla, a growing industrial city, where she promptly had six children while her husband's enterprise prospered. He had not come alone as there were brothers and cousins, an altogether hardworking lot who had abandoned their various cities in the crumbling Ottoman Empire and set up, rather courageously in that environment, as manufacturers. They, too, were birds of passage as in time, enriched and increased in numbers, they ended up in California or Florida.

I believe that my aunt pined for her own family and urged my mother in her letters to join her so that one way or another, we ended up in Barranquilla, where, as the new Spanish words became available to me, I learned to sing "*La Bandera Colombiana*" which was about the Colombian flag being red, yellow and blue.

Although I have no recollection at all of how we got there, I have a vivid memory of the shoes. They were neatly arranged in a row along the wall of a room in our new home and like all small children I must have had the capacity to ferret out such interesting objects especially when they are near the ground. Maria, my nanny, had let me put on her shoes and try to walk about with my tiny feet floating freely in those boat-like spaces, so I immediately made for the strange ones that I had found. "No! No!" they all cried. These belonged to the servants who went with the new house and I was not allowed to touch them. I remember only thinking that there must be many servants to fill all the shoes.

There seemed to have been a lot of parties in the open air. Today, when crouching by the fire in northern Europe what I see when I look back to a childhood in the tropics is parties. It is possible that these stand out in my memory only because the excitement of such events has fixed them there more firmly than other ones or that the photographs and cine-films that have still not faded seem mostly to have been intended to record these occasions. But I think that a warm climate decided the nature of our social life as I remember hordes of children, different ages intermingling, running freely and playing elaborate games.

La Cucaracha! La Cucaracha

we sang as we hopped crazily on one foot.

La Cucaracha! La Cucaracha!
Ya no puede caminar
Porque no tiene, porque le falta
La patita principal!

As we imitated the skewered steps of the wounded cockroach we did not know that it had represented the interrupted rhythm of the machine-gun firing during the Zapatista uprising.

There was a three-tier system of control as the rank of nannies supervised us while telling their stories about their own families so remote from ours, and offering their particular philosophies to explain the world to us. The nannies were mostly of peasant origin and their understanding of life, their definitions of human behaviour and of the way things are, were often presented in the form of proverbs and sayings. Mothers, some distance away, were associated only with the better and more important things. They did not deal with cleanliness or toilet or even daily meals. They were not involved with tantrums or the irritations of everyday life and some, I gathered from other children, were hardly ever there. My mother was never far away, or at least she always told me where she would be so that even when not present I felt she was available. She was young and beautiful and wonderful perfumes wafted around her as she took me in her arms so I was deeply in love with her. She had no proverbs or sayings to offer, but she read Freud and the like and gave rational explanations for everything instead. I knew that it was like her I wanted to be.

Sometimes I felt torn between these two women, my mother and my nanny Maria, as I loved them both and in my mind I tried to avoid betraying the one to the other. Even now in thoughts and memories I feel the need to maintain a balance in what was truly a surfeit of love.

To have been brought up by a peasant nanny must have given many middle-class children a particular affinity or insight that is often overlooked or forgotten, and I have attempted, at times, to explain to my students and assistants the empathy between some poor immigrant patient and myself. I, too, had spent my childhood in the arms of a peasant woman, hearing about life in her impoverished village and crying with her but I suppose the apparent distance had become too great for me to sound credible so I learned to keep my feelings to myself. Whether it made me a better doctor is not for me to say, but I have often wondered, when some patrician politician shows an exceptional grasp of the feelings of those deprived and has turned it, perhaps, to advantage, whether he owes that understanding to some peasant woman in whose arms he, too, had spent his childhood.

The fathers, on our horizon, stood even further away than the mothers and that distance endowed them with an aura of benign power. They were there, away from the rough and tumble of our day, suggesting ultimate protection as well as being the source of our survival. We were urged not to distract them with petty things that could be settled by the nannies or, at a pinch, by the mothers so that they could be left to deal with the broader strategies of life. My own father, a kind man, was never involved in any punishment but I desperately wanted to please him and he had the fortunate capacity to show pleasure and to offer praise whenever it was needed. I realised when he was in his mid-nineties that I was still bringing him news of anything I achieved much as a cat might bring a dead bird to its mistress and when he died I lost that pillar of support. Who commends old men?

All the parents seemed to spend their evenings at parties. It is the lack of any other cultural activity that forces people into making their own entertainment in this way and the warm climate of the tropics lends itself to such open air celebrations. I too enjoyed seeing my mother and aunt dress up and especially paint their finger nails red or green or even black to match their outfits. The men wore black ties and shining white jackets of a material they called "sharkskin". I have not yet found out what it was as all those who wore it are now dead but they had it also in Egypt so it must have been widespread in the tropics as formal wear. Perhaps it was silk as it certainly felt silky or it may have been an early synthetic fibre like rayon as it was so lustrous. It was these two properties that entranced me, the silkiness which I caressed with my sticky childhood hand and the fact that it shone so brightly, reflecting even the moonlight. My ambition was one day to wear a sharkskin jacket but I believe they have ceased to exist.

Although the children were often present I do not really know what sort of people my parents associated with. I suspect from later experience in what were once called colonial – and are now known as developing – countries that they would have been a collection of foreign residents as the indigenous population, if from the upper classes, would keep to themselves, while the poor would make contact only as servants.

Not all of them were particularly sophisticated as in those countries foreign circles must take in whoever is there without appearing too dismissive as they would otherwise have few people to talk to. My mother, I was to learn, enjoyed the diversity and liked to dabble in all the languages around her as she had a gift for picking them up, if only superficially. When she was an old lady in England I had tried to get her more involved in the outside world and had given her name to the social services as an interpreter. She had done very well I was told but she had created a problem by refusing payment to the dismay of the union which represented professional interpreters. I heard that she had dealt easily with a Maltese family, much to my surprise as she did not know Maltese.

"But Maltese is easy!" she had replied. "It is like Arabic and Italian with a bit of Spanish. All these Mediterranean languages are more or less the same."

There was something didactic about her and her sister and they enjoyed instructing those around them in the niceties of social behaviour even though many were Syrian pedlars, both Jewish and Christian, as well as a few Muslims of very modest origin, who had been driven to Colombia through poverty. My aunt and my mother relished their attempts at polishing them up and they seemed to inspire a certain awed devotion in those they patron-ised, perhaps because they did it with respect. I remember my aunt picking up her cutlery as we sat and calling out to a man, dressed in black tie and sharkskin jacket at the other end of the table.

"Ezekiel!" she said as she held them up in demonstration. "The knife in the right hand, the fork in the left, then you cut and eat, cut and eat."

I recall this well as I was still uncertain myself. I found her instructions useful so that they have remained as a template in my mind and when I lay the table now her words still call out silently as I mutter, "Knife on the right, fork on the left."

There was another reason why I remember that incident as, bored with the food, I had crawled under the table to play with the other children who had found their way down there. I noticed that the man had slipped out of his shoes and had also removed his socks. When I told my mother what I had seen she was not at all surprised and said that he had only recently got into the habit of wearing shoes and was even known to go out into the street barefoot. The horror of that information is still with me as I was already aware of the unbridgeable social divide between those who wore shoes and those who walked barefoot, and I could not understand my mother's equanimity even when she told me how brave these semi-literate men were. They had come all the way from the Middle East to a land whose language they did not know packing their paltry goods on the back of a mule to wander off alone, peddling them to the Indian villages on the fringes of the Amazon basin. None of this meant much to me at the time but it slowly turned into curiosity and I asked my aunt when I visited her in Beverly Hills years later what had happened to that man. At first she was not clear whom I meant but then her face lit up with recognition, after all it was so long ago and she recalled those times with pleasure.

"Oh, you mean the grandfather?" she said. "They all live in Miami now, you know. Ezekiel himself? He died, of course, a long time ago. Very, very rich, a multimillionaire!"

Not everyone who came to Barranquilla was uneducated or motivated by poverty and as the manufacturers expanded and became more ambitious they brought over graduates from the textile colleges around Manchester. Rayon, the new synthetic fibre, was produced by skilled industrial chemists and even the spinning and weaving was a different technology. The young men who came delighted the ladies with their culture and deportment, and generally raised the tone, but they did not do well.

"Why is it," my father asked rhetorically, "that educated men cannot make it here when the illiterate thrive? What is it about this country? We must get away at all costs!"

As well as the parties there were many picnics. We watched the seaplanes take off and land on the Rio Magdalena and went on excursions to Cartagena or walked along the beaches at Santa Marta. I shook Maria hard to wake her when it was still almost dawn as I could see an enthralling sight on the beach. Columns of donkeys were passing along the sands one behind the other carrying huge sacks of goods. I was amazed by the strength of these beasts but what really interested me most of all were the activities of José who followed the train of animals with a large basket.

Although he had been named after his grandfather Joseph, everyone called him *Hosé* in the Castilian manner. I had been told that he was distantly related by marriage and although he appeared quite affable to speak to he posed a serious problem to his parents as he was already in his late teens and showed no interest in or aptitude for the family business. It was not that he was not good with figures as at first his parents had rejoiced in the way he could work out in his head the complex calculations of percentage profits and discounts they had set for him, but he simply showed no interest and insisted he could not cope.

"He is mad, that boy, quite mad," I heard someone say. "They have such a good business and he just won't consider it. I pity the parents with a son like that."

I too pitied the parents as I knew something else about him but I did not spread it around out of consideration. José's behaviour in the early dawn on the beach at Santa Marta was definitely unhinged as every time a donkey defecated, which seemed to be their morning routine, he would pick up the soft, steaming dung with his bare hands and put it in his basket. What was most baffling was that Maria did not think it was odd and she often exchanged a few words with him about the roses he was trying to grow in that tropical climate though I tried to keep well away as you never know with madmen. She told me once that she had picked up dung herself to use as fertiliser in her own village near Trieste and laughed when I exclaimed with horror.

Eventually José left for the United States and I assumed he had been put away somewhere to stop him harming himself and doing outrageous things in public. No one mentioned him much but occasionally I caught words of commiseration for his parents as people were kind and those who had children themselves knew that such things can happen in any family.

"They had to let him go," I heard someone say. "There is no other way when that happens, you have to let them go."

People nodded gravely as José's mother, though sad that he had been unable to join the family business, said that he was happy at last in the place where he had gone, doing sums in his head. It was called Princeton. For many years I believed that Princeton was an asylum where the mentally deranged were happy and well looked after.

Then disaster struck as my sister and I caught whooping cough. Claudia became ill first and because she was so young the illness was very serious and my parents' anxiety was obvious. It was the first time that I sensed that they were not all-powerful but I could not quite understand how even my father was helpless and why he did not want to go to work. It is a very unpleasant realisation which every child has to go through more than once. Soon I too fell ill and after that events emerge like peaks through a haze.

It is not that I have forgotten but what I remember is of a different nature, probably because of the high temperature that this infection produces. Doctors came and went and I would wake with faces looking down at me then doze off again as fingers would percuss my back or the unfamiliar disc of the stethoscope would slide about my chest. The cough was bad and as I saw my sister struggling to breathe the voices boomed or faded as though they were coming from a faulty tuner.

"I am afraid things are worse than I expected."

Doctors in those days tended to be pessimistic, probably to exonerate themselves if things went wrong while they could always take the credit for a recovery against the odds. I know now how little they could do.

"We might be able to save one of them, perhaps the older one is more likely to make it."

I could see the despair on my father's face as my mother whimpered.

"Girls tend to be sturdier but we will have to take stronger measures, I think it has turned into pneumonia. See, Nelly, can you hear the dull sound percussion makes? That means consolidation."

There was some commotion as they turned my sister on to her front and people I had not seen before, an American doctor and nurses, arrived and then I sank again as I heard the words "strong measures" and "*ventouses scarifiées*".

The searing heat behind me brought me round and I too found myself lying on my stomach, then a strange sensation of suction, as though something was tugging at the skin of my back. Someone wiped me with a towel and I could see that it was bloody.

"Did I cut myself?" I asked but then lost consciousness before I heard the answer.

"*Ventouses*" is known in English as "cupping". Flaming tapers were held inside special small glass cups until they became very hot at which point they were applied tightly to the skin of the back making a seal. As the air in the cup cooled its volume diminished creating a vacuum which sucked on the skin. If really "strong" measures were necessary the doctor would scratch the skin before placing the cup so that the vacuum would actually draw some blood. Many reasons for cupping were given though none of them seem valid now. But people had believed very firmly in it and many patients and doctors would not give it up. I was told that just before the liberation of Paris in 1944 General de Lattre de Tassigny had cups applied. Because no one had the temerity to oppose the wishes of the commander of the French 1st Army an elderly physician had to be persuaded to do it. Cupping was abandoned when penicillin could cure pneumonia in three days.

Claudia and I gradually got better, whatever the reason, and the subsequent treatment was less dramatic. It was odoriferous, as there were soothing inhalations, healing vapours and rubbing of chests with aromatic substances and I enjoyed it all especially because it was associated with the constant presence of my mother, and often my father too. It left me with a pleasant memory of illness and treatments with a powerful olfactory content so it was a disappointment when I finally became a medical student to find that all that had gone and that medicines were now odourless pills or were intravenously administered.

We were forbidden contact with others, especially children, for an unreasonably long quarantine so we roamed the streets with Maria who took us to church after church and I have remained fond of those baroque buildings seen everywhere in Latin America and which always seem so familiar to me. She also enjoyed dramatic sights and events so she could not resist taking us to Santander Square to listen to the speeches on the occasion of the birthday of Simon Bolivar, the liberator. I protested at first as I knew that it was wrong to circulate in streets so crowded with people who might catch our illness and I told Claudia to cough as little as possible. In Maria's village quarantine was only two weeks, she said, and insisted that we were doing nothing wrong.

The crowds pushed us towards the stand that had been placed in the centre of the square and when we reached it I recognised a man who had been a guest at our house, a lawyer who had done some work for my father. He, too, saw us and greeted Maria, asking her if he could pick me up. We climbed on to the stand and he began to address the crowds pressing me to his bosom as I tried not to cough. I attempted to warn him about the dangers of whooping cough but he would not listen as he put me down to rip off his shirt.

"I too am a *descamisado!*" I heard him shout as he waved that garment in the air. He did not kick off his shoes and claim to be barefoot but his shirtlessness was definitely appealing as the crowds cheered and shouted rhythmically, "Gaetán! Gaetán!"

I later learned that he eventually became a Member of Parliament and was greatly loved by the people. As his influence grew he was shot by unknown enemies in 1948 and his funeral was the occasion for the invasion of Bogota by Indian peasants who laid waste the city with their machetes in an act of release or revenge. His name was Jorge Eliécer Gaetán but his death was several years after the whooping cough and we were long gone from South America. I am told that many poor peasants in remote parts still do not accept that Gaetán has died and believe that he will return to save them. Some say on a white horse. But then in Mexico there are those who are still waiting for Emiliano Zapata to come back to rescue them from oppression and many wait for the Messiah to sort things out, or for the First or Second Coming. Perhaps they will all come back one day to help the poor and the oppressed.

Life became unsettled at home. I had the feeling that things were kept from me as my parents would stop talking as I entered the room. My mother urged my father to stop arguing with people while at other times it was my father who insisted that she should put a stop to her accusations whatever they were as everyone was entitled to their own views. I think my father's enterprise was not doing well either as there were references to the economic situation. Maria crossed herself a good deal and appealed often to the baby Jesus which irritated my mother who said that her *Bambino Jesu* was not going to help anyone.

I began to behave badly, though when I try to look back in the hope of finding a clue to what goes on in children's heads when they do that, I can recall nothing but confusion. I suppose it is not possible for the adult to re-enter the child's mind, even if it is his own. My bad behaviour did not last long, I think because my mother read these books by Professor Freud and decided that I had to be told something. The occasion arose quite soon when a family came to spend a day with us.

There were four of them, a couple with two sons who were older than me and who kept very quiet. Actually none of them spoke much because they knew little French and no Spanish. I had heard many languages but I had never heard theirs. The two men were able to communicate as my father could speak a little of their language and the man spoke a little English. My mother could not bear to be left out and in the absence of any other means of expressing herself she began to give things, articles of food and clothing, to the woman who accepted them with no change of expression saying "*merci*" but it sounded a little odd.

Somehow I thought that I also had to give something so I ran to my room and brought some toys for the two boys. They did not know what to do as they were much too old for what I had brought and looked at their mother for guidance. I looked at my mother and saw that she had begun to cry, then both women held each other and cried together. I did not know what I had done wrong so I cried too.

A coach came to fetch the people with a policeman and my

parents said they were going back to the ship. I shook hands with the boys who said "*auf Wiedersehen*" and the woman kissed me.

The man called out to my father as they left. "You help us, ya?"

My mother was still crying. When I started to jump on the furniture as I did not know what was going on she made me sit in front of her. "These people are Jews like us only they come from Germany where they were treated badly. That is why they do not speak like us, they speak German. Now they have nowhere to go, do you understand why we are sad?"

I nodded and asked, "Why can't they stay here? The boys can sleep in my room."

"It is not possible, we were only allowed to take them home for the day. Your father and uncle and the other men asked permission for them to stay but it was refused. These poor people, our people, have been on the ship for so long."

I was very upset now and told Maria that I was afraid, as if my father could not look after us I did not know what would happen. Maybe we would have to go in the coach with the policeman, but she told me not to worry as God would help us. She said we would pray to the *bambino Jesu* and he would protect us from bad things. I was not convinced as the *bambino Jesu* was only a child and I thought it would be safer if we prayed to *Santa Maria*. We might even be better off praying to a man, like my father only stronger, *San Giuseppe* perhaps.

I behaved well after that. I think that my mother and Maria were surprised that I was so quiet but they must have been rather relieved after my previous activities. I was afraid "they" might take us away if I was not a good boy.

My mother listened to the news on the radio. In fact she left it on all the time. Just before the news a siren would sound and I had to run and call her. There was a difference of opinion and arguments between all the adults after the news.

My mother had explained that there was a Civil War in Spain. Civil meant that it was brother fighting brother. "What about

sisters?" I wanted to know as I had been forbidden to fight with
my sister though I sometimes did so surreptitiously. Sisters too, my
mother had said, Civil War was that terrible. There were the good
ones fighting the bad ones. The good ones were called Republicans. Nanny Maria kept quiet as she knew her place but she also
listened to the radio with my mother and occasionally let slip that
the Republicans were also bad as they killed priests. My mother
claimed that these stories were lies that Maria had picked up from
the Sunday church sermons. Eventually the bad ones won and it
upset my parents though my nanny crossed herself and said it was
the judgement of God.

On 1 September 1939 preparations were made for Claudia's
third birthday. This was important to me as I had watched my
mother and my aunt prepare the cakes and jellies, and I did not
know how long I would be able to resist eating them. I ran about
wildly to control the urge and they put me in the garden.

I came in after the siren. The Germans had invaded Poland and
bombs were falling as innocent people fled. My mother, my aunt
and Maria were crying. They were talking about cancelling the
party and my heart felt like lead at the prospect. I could not bear
the thought of not eating the cakes and especially the different
coloured jellies. Then to my great relief my mother said that the
living must go on living and that the birthday party would take
place.

When letters came from Egypt my mother and my aunt would
telephone each other and read them out loud, then in the evening
they would meet with lots of other people who had also received
letters and they would read them out loud again. I had now begun
to listen carefully as I knew that it affected me but I hardly
understood anything that was said so I asked questions all the time.
I became conscious that there were things called "turns of phrase"
and that it did not mean what it said but meant something else.

The one that struck me most was a letter from my grandmother
which included the expression *"on marche sur les soldats"*, one

walks on soldiers. I did not ask what that meant as I knew what they were going to say, "It is only a turn of phrase," but the questions kept coming back into my mind. Were the soldiers standing up? In which case it would be quite impossible to keep your balance while walking on their heads. They must have been lying flat on the ground side by side, or perhaps with their arms outstretched as the people walked on them; perhaps they screamed with pain when heavy persons got on top. But why did they do that? In the end I had to ask my mother and she looked at me in amazement.

"Are you mad?" she said. "What sort of imagination have you got? It is only a turn of phrase, it means there are a lot of soldiers, that's all!"

Somehow they decided that now was the time to return to Egypt and began preparations to cross the Atlantic in the wrong direction, towards the soldiers, towards the war. There were no problems in finding berths.

7

The Last Voyage of the *Esperia*

"You are white?" the Captain had said, ruffling my fair hair as he stared into my father's blue eyes. We had boarded an American ship that was to take us from Cartagena through the Panama Canal to Caracas, but as everyone else was being taken to their cabins we were told we had to be inspected by the captain first. Maria, who had an Italian passport, could go ahead. My parents were a little uneasy as we were paraded into the captain's office. Everyone was uneasy in 1940, including the captain, but when he looked at us he seemed relieved.

"Of course we are white," my father replied, now quite bewildered. "We are British."

"British by birth!" my mother added in her French accent. She was now visibly pregnant and the years spent in Colombia in what amounted to a type of anonymity had not cured her of her pride in being one of the very British Sassoons.

The captain explained that this was a segregated ship where blacks were allowed only on the lower decks and black people from the Caribbean and British Honduras who often travelled that route had British passports. When the purser had seen that, other than Maria, we were all born in Egypt he had assumed that we must be black since he was aware that Egypt was in Africa and he had, quite properly, informed the captain who had come to check for himself. Those matters, he pointed out, had to be taken seriously. Later, after we had got through the Canal, there was more trouble. Because of our place of birth we were not allowed to disembark in Venezuela. The official took one look at our passports and exclaimed: "*Turcos!*"

"*Ingles!*" my father replied.

"British by birth!" my mother said, but to no avail though this created a serious problem as we had to wait somewhere for the *Augustus*, the transatlantic which was not sailing for a few more days so my father insisted on calling the British Consul. This became one of those unpleasant situations where people dig themselves firmly into impossible positions but the consul did stop my father from attempting to force his way into Venezuela on the grounds that the official was clearly in the wrong.

"Please, please, *calma!*" he said. "In this country you just disappear. You are thrown in gaol under another name so that no one can find you and they deny that you were arrested or that you ever existed."

It appeared that the Venezuelan official, distracted by personal problems, had foolishly lost his temper but had no intention of losing face as well. He was now claiming that his Spanish ancestor, probably the only one if his features were any guide, had fought the Turks in the defence of Christendom at the Battle of Lepanto serving directly under the command of Don John of Austria himself, and he was not about to let his family down now. As for the British, Protestants all, they were no better than Turks.

There was no way that we would be allowed to enter the country, even for a few days, but the travel agent was able to arrange for us to board the *Augustus* in advance as it was already docked and undergoing minor repairs. The *Augustus* was a fine ship with two swimming pools, tennis courts and a cinema. There were games for the children and bands that played in shifts. No one complained even though they went on playing throughout the night as we understood that our lives were at stake. The ship belonged to the Italian line that also ran the *Virgilio* and as Italy was still a non-combatant country the two great vessels were among the few luxury liners to cross the Atlantic in the middle of a war.

The ocean was tracked by warships many of which approached us to take a closer look and the passengers were advised to prove their innocence by waving and shouting, "Hurrah!" One day I saw a submarine emerge from the water and its conning tower open for the officer to stare at us. Again we dutifully waved vigorously, my father holding me up to watch until it was submerged again. There may never before have been a ship bedecked with numerous Italian flags so that no mistake would be made, and as soon as dusk fell we were lit up in the green, white and red colours of Italy, still signals of neutrality.

The band played the same tunes again and again so that they became imprinted in my mind. Everyone got to know the words as they sang along with the music and we covered the repertoire of all the warring nations, presumably so as not to offend anyone. "Roll out the Barrel" was played repeatedly as well as "Lily Marlene" and "*La Mer avec ses blancs moutons, . . .*" or "*Le Fiacre*", but my favourite was "*Parla mi d'amore, Mariu*" which I still sing from time to time when the mood or the memory takes me.

Life on board, a temporary haven on an ocean riven by war and violence, was as idyllic as these out of time moments often are. My parents took walks on the deck and meals at the Captain's table as he seemed to enjoy their company and frequently invited them so that when a sailor came to tell my father that the First Officer wanted to see all of us at once we expected we would be taken on a tour of the bridge. Instead he made us line up in front of him as he sat at his desk.

"Not again!" I could hear my father whisper to my mother. "What is it this time?"

The first officer stood and took up a posture like that of Mussolini on the newsreels, his chin jutting out imperiously.

"Italy will soon join the war," he said sounding reflective, and then in a sudden change of tone he spat out, "and where will you be then? Where?"

He strutted about a little and spoke again.

"Where will your Empire be? Tell me if you please, where will your Churchill be and your Anthony Eden? Did you know that all the Hotel Edens are changing their names in Italy now? In fact the one near my home in Liguria has been renamed the Miramar!"

My father tried to point out that the hotels had been named after the Garden of Eden and not after the British Foreign Secretary but the First Officer would have none of it and insisted it was an Italian victory.

Later, my father complained to the Captain but he placed his hand across his mouth in a gesture indicating silence and begged us to forgive him as there was nothing he could do. He may have been the Captain but the second in command was a member of the Fascist party and more important than him.

The *Augustus* stopped in the Azores, in Tenerife and finally in Madeira. Each time we docked the ship's band played and a local one responded with its own tunes, those of Spain or of Portugal, and my parents were always the first to drag us down the gangways to visit the islands. I do not remember the details nor the differences between them as there were always horse-drawn carriages waiting for the tourists, and beautiful toys made by the local craftsmen. As we left the bands would again play and tears streamed down every face on land or on board. Each time "Auld Lang Syne" was played everyone sang in their own language. My mother sobbed as she sang "*Ce n'est qu'un au revoir . . .*"

It made Claudia and me cry too, and I asked why everyone was crying.

"Because the tourists are leaving," my mother said lamely.

"But won't they come back?"

"No they won't," she said, shaking her head firmly. "They may never come back again, ever!"

Every now and then, when the whim took him, the First Officer would call us in boasting of the might of Italy and the impending destruction of the British Empire. Il Duce, he said, showing my father the telegram, had had his white horse brought to Libya in preparation for his march on Alexandria. "I wanted you to be the first to know. I have not even informed the Captain of the good news yet. And you, where will you be then? Phut!" he said snapping his fingers, "Phut!"

"Wait till we enter the Mediterranean," he told us on another day as again we stood in front of his desk. "Il Duce has proclaimed it *Mare Nostrum*, like in Roman times!" He had wept a little at the thought and wiped his tears with a white lace handkerchief. He then turned to Maria.

"Shame on you," he said with a look of disgust. "An Italian woman and you serve these people!"

Sometimes children feel obliged to intervene and suddenly I spoke out, I don't know why, as my mother tried to stop me.

"She is not Italian," I said, interrupting his flow, "she is Slovene and she is not a servant, she is our nanny."

"Hah! Another one of the inferior races honoured to be incorporated by Italy. The great D'Annunzio was obviously wasting his time risking his life flying over the coast of Dalmatia! Did you know, you simple, foolish woman that yours was the homeland of the Emperor Diocletian?"

At last I saw the British Empire. We had got to Gibraltar on a sunny morning and everyone on board stood along the side of the ship. Claudia and I were held up as usual so that we could see. The straits between Europe and Africa were almost completely occupied by ships of the Royal Navy. I can remember every size from battleship to small torpedo boat, frigates and cruisers, warships by the dozen. We all stood awed before such a sight.

British soldiers boarded the ship for inspection and I saw them, too, for the first time with their spindly white legs, khaki shorts down to their knees and long socks held up by elastic bands with khaki tabs. The First Officer was out of his mind with fright. He begged my father not to report him; he wiped the bench on which the British officers would sit with his own lace-edged handkerchief. I saw him strike the waiter, then pummel him in terror as he shouted, "Bring them tea, you fool! They like tea! Bring them tea!"

And so we entered the Mediterranean on the great ship *Augustus* and made for Genoa where again the bands played cheerful Italian songs of welcome and arias from familiar operas. It was different there. It was obviously different as the bands were marching through the streets. They were called the "*Ballila*" and were a sort of Boy Scout wearing black shirts but what interested me most of all were their little black caps with tassels.

Also the way they sang was exciting as I had never seen that sort of thing before, it was very different from when we had marched in step in Barranquilla singing "*La Bandera Colombiana e Rojo, Amarillo e Azul*" Here men and boys were marching and singing, wearing uniforms and carrying banners. I remember the tunes too, even the words of one particular song which I repeated to myself over and over again:

> *Giovinezza, giovinezza*
> *Primavera di belle-e-e-ezza*
> *Nel fascismo è la salvezza*
> *della nostra libertà*

It meant: "Youth, youth / Springtime of beau-u-uty / Fascism is our saviour and our liberty."

It may look silly when I write it down now, particularly when I translate it into English but to me, sung and marched, it was wonderful especially the bit which went " . . . *belle-e-e-zza*".

We were taken over by it all. We wanted to stay a little longer. My mother thought it might be best if she had her baby, my brother, in Italy, a civilised country, rather than risk it on a ship. My father thought that he might be able to set up some business contacts. Maria wanted to visit her family in Gorizia, near Trieste. I wanted to join the *Ballila* but my mother said they would not

consider a six-year-old. I thought maybe in time, and if I practised, I might be allowed to walk behind them.

We all went together to the British Consulate to let them know
our plans. We stood behind the counter in a row, my father, my
mother, me holding my sister's hand and Maria. The clerk looked
at us with horror and said he thought he had better take my father
in to the consul.

He was there for a while and then rejoined us, tight-lipped, and
said we were leaving right away. It had all been arranged by the
consul who had himself telephoned to book us in and called a taxi
while our luggage was being sent directly by the hotel to join a
ship called the *Esperia*. There would be no other ship. My mother
was not entirely convinced and wanted to know if there was a
doctor on board. Suppose she went into labour? My father assured
her there was. Later he told me he had never asked.

When he was with the consul my father had seen much activity.
Clerks and secretaries were burning documents. The consul had
said that Italy was expected to enter the war on the side of
Germany any minute. The *Esperia* was leaving that evening and
we had better be on board as it was likely to be the last passenger
ship to leave Italy, possibly Europe.

We docked at Naples to collect passengers as we did at several
ports. We were picking up people who wanted to leave Europe.
This sort of thing was going on everywhere; people desperately
trying to get away.

We got off at Naples as my parents wanted to have a look
around. In retrospect I cannot imagine why they were so interested. I would have thought they would just have wanted to get
away as soon as possible and stayed on board in case of an accident
or something. But that is in retrospect, of course, then they could
not have known what was really about to happen.

Naples also had parades. That day it was a church procession
and it was inspiring with thousands singing hymns and following
rows of priests and penitents carrying crosses. I had never seen that

before. By the age of six I had already visited many cities as I had been to Barranquilla, Cartagena, Panama and to Caracas. Then there had been Madeira full of flowers and Tenerife where we bought wooden toys. Not great cities, of course, but I had seen no processions there, certainly nothing like Naples.

The procession led to the church of San Genaro. My parents were fascinated and wanted to go inside despite the crowds and despite my mother's pregnancy. Maria, a devout Catholic, was overwhelmed by the exceptional nature and magnitude of the happening and the general understanding that a miracle was about to take place. She insisted on coming, too, so we all went inside.

It was quite dramatic and I still remember it with awe, the hymns, the prayers, the incense, the costumes, the *'amens'*. My father explained that the little glass phial the bishop held up for us contained a dark brown substance which was the Saint's blood that had dried into a powder. Every year the bishop would hold it up and the miracle would happen, the powder would turn into liquid blood. This took place without exception in reasonable years. If the blood did not liquefy it would mean disaster for the city and for Italy, perhaps the whole world. That was why there was an atmosphere of such terrible apprehension with people crossing themselves, falling to their knees and calling out, "Maria! Maria! *Ave* Maria!" as if in pain. Many were weeping and my nanny kept crossing herself with my sister copying her. I became very frightened and whispered to my father that I thought we should fall to our knees and beg forgiveness but he said that we did not do that sort of thing. He told my mother that perhaps we should leave but she was too excited and in any case Maria was in a trance and could not be drawn away.

Finally the phial was held up again and the crowds began to pray in whispers very quickly as though trying to get in as much praying as possible. I could recognise little phrases like *"Santa Maria"* and *"Madre di dio!"* *"spiritu sancti!"*.

The blood did not liquefy. Thousands of people wept and cried out, "*Misericordia!*"

The city and the world was in for a bad time.

Maria held her hand in front of her mouth in anxiety though my mother said not to worry and that it was all rubbish and my father said to be careful not to get crushed but the crowds were restless, depressed. No one seemed to want to crush anyone.

When we finally sailed away I saw that a huge poster had been placed on the sea front so that everyone could see it as they sailed away or arrived. It had large lettering which I could not yet read but my father said it was "*Mare Nostrum*" – "Our Sea" in Latin.

We stopped at Piraeus and we went to see the Acropolis as the *Esperia* waited to pick up more passengers from Greece. I suppose that few of the passengers who boarded the ship at Genoa or Naples, Athens or elsewhere on the northern coast of the Mediterranean would have survived were it not for the last journey of the *Esperia* before Mussolini took Italy into his war.

I wonder whether the frenzy with which we and our fellow passengers visited everything we could, hiring taxis or horse-drawn carriages, visiting Pompeii or paddling in the Blue Grotto, throwing stones into the Aegean from Poseidon's temple at Sunion or just wandering about the Plaka and invariably getting back to the ship at the last minute, indicated an awareness that something terrible was going to happen and that we might never see those places again. When, in time, I put it to my parents they ridiculed the thought and claimed they only wanted to look around because they were there and the alternative was to remain on board reading a book. I am left, nevertheless, with an image of a group of people of different nationalities, their lives hanging by a thread even though they did not know it, desperately visiting places of interest along the way as they fled Europe on the *Esperia*'s last voyage.

According to the records of the Italian Navy the *Esperia* was sunk in August 1941 off the coast of Tripoli in Libya. She had been built in 1920, commissioned by the *Adriatica* line, though a new *Esperia* replaced her in 1949 and continued to ply her trade around the Mediterranean in the same manner, her name inspiring affection among the coastal cities until she too was finally scrapped in 1973.

The *Augustus* and its sister ship the *Virgilio* which had also been transformed into troopships were sunk by the Royal Navy. I often wonder if the Captain and the First Officer had been serving on board.

8

Walking on the Soldiers

We arrived in Alexandria in the spring of 1940 as the sun was setting over the sea and the inevitable bandsmen welcomed us on the quay, their white uniforms glistening with tassels and gold braid while colonial helmets made them appear even taller. By the time the *Esperia* had properly berthed the sun had set with the rapidity with which this happens in North Africa and we began to disembark in the penumbra while the *shayaleen* or porters, loaded the huge trunks, so popular at the time, on to their shoulders. They carried them down the gangway one behind the other and the band, to encourage them, began to play "It's a Long Way to Tipperary" in a lively manner. The workmen too broke into a rhythmic song which sounded less English than Arabic: "Asta Langway ta Tabarara, Asta Langway taaa gaaa."

The larger pieces of cargo were shifted by cranes powered by teams of *shayaleen* dressed in the loose blue *galabeyas* that would become so familiar a part of my childhood. As they pulled on the heavy ropes they called out the beat so as to keep together: "Ela-ela-*ho*! Ela-ela-*ho*!"

Tired from the excitement I lost track of what was happening and Claudia was now asleep in my father's arms. In the increasing darkness it was the diversity of the sounds and the smells, immediately strangely familiar, an auditory and olfactory chaos, which signalled that I had come home.

It was both the end of the day and the end of the journey and, as it turned out, it was also the end of our old world. The *Esperia* took on a few Italian passengers who wished to return home and were already waiting at the dock. The ship left the following morning at dawn but there was no band and no music.

"It's Joe!" my mother had cried when she caught sight of her brother.

"It's *ton-ton Jo-jo*," she said to me pointing to the young man standing by the car.

Joseph Sassoon was her youngest sibling and only brother, and under the pressures of modernity he was referred to as "Joe". Too young for us to call him "uncle" it was nevertheless inappropriate according to the etiquette of the time to call him by his name, a situation not uncommon at a time when families were large and the eldest was often giving birth together with her mother, generating aunts and nephews of the same age.

Such little aunts were referred to as *tantine* and I can remember women who remained *tantine* into old age, long after these terms had quietly dropped out of the vocabulary while Joe Sassoon was known as *ton-ton* until he was called up by the Royal Navy when it was deemed generally inappropriate.

Joe drove us along the desert road to Cairo. I slept through the journey and then was thrust back into the world to which I belonged as my grandparents had rented an apartment for us near to their own in Zamalek on Gezira Island, and aunts and cousins streamed in to visit us. It was a warm, welcoming world that is now called with a mixture of envy and slight contempt "an extended family". The envy is because such a structure suggests support and loyalty to those who have had none and the underlying disparagement comes with the implication that it belongs to a simpler form of society that we have outgrown. The extended family has undertones of obligations to people one may dislike, but are tied to forever by unwanted atavistic connections, and who never hesitate to take advantage of them. No doubt our family shared these traits too but they evaporated when we were scattered by the winds of revolution and nationalism, while all I can remember is the warmth and the confidence which you can never lose, whatever happens later.

Adults would touch me when I was introduced, ruffle my hair or give me a tap on the bottom and sometimes, especially the women, insist that I kiss them though when I tried to do so, perhaps encouraged by an attractive scent or perfume, they would hold me at a distance so as not to mess up their make-up. Some men had the unpleasant habit of pinching children's cheeks which was often painful, and I have never worked out what pleasure they got, or hoped to give, from that peculiar act. Fortunately I rather liked most of my cousins and it was a relief when I was told to go away and play with them.

My mother and her four sisters were complicated and difficult women who were very quick to take offence with one another. As a child I could not understand the rage and anger which their arguments inspired, especially as no one else seemed to either. Their husbands tended to be amiable men who got on reasonably well and would try to calm them down and on occasion had physically to pull them apart. It was only much later that I thought I was able to understand at least one aspect of their relationship. They were so tightly bound up with each other that they had no mechanism for leading separate lives other than to initiate a mortal dispute about some inconsequential matter or other which they could always resolve later if they wished. If one was to give a dinner party, for instance, there was no way in which she could avoid inviting her sisters as well other than to take offence about something. Once I had realised what they had been up to all their lives it clarified much of my own. The five sisters ended up living in different continents and, in their manner, remained closely attached all their lives, telephoning daily as soon as this became feasible, although they rarely visited each other. It was not that they did not travel but they tended to give their sisters' countries a wide berth on spurious excuses. I asked one of my two surviving aunts, now in her nineties, what she could possibly have to tell her sister in California every day.

"I hope you don't complain about your children!" I said.

"No," she replied rather shiftily. "We discuss our Philippino helpers."

On the other hand my mother could hardly bear the relaxed approach that the members of my father's family had towards each other.

"You see," she would say, "you see how cold they are. I would never have believed it if I had not heard it with my own ears!"

That was because two brothers, on parting after a chance meeting in the Galleria Vittorio Emanuele II in Milan, had wandered off to their distant destinations with no more than an "Au revoir." She continued to repeat this story over the years as an example of a form of behaviour she could never understand. She admitted once that she was "touchy", although she rarely admitted anything at all, but in doing so she implied that it was a good thing compared to the coolness of her in-laws.

The sisters were very competitive and their children were used as weapons, so that on the Friday nights when we were taken for supper to their parents' house we were made to bring our successful school reports to show and be congratulated by their father who would write "well done" at the bottom and sign it "Isaac Sassoon, Grandfather." If we had nothing appropriate to show, we brought a drawing or a poem to recite while the others were forced to listen. On the other hand I was never blamed for failure and never made to feel anything other than a great success, whether true or not, so I have a lot to be grateful for. I cannot be sure that this was specially good for me but it made my childhood happy and, although the world I eventually had to face was hardly as indulgent, most of the time I was able to assume that I was welcome wherever I happened to be. There can be little doubt, after all, that to feel good cannot be too bad a thing.

I believe that the sisters' competitiveness was because their mother, my grandmother Eugénie, did not think very highly of them. Her whole affection and devotion was directed towards her husband and then to her only son. On the other hand they all seemed to think that they were their father's favourite so he must have had a special way about him. I know little about their household as girls but I was told that even though the birth of each child brought in a new servant so that Eugénie should not be burdened with extra cares, my grandfather would be up at six o'clock every morning to make each daughter her favourite sandwiches himself, and packed each lunch box individually. Somehow he got away with it and compensated for their mother's distance.

Some years ago I was walking in the Flower Market in Nice with a relative who introduced me to a very old lady who was shopping there.

"I remember your mother!" she screamed at me with the loss of inhibition and the deafness that so often accompany old age, "I went to school with her, and I remember your grandmother. I hated that woman!"

She went on to tell me, as it was the first thing that came vividly into her mind, that my grandfather had had a box made in a rare type of mahogany lined with green felt to house the telephone and muffle its ringing tone so that Eugénie should not be disturbed during her siesta or when she was secluded in her room. The old lady was still flushed with rage and envy at the memory of the coddling my grandmother had received from her husband, but whether justified or not, the story was true as I remember the box very well.

By the time we had returned to Cairo some of my younger uncles and older cousins were already in uniform and the city was full of soldiers of every nationality who had to be welded into the British Eighth Army.

"*Ça ne presage rien de bon,*" my grandmother Eugénie had said dismissively. "This is a pastiche of an army, a collage of all the bits and pieces they can find to fight Rommel. Yesterday I saw some

Czech soldiers, where did they find them? At least the Maoris seem fearsome and the Indians might worry the Germans, but who will command all these people? They say that an English general's mistress was an Italian spy."

Every day Maria took us for a walk down the Rue Hassan Sabry to the Grotto Gardens where she could sit and exchange news with the other Slovene nannies. As there was not much information available they took comfort simply from each others' company. We played with the other children looked after by these women although, as we were of different nationalities and spoke different languages, we were not able to communicate at all, but it did not seem to make any difference. We each spoke in our own tongues yet understood each other perfectly well. I liked one little girl in particular as she was a round laughing blonde little thing though I could not understand a word she said. Her nanny, a cousin of Maria's, told me that her name was *Dafani*. I spoke to her in French which made her laugh and she replied in a language which had certain peculiarities. It sounded like "ch-ch-ch" as if you had to speak without unclenching your teeth. I tried to speak to her in Italian or in Spanish but that made her laugh even more.

The Rue Hassan Sabry was lined on both sides with leafy trees so the walk to the garden was protected from the sun by alternating jacarandas with their blue flowers and lace-like leaves, and trees which they called "flamboyants" which, when in season, produced the most striking crimson flowers. Despite the shady street we had so exhausted ourselves by much running at the Grotto Gardens that we could barely get back home and I begged poor Maria to let me hitch a ride on Claudia's pushchair. We would stop at my grandparents' house for a rest and be taken to kiss my grandmother very carefully as she was always impeccably made up.

One day we found her crying, her make-up streaming as she sat at the table with the newspaper *Le Journal d'Égypte* open in front of her. I could not read yet but I had some idea what those symbols meant and I had never seen such thick black headlines before.

"*La France est tombée!*" was all my grandmother could say, looking at me with such sorrow that again was new. There were too many new things and I felt confused, but what immediately went through my mind was how could a country fall, and where? Was there a hole? And what happened to the people? Did they go down the hole too? Did they die? I understood enough now not to disgrace myself by asking silly questions any more though I still had not worked out the part such imagery played in language nor, of course, could I realise the importance that the fall of France would mean for me.

Although blessed with British passports of obscure and, some insisted, dubious origin, the Doueks and the Sassoons of Cairo had chosen French for their language as had most of the Jews of Egypt, indeed as had most foreigners, including the Greeks who were the most numerous. The large Syrian Christian and Lebanese communities also took up French and so did the Italians, who were now subdued as it looked as though they would be entering the war on the wrong side. This meant that to all the foreigners in Egypt as well as upper-class Egyptians, who associated with them and went to their schools and clubs, French was the principal language. For practical purposes the main cities, Cairo, Alexandria and Port Said were mainly foreign cities where French had pride of place though Greek was also widely spoken in Alexandria.

Eugénie who had been sent to Paris for her education at the turn of the century retained her attachment to France all her life and travelled there frequently before the war though she claimed it was always for health reasons. I have been left with photographs of those trips on which she was accompanied by my mother, and they are seen invariably at watering places and spas such as Vichy and Uriages, going for walks in scenic spots or sitting chatting in cafés. Apart from useful episodes of migraine she had seemed perfectly well to me though she resumed her tour of health resorts as soon as the war was over. When I became a medical student I asked her what exactly her illness was and she showed me an extensive correspondence which had continued long after his own retirement from practice with the famous French physician Pasteur Valléry-Radot. His textbook of medicine, known among the students of my time as "PVR", had been our bible and I was amazed at the numerous and detailed letters he had written to Eugénie dealing patiently with every symptom.

My grandmother had consulted him on the occasions she had visited Paris and he had not hesitated in answering her letters by hand at great length. His script was copper-plate as legibility was seen as an asset, and his style too was the courteous one of the time.

I was unable to identify her illness although she could describe her symptoms in great detail but his sympathetic questions and kindly advice have been an example to me ever since I read his letters. I try to keep them in mind as I reply to my own patients' e-mails though I doubt that I have been able to match his patience.

The last time I saw my grandmother, when she was well into her late eighties, she had asked me to bring her some pheno-barbitone as she claimed modern sleeping pills had no effect at siesta time though she would not explain why she wanted to sleep at all in the middle of the day. She maintained a warm correspondence with her numerous children and grandchildren expressing her views on most things to the end. I know that she loved us all very much but preferred us at a certain distance except for her son.

"Walking corpses!" she called out gesturing dismissively at some old people passing by as I cringed with embarrassment. "Don't worry, they can't hear a thing. They are all deaf as a post here!"

She confessed to my sister that her memory sometimes played games and that when she sat in the café by the lake in Vevey and her eye caught sight of a man with white hair she was unable to stop herself calling out: "Isaac!"

Eugénie's influence had been so powerful that only the fall of France could have brought about such an important change as the abandonment of the French language by my family. She herself never spoke a word of English and was not at all impressed by the connections of the Sassoon family into which she had married. She had had to live in Southport, in Lancashire for a couple of years early in her marriage but had sent her older daughters to school in France and had communicated with her staff through her husband acting as interpreter.

My father, on the other hand, had at the age of sixteen got a job in the accounts department at Thomas Cook and Son in Cairo, where he had picked up enough English to get about thanks to the personal encouragement of the Chief Accountant, a Scotsman. Certainly he could write business letters faultlessly, and by the time he ended his days in London he was not only fluent in English but also enjoyed the language. My mother never lost her accent and people referred to her as "the French lady".

Soon after the fall of France my parents had come to the conclusion that if we were to survive at all it could only be through a British victory and it would be best if the children were sent to English schools. My father explained this to me carefully and told me not to worry if I did not understand anything at first as gradually what was said would become obvious like all other languages, but I was very unsure about it and asked him what it sounded like.

"It's like this," he said. "They barely open their lips and they keep their teeth clenched so that it sounds 'ch-ch-ch'. You know that little blonde girl who comes to play? The one who laughs? She is English, it sounds like her."

"Dafani!" I shouted reassured. "I will speak like Dafani!" I suspect her name was Daphne.

9

The English and their Schools

My father took me to the Alvernia Convent School where the Irish nuns accepted boys only for the first year but my parents had been told that it was a good place to start. It would give them time to look around and, hopefully, I might learn some English.

I was quite familiar with nuns who then wore elaborate and suffocating outfits, as Maria was always hanging around their institutions but I thought they all spoke Italian or Slovene. Nuns who *spoke* English were a marvel and the fact that they were not English at all just added to the complex mixture of peoples and languages that was to become my world. There is a difference between the way we acquire a foreign language in childhood and in adult life, as different parts of the brain get activated, and the same effects may take place with music and culture as a whole. This means that those exposed to diversity in childhood can never escape the consequences and I suspect that is the reason why some people are so anxious to preserve a homogenous society for their children to grow up in. That too, must be at least one of the reasons why the Egyptians who were in power at that time were so keen to be rid of us.

I was very surprised many years ago, when I met the successful cartoonist Vicky (Victor Weisz). Born in Hungary he worked in England from 1935. His inspired Macmillan as "Supermac" and his allusions to Winnie the Pooh or to characters from *The Wind in the Willows* had touched the heart of the English to an extraordinary degree.

"To understand people you have to read what they read as children, not what they are reading now," he told me.

A foreigner who comes to England at the beginning of the twenty-first century would be wise to watch "Blue Peter" as a first step to understanding its present young adults.

I remember holding my father's hand as he handed me over to Sister Mary Urban but I was not frightened, only excited at all the new sounds, the nuns in their habits, and the numerous little girls who were playing hopscotch and other extremely elaborate games involving steps, clapping and rhyming recitation. Everyone spoke French .

A group of children had formed a circle and were clapping hands rhythmically and chanting:

> *Diable, diable, sous la terre*
> *Fait tomber Jacqueline parterre!*

while the eponymous girl performed complex acrobatics in the centre, contortions that only girls can do, easily overcoming the hostile words of the incantation.

> *Am stram dram*
> *Piké-Piké kolégram!*

came from another corner where I saw a group of girls hopping, skipping, alternately slapping hands following a pattern so intricate that no one could afford to miss a beat or a step, and which I could just watch in admiration. I, who had never seen such things before, had entered a magical world of ritual and spells dominated by girls.

Then Sister Mary Cecilia came in wielding a bell. She was rather heavy set and wore glasses so we assumed she would be very severe and we tried to comply at once.

"Now children," she said, "everyone speaks English from now on! You two, what are your names?"

She had addressed two little Coptic girls who were holding

hands. Sisters, they wore blue overalls over their dresses and their hair had been carefully woven into heavy brown plaits by a loving nanny. They did not hesitate for even a moment and curtsied in a beautifully choreographed movement saying in one voice: *"Nous ne parlons pas l'anglais,"* very calmly, scanning the meter in order to keep in time. When the nun asked them something else they simply repeated the procedure. *"Nous ne parlons pas l'anglais,"* as they curtseyed impeccably again.

We were ushered into the reception class where Sister Mary Urban had placed a huge chart on the wall and as she indicated with a long pointer we were immediately taught to chant: "A is for apple; B is for . . ." and so on to "Z" which was for zebra.

In time we were also singing out loud: "Two twos are four, threes twos are six . . ."

We learned everything by heart, and I can still recite it all without hesitation when the need arises, and my only regret is that I did not learn more in this way. My year at the Alvernia Convent School for Girls was very happy and I made many friends with whom I am still in touch, old ladies now. At the end of the year everyone in that mixed-ability class spoke English, could read and write and got as far as multiplication if not division.

I was now quite ready to join the Gezira Preparatory School and though I was sorry to leave Sister Mary Urban I was relieved that I would have nothing to do with the strict Sister Mary Cecilia who taught the next class and I knew, too, that it was right that I should move on.

The Gezira Preparatory School stood near the corner between the Rue Hassan Sabry and the Rue Fouad I. Or rather I should say stands, as it is still there, virtually unchanged – including Mrs Whitfield's kindergarten extension and the netball pole – except for the peeling walls and the general signs of decay it shares with the rest of the city. When I took my wife to see where my school had been we were amazed to find it there though on reflection it is not at all remarkable in Cairo. Buildings are simply allowed to disintegrate over the centuries, gracefully or not, taking on different uses as needs change. Occasionally a fateful moment comes, usually when someone attempts to add on extra floors against regulations and beyond the capacity of the foundations, or when an equally prohibited extension digs away at a weight-bearing wall. That is when the building finally surrenders and crumbles into its original dust, invariably with considerable loss of life as there is always a multitude of people around.

Names of streets change but only up to a point. Sharia was translated into Avenue, Street or even Boulevard according to the grandeur or the modesty of the person who lived there as the word Sharia simply indicates that it is a passageway of sorts. In the early 1950s, Sharia or Rue Fouad I became the Avenue of the 26th of July to commemorate the military coup which the perpetrators claimed was a revolution. Few have any particular respect for the memory of King Fouad and much less for his son King Farouk. I suspect that not a single person regretted the latter's departure, and yet there was something wrong about the whole episode. Gamal Abdel Nasser and his fellow officers were no doubt right to get rid of him but it was not the popular revolution they claimed it to be. However well-meaning they were, they remain just another group that seized power by force as has happened throughout history, only this time claiming legitimacy from a new god – The People.

Perhaps that is why a Cairo taxi driver will take you to Sharia Fouad without further clarification even though its name has been expunged for fifty years and he himself is likely to have been born after that.

The Gezira Preparatory School was for both boys and girls and had been founded and run by a Mr and Mrs Bullen, with the help of an excellent teacher, Mrs Wilson, who also dominated the "English Children's Corner" on Cairo Radio under the name of "Auntie Barbara".

I was an avid listener of that programme, of the stories told and of the requests they played but I was not entirely pleased when I finally discovered that all the "Aunties" were also the teachers at school. After all, the "English Children's Corner" had acted as an alternative source of information about English things for me and the thought that there was only one single origin for everything I knew was disconcerting. It was as though I had discovered that both right- and left-wing newspapers were written by the same people using different pseudonyms or that the Republican and Democratic party leaders in America had been one and the same all along offering alternative policies under different names. Ever since then I have had doubts as to whether oppositions really existed.

Going to an English school meant that I was aware of things that my parents were not and gradually began to interpret for them and even explain to them things that they had not quite grasped. Needless to say I grew in their eyes, as the British and then the Americans emerged as our sole defence against extinction. Although my familiarity with the English-speaking world gave me an increasing sense of power over my parents, I did not relish it and quickly became aware that I would have preferred to rely on them intellectually rather than grasp the independence that so many young people seek.

The school not only had British teachers but I met and befriended many British children too. I say British rather than English as I began to recognise the subdivisions of what to us had been "*les Anglais*". These children were very insistent that they should be counted as Scots, Welsh or Irish while those who allowed themselves to be classified as English seemed to concede to them an extra dimension which, in a subtle way, gave them an element of superiority. The rarer the sub-group the greater seemed to be the respect accorded to it as I found when one boy announced himself to be Manx to universal acclaim. I think that this exceptional affection for minorities is peculiarly British though it has spilled over a little into the United States. I learned that whereas the French were appreciative of any effort to become as French as possible and were anxious to confer "Frenchness" to anyone willing to ape their culture and style while directing their xenophobia towards those who resisted, this did not apply to the British where any effort to claim unjustified "Britishness" was regarded with suspicion if not open hostility. I cannot pretend that I understood all that as soon as I arrived at the Gezira Preparatory School but I developed an awareness of the structure relatively early which served me well in life.

I found the English girls extremely attractive from every point of view and I have never lost my admiration. In the days before dental braces they mostly had protruding upper incisors and I found that genetic trait a sign of great and exotic beauty. When my own niece came to Guy's Hospital for her orthodontics I recalled the little girls at school and begged the surgeon concerned not to push her front teeth too far back. I have never discussed this with her and hope she is happy with what we gave her. The girls I knew had ordinary and banal names like Colette or Francine but the English girls evoked dreams. They were called Mary Kate or Peggy and there were the really dramatic ones like Pamela and Penelope and, of course, there was Daphne.

The boys too had impressive names like Dickie Chapman and Michael Teague though my favourite was Neville Ravensdale and I wanted to change my name to his. I raised it with my mother but she was horrified and insisted that the Douek and Sassoon names were of much greater distinction and that you cannot just go and be someone else whenever you like, so I dropped the matter. Many years later when I eventually came to live in England, a Home Office official suggested I alter my name to something which sounded more English. I was surprised as I did not see the point of his suggestion but I asked what he had in mind.

"Well," he said, "something like Davis, for instance."

I did not think I wanted that, so our name has remained the

same for another half century or more, but I wonder what I would have done had he suggested Neville Ravensdale.

Mr Bullen taught us Latin and it is these lessons that I remember best as again we simply learnt everything by heart. "Amo, amas, amat . . ." we would chant together as he beat the rhythm on his desk and I can still recite the verbs and the declensions now.

In his spare time Mr Bullen ran a magazine which brought together British writers and poets who were in Egypt during the war such as Lawrence Durrell and artists like Edward Bawden, though all I knew of him then was that he was a large red-faced man who died of a stroke one day, after a huge meal they said, as people nodded adding gravely: "Blood pressure" or "gin".

We wore grey shorts and white shirts with a pale blue tie and a grey cap which we were expected to doff when we passed a lady. This habit became so ingrained that even now, when driven by the cold to wear some sort of headgear I feel the urge to raise my hat though I have learnt to restrain myself as it may be seen as a mocking gesture and cause offence.

As the heat of the Egyptian spring took hold we changed to summer uniform and our shorts became light khaki twill while the crisp, white, cotton shirts were now short-sleeved and open-necked. We were not the only ones to change in this way. The police who had been wearing black felt uniforms suddenly turned out in gleaming white though the red tarbooshes remained the same, contrasting even more vividly with the rest of the uniform.

To me these seasonal changes seemed of the same order as those of nature. The jacaranda trees and the flamboyants along Rue Hassan Sabry produced their strikingly coloured flowers and then shed them, the Nile visibly rose into flood amid great festivities only to fall again, so the change of uniforms and the displacement of the whole government as well as the King to Alexandria in the summer were clearly ordained.

I took easily to the English language and to English ways and when the moment came for a visit from Sir Miles Lampson, later

Lord Killearn, the British Ambassador, I was chosen to dance round the maypole together with other fair-haired and blue-eyed children as we sang: "Come lasses and lads!" We were greatly impressed by Sir Miles Lampson as even we children knew that he had had Abdin Palace surrounded by tanks and placed King Farouk under something like house arrest. He had presented the King with an ultimatum and although I did not know what the word meant I realised from its unusual sound that it was something very serious.

We had danced well, weaving the coloured strands into a regular pattern that had come right down the maypole, so the Ambassador had asked for us to be introduced individually. He shook my hand and said: "Well done boy!" There could have been no doubt that I was a good representative of the British race and like them I began to yearn for "home" when it was "all over". I completely identified with Britain, that little island coloured red when I stuck the cut outs in my book on "Children of Different Lands". John, the English boy, lived in London and went to school in wellington boots because it rained so much. He was my dream and my ambition, and his picture in the rain came back to me every time I dropped my own children off at school in Hampstead, retelling them my story.

My parents were perplexed by all this as it had certainly not been their intention to live in England. On the other hand they did not want to confuse me and they listened to me declaim and yearningly describe this "home" with some amusement though I suspect they realised they had let loose an unexpected genii. After all, the French who had educated them had made all the little children in their class, however dark in complexion, recite to-gether: "*Nos ancêtres les Gaulois avaient de longues moustaches blondes.*" And they had a picture of a Gaul on the wall with long blond moustaches with whom they could identify, or at least accept as their ancestor.

I have seen many examples since of the power of this embracing

French habit. A friend from the Cameroons, at a time of protest while we were students in Paris, insisted that our ancestors had fought for our rights in the Revolution of 1789. When I pointed out that my ancestors had lived comfortably in the bosom of the Ottoman world and his were living in Africa at that time, he was profoundly taken aback. As far as he was concerned, he said, our cultural ancestors had fought for us even though not our genetic ones.

Although I was able to identify with the English, on the whole they held us at a distance. As I moved on from the Gezira Preparatory School to the English School in Heliopolis the discussions became more detailed. It was a wonderful school which took both boys and girls, and although we were separated in the classroom we enjoyed each other's company in the playground as well as in other activities.

Like other English schools we were divided into houses represented by different colours and named after individuals. Ours were the admirals of Queen Elizabeth (mine was Frobisher) and we were taught both to support our house and to be moderately hostile to the others. I was uncertain as to the purpose of this officially generated petty competitiveness but eventually, together with all the other puzzled nationalities, the Egyptians, the Chinese, the Syrians, the Lebanese and so on, I learned to join in enthusiastically both in love of Frobisher House and contempt for Drake, Raleigh and the others.

It was Mr Huntley who taught us about ancient Rome. Most of it is now forgotten except for this small comment. When talking about the end of the Roman Empire Mr Huntley said he believed that as the Barbarian hoards burst through the boundaries, the population along the fringes sought refuge in the heartland of Rome. His theory was that by the time the great City itself was threatened its population had become a motley lot. The Emperors themselves seemed to have been of mixed blood. After all, Justinian was a Goth hiding under a Roman name. Wasn't

Septimus Severus a Libyan? "A Libyan!" he would repeat rolling his eyes. As for Heliogabalus with his eccentric un-Roman deities, he was a Syrian, a Lebanese. What had happened, Mr Huntley explained sadly, was that this subtle incursion, this thinning of the original blood and adulteration of the Roman stock had weakened the moral fibre of the Empire and he looked straight at us when he said that, leaving me slightly uneasy.

When I first went to London aged fifteen, I rushed at once to Piccadilly Circus, to the lights and the crowds, to feel myself at last at home, in what I had been told was the very centre of the British Empire, my Empire. That was when the uneasiness came back as I remembered Mr Huntley looking at us, and I had to question whether my arrival was about to weaken the moral fibre.

10

Djins, Demons and Helpful Spirits

Egypt in my childhood consisted of two co-existing worlds. There was the obvious one of the men, women and children, a colourful world which included Paris fashions and men in European suits though some still wore the cylindrical red fez or tarboosh on their heads. There were the poorer folk where the girls wore the vivid pink, sky blue and pistachio green, what we called "baladi" or common colours. Their men would still wear the long robes or *galabeyas* that indicated not so much working-class status as many manual labourers already wore the more convenient trousers, but a determination to hang on to things past and a respect for simplicity and for traditional values.

The obvious world of Cairo and Alexandria was polyglot. It was normal to speak to the telephone operator in French or Italian, to the grocer in Greek or, again, French whose sounds dominated the cities, while all these languages took words from each other when appropriate. Even the Arabic spoken by the general population was infused with borrowed words, its impurities irritating the linguistically fastidious. The English spoke English though even they had begun to acquire expressions from other sources such as *bakshish*, which meant a tip, from Turkish. *Ma'alesh* too, which came from the Arabic, had become a ubiquitous, indeed essential word, which is sorely lacking in most other languages so everyone used it all the time. It is supposed to mean "never mind", but there is much more to it as it implies that some things do not really matter and also that you should take a more relaxed view of the unimportant things in life. All that could be understood from a single word, which, infuriating as it was to the Western mind, would make Europeans feel that they were, perhaps, over-reacting to trivial events such as the plumber not turning up, or a job not being completed. Nowhere was linguistic fusion so elaborate as in children's conversation and particularly in the rhythmic songs which were usually accompanied by hand clapping in Arabic style, with the hands held wide open and the fingers spread out.

Fatma veux-tu une gazma g'dida pour aller en foss-ha b'ida?
La! La! La ya omi la! Ce n'est pas ça ma mala'tia.
You! You! *Quelle mère j'ai qui n'entend pas le doux mal de sa Fatma!*
You! You! *Quelle mère j'ai qui n'entend pas le doux mal que j'ai!*

Even a working knowledge of both Arabic and French and some Italian would not have made this ditty entirely comprehensible and yet as children we understood it all perfectly well as if it was in a secret language of our own.

The variety of sounds and languages exhibited by this visible world was accompanied by a varied range of skin colour seldom seen elsewhere, from the pink face of my Panama-hatted *Oncle* Victor to the shiny black Nilotic features of Gamal, the dignified concierge at the Baehler Buildings.

This was the busy world we could see but everyone was conscious of other unseen worlds filled with equally busy and equally colourful spirits as the spirit world was itself a reflection of the mixed and multi-lingual visible one. It was full of *djins* and demons and *afreets* of every description and there were also benign, protective and healing spirits roaming around.

Though, of course, fearsome and dangerous, there was nothing too mysterious about this second world. Its inhabitants, good and bad were well known and lived amongst us and the *babula* was often discussed privately by us children as we knew that our parents would barefacedly deny its existence if the subject were raised.

"Do you believe in the *babula*?" I was asked as often as, in later years, I was questioned about my belief in God.

We agreed that it came out mostly at night, lurking during the day in secret places, though we could never come to a consensus regarding what it might do to us or what it looked like. Teenagers amused themselves by frightening little children and nannies saw it as a useful threat for keeping their charges in order. Maria was not like that – the Catholic priests made her wary of such pagan ideas – but even she could not resist some curiosity when the neighbours' maid showed signs of instability.

Adila, who had always exhibited hysterical tendencies had now actually seen an *afreet* – it had sat on her shoulder and she had even noted that it wore a *tartur*, a type of round headgear. The servants were certain that the only thing that could help her was an exorcism – a *zahr* – but her mistress had refused permission to hold it in her apartment. She was a rather superior Swiss lady, scornful of such primitive beliefs and besides it was quackery and against the law even though the lower ranks of the police usually turned a blind eye. Eventually it was agreed that a *zahr* would take place but upstairs in Adila's tiny room in the servants' quarters so that the Swiss lady need have nothing to do with it. I was intrigued and Maria herself interested enough to take me upstairs to observe the ritual though we both knew that we should not mention it to my mother.

The door was open and I peeped in to see Adila throwing herself about, screaming that she was possessed and slapping her own tear-stained face in despair.

The organisers arrived: a man with a drum, another with a sort of trumpet, and the third was a fat, lugubrious Nubian woman, hung with necklaces and trinkets. Adila's room was very small and half the servants of the district seemed to have congregated there to watch the exorcism. They clustered around the door taking turns to peep at the ceremony going on inside.

The leader began to beat the drum and the procedure started at once. The trio had other clients to attend to – there were all sorts of *afreets* to exorcise. Because of the lack of space the drummer stood outside and beating slowly and rhythmically, while the Nubian woman got Adila to stand by her side, arms hanging loosely. With every beat the two women, eyes shut, flopped to one side and then to the other. Very gradually the beat got faster and the movement to right and left became more convulsive as the women breathed faster still. The crowd pressed closer to try and get a look and I managed to squeeze between people's legs, looking upwards at the enormous breasts and potbelly of the Nubian flopping from side to side. Adila, young and slim, was copying but her motion was more of a twist at the waist and more extreme, until she literally threw herself from side to side.

Suddenly the trumpeter gave a long squeak – everyone had forgotten his existence so the sound was unexpected. The Nubian stopped and began to shudder, her eyes opened wide, rolled upwards so that the irises disappeared, and looked completely white. I was transfixed by the sight but then Adila fell to the ground and, foaming at the mouth, her limbs contorted and she began to fit. As the drum beats slowed down in time with each of her convulsions the drummer controlled the rhythm of her move-ments from faster to slower jerks. At last, exhausted, Adila was lifted up and placed on her bed while the trio was paid off by one of the servants.

Although my mother expressed disgust at such practices she was as tainted as everyone else in the country. She read Freud avidly and knew about vitamins as soon as they were discovered but she allowed our more credulous relatives to pin little pieces of jewellery incorporating blue pearls on to our clothing provided they were discreetly placed and looked decorative in their own right. Blue pearls were protective against the Evil Eye.

My mother had taken me for a walk in the Esbekieh Gardens, then in their full glory as the numerous roads and bypasses had not yet cut them into shreds of patchy turf. I remember my warm contentment as there was just her and me. She sat on a bench next to an Egyptian woman who also had a small boy with whom I quickly began to turn somersaults on the grass.

The woman wore traditional clothes, a pink dress of a tone which my mother called *"rose bonbon"* after the French sugared almonds that one can still buy in Paris, and was swathed in a finely-woven black *abaya* which also modestly covered her head. In retrospect I think she was probably well-to-do as her arms and ankles were encased in gold bangles. She must have been keen to move with the times as her face was not covered by a veil, but the blue tattoos on her lower lip and chin revealed her background. She had come to town from the villages, the wife of a successful peasant.

"Sabakh el-kheir!"

The ladies talked formally to each other – thanking God in the expectation of a happy morning and a fruitful day. Then the woman turned her attention to me. "How old is your little girl?" she asked. I stopped my somersaults in dismay and shouted that I was a boy but my mother shushed me with her hand.

"It is a pity she is so plain, you will never get her married off."

My mother responded with equally insulting remarks about the woman's daughter as I shouted: "He's a boy! He's a boy!"

I was silenced by the enormity of the adult conflict only to see the two mothers part company smiling at each other and loudly thanking God for his bounty and his clemency.

Later my mother had tried to explain the Egyptians' fear of the Evil Eye and how drawing attention to a beloved boy would attract the malicious demons, *djins* and *afreets* to damage or even destroy him. Then, as an afterthought as she knew she had to explain away my baby sister, she added that a plain girl could be a burden on a village family so the demons would lose interest. Not, of course, that this could apply to our own pretty baby.

I became familiar with this widespread belief though it did not affect our neighbours on the third floor of the Baehler Buildings in Zamalek as they had had five daughters with curly hair in quick succession and they seemed to love them all equally. The fifth birthday of the fifth girl was an auspicious occasion as the figure five also had magical properties. It represented the hand warding off evil intent, and to say *"Hamsa alek"* or "five be upon you" was protective. We were invited to the party and the mother had added in her invitation that there would be five times five children so we would be well-covered. The birthday girl, who was actually called Hamsa, which also means five, did not seem to be around and when the fateful moment came, the cake and candles were presented to a familiar looking boy, whom we had at first taken to be a cousin. He was Hamsa, now called Samir, shorn of his curly hair.

The parents, with some embarrassment at being caught in this clash of cultures, explained that things had gone too well for them. They had four pretty daughters and the husband had been appointed managing director when, to their indescribable joy, she had given birth to a boy. Their anxiety about the Evil Eye was such that they had followed the advice of a specialist in such matters on the recommendation of a grandmother, to the extent of deceiving anyone who might cast the Eye, as envious relatives were far from excluded from evil intent.

Not all spirits were bad, however. Many were very helpful, sharing the occult world with the *djins* and *afreets* and the visible one with us. The Jews, for instance, venerated what they called the tomb of the sage Moses Maimonides. In fact it was not his tomb at all but the little room where the great twelfth-century physician had carried out his business, though his body had been placed there before being taken to Jerusalem for burial so a case could be made for his healing spirit to be still there. This famous doctor and rabbi referred to generally as *Rab Moshé* or Rabbi Moses, a rationalist who had dismissed magic and amulets in his writings on the practice of medicine, was also known for his hard work. He would take off on his donkey at dawn, riding to the

Citadel to carry out his clinical duties at the Court of Saladin, and then all the way back to the queue of patients waiting for him until the Sultan presented him with a white steed to hurry him on, presumably in case of emergencies.

Many Jews, as well as Christians and Moslems, when seriously ill would spend the night in this room desperately hoping that his curative essence was still around. When King Fouad was terminally ill and could not be moved, his pyjamas were placed overnight in Maimonides' room. This was a feather in the cap for the Jews but unfortunately the Rabbi's spirit could not help the king and he died.

There were other holy places where one could make requests and Matariya was one such. It was there the Christians revered an old tree where the Holy family was believed to have taken shelter when crossing the desert on the flight to Egypt. Pilgrims, Jews and Moslems as well as Christians made their way to Matariya on special occasions. Again there was no ethnic or religious divide among the superstitious in Egypt. My nanny Maria, a devout Catholic, held this Tree of the Holy Family in deep reverence. From time to time she went on the pilgrimage accompanying a group of Italian nuns from the Convent of San Francesco. She told me that she prayed for forgiveness though what she had done wrong remained a mystery to me. She was a most upright, faultless and deeply religious woman.

Nevertheless, prayer to the saints definitely helped her, especially if they were depicted in tangible form such as a statue. The Moslems and Jews who were forbidden statues, found the tree which had given shelter to the Holy Family generally acceptable. Everyone was in agreement that spirits like the *afreet* that had frightened Adila, which had intruded into the visible world, were harmful and demanded exorcism. Good spirits, everyone also agreed, were creatures of the mind and of the emotions though sometimes they presented themselves in a peculiar manner as in the case of a *marabout*, the tomb of a holy sheikh outside Alexandria. His life and qualities had been forgotten with time but for some reason his tomb was believed to help with infertility.

In a country where polygamy was still practised in the villages and where infertility was generally accepted to be the fault of the woman, a childless marriage was a serious threat to the status of a wife and this had led to a steady stream of anxious girls making their way to the *marabout*. Despite its sexual connotations I had always assumed they just prayed for a baby but when I was fourteen and we spent our summer holiday in Alexandria I heard a different story from a rather unsavoury boy called Momo. The *marabout* had a keeper, a young man who had epileptic fits and whose brain functioned only slowly. His main pleasure was to spin himself round and round, his arms outstretched, until he became dizzy and fell to the ground. It was he who collected the money from the visitors and he was called Aboud. Momo claimed that for an extra fee Aboud would lift up his *galabeya* exposing his penis and allow the women to masturbate him.

"No!" I shouted in titillated horror. "Impossible!" But his story was confirmed by Yorgo, a Greek boy, who said he had heard about this and other worse things going on at the *marabout*. He would not say what but as he was not coy we assumed he did not really know and was repeating the fragments of conversations he had overheard.

Led by Momo we went to the *marabout* but there were no infertile women there, only Aboud twirling round and round like a dervish.

"Hey! Aboud!" shouted Momo. "Show us your willy, we'll pay you."

But Aboud threw stones at us and we never learned the truth. Momo said philosophically that one way or another they must get babies or they would not keep going there.

I also do not know if the spirits, benign or malignant, came with us to Europe. I am certainly no longer frightened of the *babula*, which we had feared when as children we had played at the Grotto Gardens in Zamalek, and which we firmly believed lived in the cavern, behind the metal door in the aquarium. I once saw the gardener open it though, and it was only a broom cupboard. This had worried me at the time as now I did not even know where the *babula* rested while getting ready to pounce and eat me.

Yet there are still puzzling things that we cannot control in the visible world and I pondered on this many decades later when listening to the young doctors at Guy's Hospital trying to explain the death of a patient. They had intervened with every tool that our advanced technology could provide and yet relentlessly, irrevocably, the patient had gone downhill. They turned to us, the older experienced ones asking for a reason and we had none to give.

Then my colleague and old friend from the English School, Omar Shaheen, the cancer surgeon, whispered in my ear: "You know, in the country we both come from, they would have said: it was written."

11

Touching the War

In the year 2000 I was invited to explain the nature of noise-induced hearing loss on television. I had become an expert on the subject and had been called on many times, but this interview was part of the news and had a political content which was to try to elucidate the facts behind the government's decision not to increase the pensions of men who had been deafened by gunfire during the war. I was grateful for our Civil Servants' zeal in containing expenditure but this seemed unnecessary as these were extremely old men who were rapidly dying off and the saving would have been negligible.

Looking for an illustration, I explained that as a small child I had heard the bombardment of the battle of Alamein day and night from as far away as Cairo. I could even remember the vibrations under my feet.

"Imagine the noise level for those actually involved!" I said passionately, gesticulating into the camera. "All that is left of these people now are the deaf old men who can benefit from digital hearing aids if only to talk to their grandchildren for just a few years or months. These men saved my life!"

That passage was cut from the broadcast. "Too emotional," the producer had said. "An expert should stick to the facts."

That battle in 1942 had been a reality for me as our lives altered abruptly. Although I could not have been fully aware of the implications for us if the Germans had been victorious, it was very clear to everyone, even the children, that a momentous turn for the better had taken place.

What I remember from before the battle was mainly gloom. From time to time small contingents of dejected soldiers walked along Rue Fouad I exhausted and out of step, occasionally requesting a glass of water from the Europeans who approached asking for news from the front. Thumbs-down signs soon became familiar. Once I was lifted into a tank that had broken down and spoke to the crew in English. It was hot and smelly and I experienced my first feeling of claustrophobia so I decided there and then that I would not become a tank commander. Such a decision was not just childishness as in time of war all children take part, at least in their minds. We played with guns, we took turns to be the Germans which meant exerting a degree of self-control difficult for children as we could not get carried away and win. We focussed our fear and hate on images of Hitler, Mussolini and Hirohito which we used for target practice with the dangerous projectile toys we had, now fortunately forbidden. We knew we could depend on Churchill, and in time on Stalin and Roosevelt, as we could rely on our parents to protect us.

We had silhouettes of military aeroplanes everywhere, even on classroom walls, so that we could learn to identify them and take cover if necessary. Even now when film footage of the war appears on television I can recognise a Stuka or a Heinkel, a Lancaster bomber or a Flying Fortress although my wife seems uncertain as to whether she should believe me.

I remember the manner in which a couple of pieces of wood tied together with string could become a weapon. I can recall the sense that it was a gun and yet it wasn't and it is that memory which helped me as a doctor when I first began to participate in developing play to help children with communication problems though not, obviously, with firearms.

Our parents were clearly awed by the intensity of our war play and re-enactment of battles, especially with the sounds we made as we imitated sirens and the noise of bombs falling, and best of all, pretending to be choking and dying. Somewhat embarrassed they watched our activities. I realise now that, as with so many other forms of behaviour, there are some things that are all right for children but not for adults. When I watch the news and see people burning effigies of their perceived enemies and going through war-like motions with useless weapons, I wonder whether this is an adult example of play-acting and what it means when displaced in this way.

We were joined at school by refugee children, but we ourselves were not subjected to real war. Alexandria, a port, was regularly bombed but Cairo was attacked only occasionally and to no major effect. We went through the motions though, and were issued with gas masks which became toys. All mirrors had sticky tapes criss-crossing them and thin blue muslin net was stuck on to all glass window panes to prevent the light being too bright at night as well as to prevent shattering. I grew up in that world so that when the danger was over and the tapes and the blue material were joyfully scraped off by my mother and Maria leading the servants in what was a party atmosphere, the house seemed unpleasant and naked to me.

During the alerts at night all of the Baehler Building's residents would troop down to the basement and as nothing bad ever happened it was very exciting. My grandfather would go out in his pyjamas and dressing gown visiting his children's families in their basements. I was amazed that it was in order to wander about in the street in one's dressing gown, so I learned that if necessary, conventions could be abandoned and everything became possible.

I have always felt that I know what war was about, what people had to do in such circumstances and I believe it coloured my later actions. When I was called up for National Service I did not seek exemption as did so many young doctors. It was peacetime then, of course, but I think that even if it had been war I would have wanted to go simply to be part of the twentieth century, my century.

Maria still took us for walks to the Grotto Gardens, but now they were full of soldiers on leave, some of them so young they delighted in playing ball with us. We soon learned to recognise the innumerable nationalities that now formed the Eighth Army, New Zealanders and Australians, turbaned Indian soldiers and black regiments from Africa. Then there were remnants of the defeated armies of Europe with shoulder tabs indicating Greece, Czechoslovakia, Belgium and so many others that we learnt to look up in our atlas.

Whenever we found soldiers who bore "Yugoslavia" we would grasp them by the hand dragging them to where the Slovene nannies were sitting in the hope that they had information to exchange. In time we realised that things were more complex in Yugoslavia and that the nannies were not fond of the Croats and particularly not of the Serbs. There was another complication though that did not bother the nannies; some soldiers had a red star on their caps for Tito while others had a gold crown for Mihailovitch. Words like *communists* and *France Libre* began to appear on my horizon for the first time.

A Free Frenchman brought a cheese as a present to my Aunt Germaine and she invited all her sisters and their husbands to share it. How he had come by it in North Africa where he had been fighting no one knew but the cheese was supposed to be such an experience that I wanted to taste it too.

"Absolutely not," the sisters had said, for once in one voice. "That cheese is not for children, it is extremely rare. Besides you would hate it, it smells so bad."

"Like unwashed feet," Aunt Giselle had added.

"Disgusting, you could not bear to be anywhere near, ugh!" said Aunt Marcelle who was prone to exaggeration.

Of course I did not believe them. If it was so bad why did they want to eat it so much? I could recognise unfairness when I saw it and I retained the name of that cheese, it was called *camembert*.

There are always adult mysteries in time of stress and I was often told that my ears were too big and that I should not be listening to their conversation though my parents took the view that it was better for me to hear what was going on provided I did not ask too many stupid questions.

"Why does Dr Picard . . . ?" I had begun

"Professor!" my mother interrupted, "Professor Picard. You know how he gets offended if we call him doctor."

Professor Picard had been the senior surgeon in a Berlin hospital and when he lost his job he was lucky to be offered a post at the Jewish Hospital in Cairo. Although this invitation had saved his life he took out his mortification at this demotion on the local Jews. He had had no interest in Jewish things, his wife was not Jewish, and he had made it in the gentile world with a top professorship only to be kicked out without ceremony and replaced by a less competent Aryan, a "Nazi imbecile", as he kept insisting whenever the matter came up.

The Jewish community of Cairo was conscious of their good fortune at having acquired such a renowned surgeon for their hospital even though the way it happened had been so unfortunate. But, as Dr Riso-Levy had put it, where medicine is concerned one country's loss is always another's gain. Though Professor Picard was treated with great deference this seemed only to rankle further and make him even more embittered at his reduced circumstances.

"Why," I repeated correcting myself, "does Professor Picard want the Germans to win?"

"Of course he doesn't!" my mother exploded. "How can you say such an idiotic thing? He ran away from Germany, if they catch him they will kill him!"

Professor Picard had retained his admiration for the Germans, for German culture, which he considered superior to all others, and for German efficiency. It was obvious that he would really have liked to have been one of them and I wondered how he explained his own fall from grace. Did he feel that a terrible mistake had been made in his case or did he actually sympathise with their decision to get rid of him? Did he feel, perhaps, that he would have done the same as them in different circumstances? I may, in retrospect, be judging him unfairly but that is the impression he made on me and I have been reminded of this on many occasions when I have observed people, often very distinguished people, trying to ingratiate themselves with those who despise them.

"You do not understand their efficiency, their strength of purpose," he would say, exasperated. "They will make mincemeat of this raggle-taggle army. As for the British commanders, just look at them. They are so relaxed they won't know what hit them. I assure you, you have not seen such a military machine."

"But," someone timidly intervened, as few would question Professor Picard's knowledge of the German Army, "we have a new commander."

"What?" Professor Picard interrupted contemptuously "Are you comparing Montgomery with Rommel? Rommel is a genius, Montgomery a clown."

That was also a time when people prayed a good deal. There were services at All Saints, the Anglican cathedral in which the schools participated. Although my own family was not religious they thought it was time for me to start Hebrew lessons. "If we go, we will have to go with our own people," my father had said "so he might as well know what it is about."

"Go where?" I asked, but I was now old enough to add, "I know, I know. No more stupid questions."

My teacher was a Mr Chichek, a Bulgarian with a beautiful tenor voice who was also the cantor at *Le Grand Temple* in the Rue Adly. I learned the Hebrew alphabet and I must have learnt the rudiments of Judaism from him. I talked a lot with Mr Chichek and he tried to teach me to sing the Psalms but I had no voice and he soon gave up. He seemed so despondent about this that I wanted to divert his attention by praising him instead and commented on his own wonderful voice. I said he could have been an opera singer. His eyes misted up and he told me about the time he had been in the trenches in the First World War and they had received such a terrible battering that the soldiers were totally demoralised. At that moment he had begun to sing an uplifting song and gradually the soldiers had joined in. The King of Bulgaria, King Boris was at the front and asked for him to come forward.

"And what is your name, singing soldier?" the King had asked.

"Chichekov, Your Majesty, I replied." Mr Chichek remembered. "In Bulgarian my name was Chichekov and I dropped the '-ov' later. But we lost and, well perhaps things could have been different."

"But what side were you on then, Mr Chichek?" I asked.

"On the side of those monsters!" he said, but his tears had now turned to anger.

My parents told me much later that everyone had different thoughts on what to do in case of German victory and they discussed it all the time. It was too late to contemplate evacuation by sea to South Africa as after the last ship to leave had been sunk no further departures were planned. Everyone knew that if Egypt fell there would be no defence beyond the Suez Canal and the Germans would be in Palestine within hours, so fleeing there was pointless. Besides there would inevitably be an Arab uprising as the Grand Mufti of Jerusalem, now safe in Berlin, was calling for a massacre of all the Jews. In the end they thought they would leave us with Maria, who had an Italian passport, with false papers indicating we were her children, while my parents would get hold of poison. Though this was obviously kept from me, I was well aware that they were very depressed.

When the Day of Atonement came in 1942 *Le Grand Temple* was so crowded that the congregation spilled over on to the pavement and into Rue Adly itself. My mother, whose family liked to profess disdain for the religious, noticed Dr Riso-Levy as we entered.

"Guido!" she called out. "I thought you were an atheist? What are you doing here?"

"It is neither here nor there," he said. "No one will care who is an atheist and who is not when we go. I want to be with the rest of you while we wait."

The Chief Rabbi, Haim Nahum Effendi, had been a renowned Turkish scholar when the Egyptian Jewish community begged him to be their rabbi, more because he had been a diplomat connected to the Young Turk Party than for his rabbinical reputation. He was almost blind and wore dark glasses to protect his remaining eyesight. He knew that his diplomatic skills would now, more than ever before, be tested. King Fouad had been very fond of him and always dropped in to the synagogue on the Day of Atonement. There was always a little scuffle as the King tried to kiss the rabbi's hand and Haim Nahum pulled it away in modesty, as they talked in Turkish. There would be nothing like that now as Farouk had sent only the lowliest official he decently could to acknowledge the Day, yet another sign that things were not good for the Jews.

There was one aspect which was not crushing in its hopelessness and that was the large number of soldiers wearing prayer shawls over their khaki uniforms – this had never been seen before. The Jews of Egypt were amazed as these were not only British soldiers, but also Australians and New Zealanders with strange broad-brimmed hats. There seemed to be Jews in all the various contingents of the Eighth Army.

"They will defend us, you'll see," my mother said quietly.

When it came to the Kol Nidrei, perhaps the holiest point in the liturgy, I waited to hear Mr Chicheck but instead he led a young Australian soldier to the pulpit. Everyone stood silent as this should have been Mr Chicheck's greatest moment of the whole year. Instead he said: "This soldier will sing the Kol Nidrei."

"He looks like a child!" my mother said.

The young soldier sang beautifully, encouraged by Mr Chicheck, as people wept for our fate.

"Why do we sing '*Kol* Nidrei' when it is written '*Kal*'" I asked my father quietly, as I could read the letters now.

"I think it is Aramaic," he replied, uncertain.

What was Aramaic? That was new to me, I would have to ask Mr Chicheck. I hoped the Germans would not come and kill us, not because I was frightened, but because Aramaic was so old and it would cease if we died.

As we left *Le Grand Temple* and walked along Rue Adly people taunted us.

"Soon the Germans will come and they will cut your throats!"

"Once the British are gone you can say goodbye, we will finish you off!"

The next day the Italian ladies who lived in the building across the road began to hang Italian flags on the balcony as everyone had heard that the Germans had arrived at Amriyeh, in the suburbs of Cairo. Then it turned out that it was only a single unit that had got lost in the desert behind British lines and had surrendered at once as they were thirsty and starving. My father called the Military Police who came and took away the flags but left the women alone.

"They are harmless," the officer told my father.

That was the time when I first realised that not everyone was on our side or cared what might happen to us. I was troubled enough to put it to my father. How could anyone want these evil people to win? How could ordinary persons in the street, or these nice Italian ladies whom we knew, not care whether we were taken away and killed, as no one had any doubts about what would happen? But he shrugged his shoulders as he had no answer.

"It is just the way of the world," he said.

Every night my parents went out to friends and Maria sat by the radio in the dark. She toyed with the tuner until we could hear:

"Boum-boum-boum-boum! Boum-boum-boum-boum!" the resonant tones of Beethoven's 5th Symphony and then the chimes of Big Ben which went on to the bitter end to give a chance to the listeners to compose themselves. "London calling!" Then incomprehensible words came out as Maria glued her ear to the set, for it was the news in Slovene.

"What does it say?"

"Shh! I can't hear with the static, but Tito is fighting in the mountains above Batuje!"

Then one night my mother called. I did not know where they were but there was a party going on, I could hear the music and the sound of excited voices.

"We have won!" she said. "The battle of el-Alamein is finally won, the Germans have been completely defeated!"

"Are you sure?" I asked.

"Yes," she said, "quite sure. It will be all right now. We'll survive!"

12

Sugaring the Women

There are moments, though they are usually brief, when for some people in a particular place, life seems like an earthly paradise. That was our good fortune after the battle of el-Alamein and our luck lasted about four or five years. For a child, though, it seems like a whole life and as one grows older and looks back it is an entire childhood that glows in this contented light. On the whole I feel that a good time is worth having whatever people say about bad experiences strengthening the character. As far as I am concerned, a certain optimistic note has been added to my nature for which I am grateful and I hope that I have passed it on to those I have touched. Of course there are many other factors involved and in my case my nanny Maria was an important one.

Her own philosophy has been shared by many poor peasants, reassured by the local priest, that their present misery would see them settled in heaven when the time came. Maria had a special problem, however, as she had long ceased to be the poverty-stricken peasant for whom her philosophy had been designed and, although technically poor herself, she shared all the advantages of a middle-class, even colonial existence, as all the comforts of good food and the service of others were available to her. Once we were at school she had literally nothing to do as Awad did the cooking and the cleaner cleaned, Gamal the concierge carried her bags and Om Labib came to do the washing, leaving Maria to struggle against the gluttony and laziness which she recognised and feared as deadly sins.

It was not that the priests were dismissive as they understood her predicament only too well and they took her confessions seriously, giving her helpful little prayers to recite. In the circumstances she was content regarding her present existence but uneasy about her chances in the afterlife. As I grew older, we had long talks about her anxieties and I do not see how, at such a young age, I could have escaped being influenced.

She had, of course, evolved her own philosophy that we are born with a total amount of happiness and suffering which has to last us for both the present and the life to come. She saw suffering and misery as vouchers which could be exchanged, when all things came to the reckoning. This meant that every miserable period in her life was to be welcomed as it would contribute to the final discount. A number of minor unhappy episodes was the ideal as each counted in her favour while none need be unacceptably destructive in its own right. Although I grew to become affectionately amused by her way of facing life, when I look back now I have to recognise the origin of much of what has been my own approach.

I suspect that Maria may be responsible for the surge of optimism, almost of satisfaction, which I still experience when struck by adversity – she brought me up to expect a plus in return for each minus, even though for me it has had to be limited to this life, as I do not have the benefit of the necessary dimension to extend my own accounts into the next.

Some years ago my sister Claudia contributed an article "The Most Influential Character in my Life" to a weekend colour supplement. She described Maria. No doubt my mother would have been mortified had she been alive and she would never have imagined that the influence of such a simple and unsophisticated woman could stretch so far into our later lives.

After the battle of el-Alamein, home life relaxed at once and the newspapers generally brought good news. My parents went out a great deal and there were many parties, card games and the entertainment of troops whose own futures were unlikely to be as idyllic as ours as they were yet to be deployed in the invasions of Sicily and later Normandy. To us children the release of tension was tangible and though I was kept informed of what was happening elsewhere, I think that was when I first understood how exciting victory is.

Egypt was a land of plenty and though there were some shortages this did not apply to the moneyed classes. It was the only instance that I know of where rationing was based on income. The rich, for instance could have as much oil and sugar as they wished whereas the poor were only entitled to a lesser amount. When, in adult life, I could hardly believe the enormity of such a system and enquired further, it was explained that the poor were entitled to as much as they could buy anyway. If they were given a bigger ration than they could afford they would only sell it to those who could, giving rise to a black market.

As children it was not so much oil that mattered to us as sugar. What had been used before sugar? I suppose it was honey, but for us it was the sucrose that came from the cane, the only source until the northern Europeans destroyed the livelihood of so many people who lived in warm sunny climates by growing sugar beet. We were insatiable for sugar in any form.

Our favourite was a segment of the cane itself which was chopped into manageable lengths, and the hard chittinous skin peeled off with a sharp knife leaving the fibrous core to chew and spit out. With each bite the miraculously sweet sap would fill the mouth, trickling out at the corners, leaving a white residue on cheeks and chin. Not to lose even that, we licked it off with our agile childish tongues.

Cane fields would beckon and seduce everywhere in the season, siren songs of the fields, but my greatest cravings came during the train journeys to Alexandria or Helwan. At every stop in the little towns and villages of lower Egypt with names such as

Benha and Tantah, Damanhur and Kafr el-Dawar, vendors would push their wares through the windows of the train. Sticky cakes and home-made sweets, Coca-Cola and Pepsi, but most enticing of all, the sticks of cane peeled and moistened in suspect water. I was jealous of the children who were allowed to buy them, a dozen for a single piastre, and they generously offered me a share. I bitterly resented my mother's fastidiousness which forced me to refuse. I never told the other boys that she steeped all our fruit in potassium permanganate to disinfect it, then rinsed off the purple colour with boiled water herself as, despite his protestations, she was convinced that Awad did not really accept her concepts of bacteriology. The unsatisfied craving still rankles like an incubus and the memory of the proffered sugar cane remains vivid even now.

There was another, unexpected, use for sugar. It was *halawah*. *Halawah* is the crushed sugary sesame seed cake that comes from the eastern Mediterranean, its strong sweet taste belying the dull grey colour. But when Om Labib, the washerwoman, came to do the *halawah* it meant something else. It meant the sugaring of the women and it was a great occasion for the children.

I cannot remember how often it was done. Certainly not often enough to become commonplace as my mother and her sisters were fair-haired and light-skinned. On those days these young women would gather together, in a party atmosphere and Om Labib would come in a different capacity, arriving at the front door and not the back as when she came to do the washing. She was punctual and when the doorbell rang the excitement was great as the children jumped up and down shouting "Om Labib! Om Labib!" She entered like a queen, a half-smile on her face.

Om Labib tended on the whole to be rather cross. Normally she would collect the washing once a week and take it to the roof of the building where it was all done by hand. She would add the little muslin bag containing the blue dye which in some mysterious way would bleach the clothes as they were dried by the sun in the unpolluted air of the time and end up crisp and white.

She did the sugaring as a sideline, her natural bossiness exposed by the opportunity to give orders to the sisters, pushing them around, determining whose turn it was next, even making personal comments on their appearance. In that manifestation Om Labib was a different person and when, so much later, I came to read novels on the early years of Soviet Russia by Igor Gouzenko, Arthur Koestler and Boris Pasternak the unforgiving figure of the servant turned commissar invariably evoked the image of Om Labib when she came to do the sugaring.

To the children the whole process was fascinating especially as it involved the handling of sweets. The sugar itself was purchased in bulk, in the shape of cones about a foot high, wrapped in thick dark-blue paper which we were allowed to help unwrap.

The excitement mounted as the sugar was heated into a sticky mess and then applied to the skin as the young women yelped in apprehension. At that point Om Labib came into her element, exposing a streak of cruelty as she tore off the hardened sugar, and an impertinence which was only just permissible because of the need to keep the women under control.

"*Eskot ya Set!*" she would hiss between gritted teeth. "Shut up, O Lady!" Some of my aunts affected a stoic unconcern while others, according to their nature, demonstrated an exaggerated fear. The odd one even showed the signs of the hysteria which would dominate her later years.

The delight of the children and the reason for our presence was not to hear our mothers scream although that too had its interest. It was the sugar which we gleaned, stuffing the drops which splashed around us into our mouth, gradually collecting the rivulets which had formed and then hardened. As greed promoted competition we stole bigger pieces so the mothers complained and Om Labib would shout "*Bas ya walad!*" "Enough O Boy!"

Awad, disliked Om Labib. She was argumentative and confrontational and always got the better of him. "I remember her," he mused, "when she was only called Fatmah and crawled along the edge of the pavement, eyes down. Since Labib was born she is a different woman." He imitated the way she walked now, head high, her look contemptuous, her hips thrust from side to side, pushing anyone in her way.

Poor Egyptian women, even those who were married, had little security as the husband could divorce them on a whim. The birth of a son completely changed their position, he brought status, he meant power, and he could not divorce his mother. That was why they insisted on being known, not by their own name, certainly not by that of an unreliable husband, but triumphantly as the mother of their son and that was why the mousy little Fatmah had been reincarnated as the proud mother of Labib.

This Labib, whose presence gave such importance and security to his mother that she could browbeat Awad and speak insolently to the sisters, assumed growing proportions in my mind. He must be tall and strong, perhaps a soldier or a policeman. When my mother one day said that Labib had come and was up on the roof with his mother and would I like to go and see him, I rushed up in excitement. There he was in Om Labib's arms as she showed him around with pride, the source of all her authority. Labib was two and a half years old.

Awad, too, had had his problems as one day he had asked unexpectedly for time off to return to his village for a few days. He had not so much requested as demanded leave tersely without giving a reason and making it clear that he was going anyway. Indeed his demeanour was so out of character that my mother became suspicious, eventually prying the real story out of him. It seemed that his mother had summoned him back as the village 'omdeh, a bully who had proclaimed himself the local authority, had encroached on a few metres of the poor widow's tiny land-holding and had refused to give way.

My mother, seeing Awad's look of despair, realised that one

way or another murder would be the likely outcome, if not a blood feud, and she forbad him to go, insisting that she would deal with the matter herself. In front of Awad she telephoned Ibrahim Pasha Amer, a close family friend, whose son-in-law was a member of parliament and who in turn agreed to put in a request for the Minister of Agriculture, himself an old school friend, to enquire as to what was going on in the village. Everything was quickly sorted out with the 'omdeh withdrawing his claim, and Ahmad, Awad's cousin reported that his power had collapsed as if by magic.

"That Awad," everyone in the village said, "has a long hand. What a comfort it is to have a son like that!"

Awad's problems came back to me decades later when, as a Captain in the British Army, I had to face an eighteen-year-old National Serviceman brought to me by his friends to stop him deserting and returning back home to Liverpool.

"Because Major Garelly wouldn't give me leave," he had replied when I had asked him why he was risking prison by running away.

I, too, as my mother had with Awad, found out what had happened when he handed me a scruffy piece of paper on which was written in capital letters: "YOUR WIFE TRACY IS HAVIN IT OFF WITH HER OLD BOYFRIEND JOHN."

He may have been only eighteen and weeping but then I was only twenty-four though I knew that somehow or other it was for me to sort out.

The Sudanese and the Nubians, who were very good looking and very black, were considered by my family to be outstandingly honourable, morally a cut above the Egyptians of the region of the delta and my parents' confidence grew the further south they came from. 'Abdu, the chauffeur, who had been hired initially to take my grandmother about, was a Nubian.

As soon as the war had ended and cars could again be imported my father bought a modest little Morris Minor as he eschewed the garish or obtrusive but I was deeply mortified. All the fathers of my fellow pupils were buying cars after those years of deprivation and the talk among the boys was almost exclusively about the relative merits of the various makes. American cars were by far the most admired but when I had timidly suggested we buy a Studebaker with which I was in love because its silver tail fins made it look like science fiction, my parents stared at me in disbelief.

"Are you mad?" my father had said witheringly, not hiding his amazement at my lack of taste. "It is made of tin. The Morris is a good make."

Although I never had the courage to raise the matter again, I dreaded their picking me up at school particularly because 'Abdu was a very large man who seemed to overflow into the rest of the car, crowding us tightly together. Someone always had to sit next to him which countered the whole effect of being driven by a chauffeur. In time they had bought an Opel which though larger and more advanced in design was nevertheless sufficiently modest for them. My mother had decided to drive herself in order to move with the times, so there was the problem of acquiring a driving licence but this was quickly solved by simply sending 'Abdu, armed with a few pounds, to collect one.

She did, in the end, have to pass a driving test when she finally came to live in London but she failed it on five occasions despite numerous lessons from a driving school. Eventually she was advised to take the test in St Albans as the inspectors were said to be kinder there and she did at last pass.

By then her circumstances had again improved and I asked her whether she would like to employ a housekeeper. She had looked at me in horror.

"I could not bear to have anyone living with us," she had said shuddering.

"But you had all these people," I insisted. "There was Maria and Awad and . . . "

"I don't know how I did it, I really don't," she replied, interrupting.

I am still not clear whether an earthly paradise for some requires the servitude of others or whether it is the freedom from servants that creates the earthly paradise just as much as the freedom from servitude.

Weekends in Cairo were spent at the various sporting clubs where we swam in the pool all day. In the evenings when it was too dark for swimming or tennis, large groups of children or teenagers sat talking as our mothers played canasta or kumkam and our fathers played poker at the Tewfikieh Tennis Club.

On Sundays we would often be taken to have tea at the Mena House Hotel where professional dancers demonstrated technique in the shadow of the great pyramid, but it was to my cousin Irene to whom I was grateful as she showed me how to dance despite my basic ineptitude. She did it by numbers, making me count the time out loud and then in my head. "*Le tango c'est un deux un, la valse un deux trois, un deux trois.*" I confess that although since then I have always enjoyed dancing I still have to count in my head. My repertoire was enlarged at school where we were taught the slow waltz and foxtrot though my favourites have remained the tango and the waltz.

We also went to the Fayoum for weekends. There were only two hotels, one on either side of a large expanse of water with wild geese rising up in droves from the reeds in response to some secret signal. One was called *Bigel* and the other, of course, *L'Auberge du Lac.*

When, recently, I took my wife there to show her the beauty of the lake we were given police protection as the Fayoum, we were told, was full of fundamentalists who objected to foreigners, and the fine hotels had disappeared.

13

An Earthly Paradise

It has always been the custom in countries which touch on the tropics that those who could afford it would flee the inland cities for the mountains or the coast during the summer.

Unlike the English and the French who own country houses or *châteaux*, the well-to-do Cairenes had not yet reached that degree of attachment to the land. They were, after all, immigrants from Europe, Syria or Greece who had been there for one or at most two generations. While Egyptian absentee landlords and what was now the less distinctly identifiable Ottoman gentry may have had farms or *ezbas*, they were usually in the low-lying Nile Valley of the delta. Though fertile and picturesque these were hardly places to take refuge in the summer.

Port Said, had its vogue but to my recollection "no one" went there in the 1940s and there was also Ras el-Bahr, which was at the head of the Nile, where its tributaries had split up into further branches after the main divisions of Rosetta and Damietta. Ras el-Bahr was a temporary village, as when the flood came in the autumn most of its structures were washed away so that conditions were unlikely to have been luxurious. Nevertheless those who did go told stories of an idyllic life of boat trips by moonlight, of the romantic music of the ʿoud and the tambourines and tragic tones of a singer.

My father had been there regularly in his youth and it is his version that I repeat though he only spoke of superficial things and most of what brought mist to his eyes remained unsaid. My mother felt it was downmarket. She had never set foot in Ras el-Bahr and had no intention of ever doing so however fondly my father remembered his youthful days. It was one of the few bones of contention in that long and happy marriage that he had had to give up the notion of going to that romantic place. I commiserated with him as we sat in the setting sun, long after the war, on the terrace at the Villa d'Este overlooking Lake Como. How could that view compare with the reflection of the moon on the Nile at Ras el-Bahr? Where was the glittering fish grilled on a skewer, the taste of which he had never found since, while arak flowed to content the spirit – an experience from which I felt bitterly I had been excluded through my mother's snobbish intransigence?

He recalled the scene again, as we watched the lights twinkle on the Seine in the evening and he fingered the menu at the *Tour d'Argent* vainly seeking the smoky scent of dried twigs and charcoal as he remembered each of the herbs and spices and repeated their Arabic names. He was in his mid-nineties when I heard him disconsolately talking to my mother as they sat wrapped up in their woollen dressing gowns during the London winter.

"You would have liked Ras el-Bahr, you know. You would have enjoyed it, the people were not as bad as you think."

"Go!" I heard her reply as usual. "Go on, who is stopping you?"

Although they had spent their honeymoon at the Cecil Hotel in Alexandria, she now favoured the Beau Rivage by the sea. What I remember best is the garden where tea was served in the cool of the late afternoon. There was always a somewhat dressed-up atmosphere as those who had returned from the beach at Sidi Bishr, as well as those who had avoided the middle of the day altogether by taking refuge in fitful somnolence under the rotating fans, would have had their shower and come down lightly clothed in crisp cottons and linens.

There was also the advantage that the children, once they had finished their ice creams, could roam about among the bushes in an illusion of independence leaving the adults free to discuss the latest rumours of the war as they relaxed on green Lloyd-Loom chairs. The urge to collect what I can still find of these indestructible objects has never let go even though, as I paint and re-paint them, I can sense that it is only a misguided attempt at reproducing a mood which has no place in Hampstead Garden Suburb and, like me, they remain rather forlorn on the terrace which overlooks the back garden.

My grandmother Eugénie would often join us. She would arrive shaded by a wide brimmed hat, a parasol and white lace gloves not too much unlike her namesake, the Empress who had briefly been her contemporary, at the end of one life and the beginning of the other. It was protection from the sun that she sought and although Ambre Solaire as well as Nivea were already available to the fastidious, those early sunscreens had an oily consistency which, though attractive to some, was unappealing to others. She would give a look of disgust when they were proffered and told us that in her day, in Istanbul, the ladies of the harems of the Sultan Abdul Hamid and of his Pashas used a cream made from ground rice and mother-of-pearl to ensure a translucent pallor as tanned skin was indicative of an inferior background.

Even in childhood I was sufficiently aware of the health-giving properties that were already being attributed to the sun. After all, everyone had seen Dr Schwartz, the paediatrician, holding apart his own children's thighs so as to expose their bottoms directly to its beneficient rays, an act which would be looked upon with horror today. And yet, as I approach the later part of my life, one of the facts I have learnt of the human condition is that all things to do with belief and opinion will turn full circle if we wait long enough.

One summer we rented a flat near the beach at Glymenopoulo. It was large enough to share with my Aunt Germaine and her family as well as Maria and our cousins' Greek nanny, Stella. The

Egyptian servants Awad and Ahmad were related to each other as it was common then for families to work for other families, and although Ahmad tended to be quick tempered and picked quarrels in the market place, Awad was wiser and could keep his cousin under control.

The fathers had remained in Cairo and came for the weekends with other men unable to absent themselves for the full three months. They travelled together by car along the desert road stopping only at the military check points and at the Rest House, an establishment mid-way between the two cities which served Turkish coffee or a bottle of Spathis or Stella beer. Much later I discovered that the British Empire had been dotted with similar Rest Houses and that a short stop for the toilet or a drink represented our participation in a network that straddled the earth.

The government also transferred itself every summer from Cairo to Alexandria in order to enjoy the cooler climate and so the city was allowed the satisfaction of calling itself '*Alexandrie, Seconde Capitale*' which entitled it also to a special page in the daily newspapers. King Farouk was installed in his palace at Ras-el-Tin where, comforted by the breeze that drifted in from the sea, he could brood over the site of the Battle of Abukir as it was here that Nelson's defeat of the Napoleonic fleet had laid the foundations of the British protection we now enjoyed. Farouk's loyalties were well known, however, and as children we had little doubt that he spent his nights signalling vital information to German submarines. We demanded action, but our parents were less worried by his activities, no doubt reassured by the fact that he was seen every evening without exception gambling at the Casino San Stefano, or carousing with loose women and other men's wives.

"A court of pimps and brothel-keepers!" *Oncle* Victor had pronounced, stressing each syllable with a wild stroke of his horsehair fly swatter. As a lawyer accredited to the Bar of the *Tribunaux Mixtes*, it was understood that he had contacts in high places so he would know what was going on.

I heard a loud knock early one morning when only the younger children were awake and the nannies were still pretending to be asleep so I went to answer the door. It was the Greek grocer from downstairs, quivering with emotion.

"Wake your parents!" he said embracing me tightly and kissing me on both cheeks "Tell them that Mussolini has been thrown out! At last we can see the end!" It was 1943.

During that long summer newspaper and radio reports multiplied, coloured by the rumours said to come directly from contacts with the military, which acted as a sort of accompanying elaboration or interpretation of the facts. It seemed that the unbelievable had happened and that the Grand Council of the Fascist Party itself, led by Count Ciano, had simply sacked Mussolini on 24 July, in the very middle of our holidays. The dictator, it was said, at first had paid no attention but then he was arrested on the steps of the Villa Savoia where he had gone to speak to the King.

I was amazed by this event as I thought that such powerful men could not be overthrown so easily. They had to be fought to the end and presumably killed, so I was more comfortable with Hitler's demise two years later as it conformed much better with my childish preconceptions. However, Mussolini was not quite finished that summer. I followed his story with interest and was most preoccupied with what they would do with him. When names such as that of General Badoglio who became prime minister following Mussolini's fall and whom I had understood to be a bad man, were suddenly spoken of as belonging to the good side I was left somewhat uneasy.

Mussolini, everyone told me, had been imprisoned high on an inaccessible mountain in the Abruzzi and I imagined this to be like the Chateau d'If in *The Count of Monte Cristo* which I was enjoying at the time so I was deeply shocked when I heard that he had got away, rescued by German commandos who had landed by glider. I was disconcerted at such a daring act by people who, as a nine-year-old boy, I would have preferred not to admire. I could not know, of course, that this rescue was the start of a chain of events that would ultimately lead directly to his demise and if he had been left to see the war out quietly in jail he may well have survived.

The subtlety of these unfolding events escaped me completely when I was told how he had established his new headquarters at Salò, near Como, and that he had executed those who had betrayed him. I remember that what I had found incredible beyond belief was that he had executed Count Ciano who was his own son-in-law. I was not yet familiar with Greek tragedies and I could not envisage such behaviour towards family members.

When, as the war was coming to its end, he was captured and shot after a summary trial by communist partisans I cheered as loudly as the Milanese crowds I saw in the cinema news. As they pelted with stones the dead bodies of Mussolini and Claretta Petacci, hanging limply upside down from meat hooks in the piazza, I had no concern other than that justice had been seen to have been done. I have been left, however, with what may seem to those around me as an inappropriate and unexplained interest in the events surrounding the fate of Mussolini.

The flood came earlier than usual at the end of that summer. The Nile rose fast, filling the irrigation canals overnight, and even penetrating the basements of the buildings, and the waters were almost blood red.

"Like Exodus!" the superstitious whispered. "It is good news! Blessed be the Name of the Lord."

The sceptics sneered, of course. It had to do with the rainfall in the mountains of Abyssinia, they said, or perhaps with the confluence of the Blue and the White Nile. Either way it signalled the end of the summer and it was, one way or the other, going to be a good year.

There was always much more to do in Alexandria than going to the beach and when we were younger and willing to be led, Maria would take us on walks round the city. Sometimes we would travel on the Smouha City double-decker tram and go further still. She would buy us the prickly pears which we were allowed to eat as their thick skin was peeled off in front of us, or corn on the cob sterilised by the burning embers of a charcoal fire. Although we covered every district of the city we always ended up in a Roman Catholic cemetery wandering among the grave-stones. There we were allowed to roam about and look for the tomb of "Maria Koron".

That was also the name of our own nanny but it was for her mother's tombstone that we searched and she had been given the same name. In time I was able to piece together that poor woman's story. Still in her early thirties, she was already the mother of four children when our own Maria was born just as one of the many natural calamities which regularly afflicted the villages around Gorizia struck again. The peasant families of Batuje now faced starvation and they had only one resource still available, but it was one that had saved them from destitution or famine many times before and they knew what they had to do. All they had to offer the outside world was their lactating mothers.

These Slavic peasant women had been held in high regard for many centuries by the well-to-do families of the Ottoman Empire. They were said to be healthy, scrupulously clean, of equable temperament and totally honest so they sought them out as nannies for their own children and the Slovenes in turn had become accustomed to travelling to Egypt, Lebanon and Turkey itself. As their board and lodging were free they were able to send all their earnings back home and at times this might have been the only source of income which allowed their families to survive.

It is only relatively recently that milk replacements and formula have been available and before this if a mother had no milk or had died in childbirth the infant would be lost too unless another woman was found to breastfeed it. This was not rare and many aunts or friends of the mother who had plenty of milk would take on this role. I knew a number of people who had told me that they were *frères de lait* or "brothers in milk" which meant that they had been fed at the same breast. I believe that they often seemed to have retained a special, almost sibling bond even though they could have no memory of the time. A wet-nurse was therefore always in great demand and highly paid by their standards.

Her own daughter, successfully weaned and thriving, Maria Koron collected her pre-paid, one-way ticket from the shipping office of the *Adriatica* line in Trieste, and sailed for Alexandria in 1898. As the crossing took a few days, she would have had to continue drawing out the rich milk from her swollen breasts using a glass receptacle attached to a rubber suction pump to prevent it drying up. She had notified her husband by telegram of her safe arrival but her family had had no further news until they were informed by her employers some months later that she had died of typhoid. They had added that they had used the salary they owed her to pay for a decent burial in the Catholic cemetery and although the sum had not covered the expenses entirely they were prepared to waive the excess as they were aware of the straitened circumstances in which her husband now found himself.

My nanny Maria had considered this to be a very generous gesture on the part of her mother's employers as it meant that the mother she had never known would have a marked grave rather than be thrown in anonymously among the paupers. She would, she felt, one day find the grave although they had not given any details as to the location, so that she might pay her respects and say a prayer for her. On the other hand it may be that it was the quest itself which had the greatest significance. She never did find her mother's final resting place although she continued to search until finally leaving Egypt and returning to what had become Yugoslavia.

It is the beaches of Sidi Bishr that I remember most clearly. They

1 My great grandfather, Hacham Abraham Douek HaCohen, the Chief Rabbi of Aleppo and the Ottoman Empire c.1890

2 Joseph Alphandary, my other great grandfather (*front row, centre*), headmaster of the *Alliance Israélite Universelle* school in Tanta, Egypt 1910

3 My grandfather Elie Douek with some of his daughters and my grandmother Sara, Egypt 1924

4 Nelly (my mother) as a girl 1928

5 Nelly and my grandmother Eugénie in Venice on one of their European tours 1932

6 Cesar and Nelly on honeymoon in Alexandria 1933

7 Nelly, Nanny Maria and me 1934

8 My grandparents Isaac and Eugénie Sassoon, Vichy 1937

9 Nelly, Claudia and me at the Grotto Gardens in Zamalek, February 1937

10 Aged 15 months with my father's pith helmet

11 With Claudia on board the *Augustus* 1940

12 Nelly and Cesar in Cairo 1941

13 Cesar, Nelly and Claudia with soldiers 1942

14

16

15

17

were numbered one, two and three and were quite different from each other. Sidi Bishr Number One consisted of dangerous rocks only while Number Three is today probably considered appropriate for surfing. So it was on Number Two that we rented a little cabin where we could take shelter from the sun and have our picnic lunch on its wooden terrace. Conditions were ideal for families as the waters were calm and safe, protected from the open sea by an island which we called Cleopatra's Island. It is unlikely that it had ever had anything to do with her but it was the only name we knew of the ancient queens and a rectangular basin cut in the stone was firmly believed to have been her bath. We told each other stories of the fabulous wealth covering the island. Some children held that it had been entirely coated with gold and silver, and encrusted with rubies, emeralds and sapphires hence its present lack of vegetation. Occasionally this led to searches among the rocks for any precious stone that may have survived the centuries but the bath was the only tangible evidence we had. Some imagined it filled with perfumes while others insisted it overflowed with asses' milk. The more technically minded wondered whether the milk was brought to the island in buckets or, whether in order to avoid it turning sour in the heat, the donkeys themselves were transported there to be milked directly into the stone basin and ensure absolute freshness. This led to all sorts of calculations and arguments regarding how many donkeys would be required and whether they could be kept on the island for that purpose. What happened to the refuse when they relieved themselves? All that dung and urine all over the place? As far as I remember no one suggested an alternative possibility such as that fishermen had cut the basin to keep the fish alive in sea water until they were ready to take them to the shore.

It was on 6 August 1945 while reflecting on such ancient practices, on beautiful queens and their toilet habits, that we noticed something strange on the beach across the bay. Paper floated everywhere, wafted by the gusts of wind created in the channel between the island and land. Large sheets of what seemed to be newspaper wrapped themselves round objects and people who tried vainly to fold them or at least gain some sort of control. As the wind grew stronger so the sheets rose higher in the air. This was certainly not the usual time for newspaper vendors to arrive.

As we swam back to the beach the newspapers were floating on the sea itself and we picked up the mysterious message from the pieces of soggy print. "*La bombe atomique*" said the red headline of *Le Journal d'Égypte*: "Atomic Bomb over Japan" in the thickest type of the *Egyptian Gazette*, and even *Le Progrès Égyptien* as well as all the Arabic papers had produced special editions which profited the vendors who had invaded the crowded beaches.

The explanation was given by *Tante* Marcelle, an aunt driven by drama and hysteria. She could not resist being the first to tell us of this tiny bomb, the size of an egg it was said, which had vaporised a whole city. At first I could not believe her. The story of the frogmen was still too fresh.

In the earlier days of the war when we were younger and willing to believe anything our aunts told us, she had announced that frogmen had been attacking Italian submarines. The name "frogmen" inspired fear in our young minds with images of monsters from the deep with webbed feet and horrific faces, and she had played on our infantile anxieties to make her dramatic impact. She never really explained what frogmen were and it was only in later years that the mockery of our school friends dispelled the myth. Even now, when the term is used, I experience a sudden moment of apprehension before I can pull myself together.

It was only when my parents confirmed that the atomic bomb was small and that the main ingredient, the radioactive uranium U235 amounted to no more than the volume of an egg, that I accepted the story. I later studied the diagrams in the newspapers for myself, and understood the need for a detonator.

We were not the only ones to be confused and *Tante* Marcelle was not the only one to over-dramatise. My older cousin, Albert, a rather silent and sporty young man, was arrested while returning from the Tewfikieh Tennis Club by a policeman guarding Kasr el-Nil Bridge. He was handcuffed and taken to the crowded police station which, in the heat of the summer, was full of complainants, supplicants and minor criminals but the matter was soon resolved by the harassed *kaimakam*, the captain. It seemed that the policeman, having discussed the size of the bomb with his friends and never having played or even watched tennis in his life, had feared that the tennis balls might well be atomic bombs. Albert was released immediately and gave ten piastres to the apologetic policeman as a sign of goodwill.

When we reached our early teens my parents took a summer membership at the Sporting Club in Alexandria as we needed to be with people of our own age – going out with our parents to eat falafel at Athineos or to watch the matinee performance of acrobats and tango dancers at the Casino Chatby was no longer enough.

There we made new friends not only with fellow visitors from Cairo but with young Alexandrians. The latter turned out to be subtly different from us though it is difficult to identify the nature of this difference. It was a very mixed society of Jews, Copts, Syrian Christians, Greeks, English as well as some Europeanised Moslems and others. Though a mainly French-speaking group, English had begun to creep in as so many now attended English schools but we all had a smattering of each other's languages. Cairene society was of a similar composition if with slightly different proportions but there was something particularly exciting and attractive about the Alexandrians.

In a way they were slightly racy, as though the boundary that kept us hidden behind a rather staid façade in Cairo was suddenly loosened when we got to the Sporting Club. For example, there was always a boy whose contacts allowed him to collect our bets and slip under the barrier at the racing track. One way or another they were more fun than our friends in Cairo.

The girls, too, seemed to be more forthcoming, even flirtatious, in Alexandria when such considerations were becoming important and we had begun to enjoy dancing in the evenings. Bakelite 78 rpm record collections gave great status to those who managed to accumulate them, especially to those who had access to the most recent issues through suppliers or even the American Army, and we played them outdoors on gramophones that still had to be wound up by hand. The "pick-up", however had made its appearance initiating the march to louder and louder music. This was a turn-table powered by an electric motor which was connected to a radio which "picked up" the sound, broadcasting it through its own loudspeaker. Soon models appeared where the records could be piled one on top of the other in groups of five or six, released by a complex mechanism to fall, one by one we hoped, as soon as the previous disc was finished. When all of them had been played we would turn them over so as to hear the other side.

My interest in girls seemed to have come suddenly and un-expectedly, or at least to have been given a new direction which I found slightly embarrassing, so I was surprised by the amused encouragement I received from my mother who must have observed the changes in my behaviour. We had played together with the girls in the sea and in swimming-pools almost every day as we grew up so I had scarcely noticed the developmental changes that altered the contours of their figures. It was Christian Dior's New Look that drew my attention to them so perhaps, as far as I was concerned, it was the First Look.

Although I realise that it could not possibly have been like that, the girls and their mothers all looked different on the same day. They appeared with long flowing skirts and the girls looked like ballerinas as they twirled around irresistibly. They wore embroidered blouses which they referred to as "peasant", high heels and even their hair was worn enticingly differently.

My father, as a cotton merchant, had a great suspicion of fashion and dreaded it. He had come to the conclusion that his safest course of action was to deal exclusively in the raw unbleached grey material or in white textile cloth. Arguing, as teenagers do, I insisted that there was no harm in importing pink shirts, for instance if that was what people wanted.

"They change their minds," he said. "You stock pink and then they want only blue for reasons that you cannot work out and it can simply ruin you."

Some merchants handled it and did very well, but in his uncomprehending innocence my father knew he was out of his depth and limited himself to white, which people would always want. He also did well, as naturally there is no single way.

In 1947, with a group of businessmen, he was flown by military aeroplane to Italy in a successful attempt to kick-start trade in that devastated country. By 1949 commercial flights were available and we began to spend our long holidays in Europe, but when I look back it is the memory of Alexandria during the summers between the Battle of Alamein in 1942 and 1949 that have remained in my mind as the earthly paradise that was Egypt during that brief period. From that moment, too, I realised that there was something very important about fashion.

14

A Last Taste of Sweets

They say that a thousand years before the birth of Christ a Libyan warrior called Sheshonq swept into Egypt and proclaimed himself Pharaoh. At first he did not venture too far and built himself a capital in the eastern delta near the present town of Zagazig where the cat-goddess Bastet was worshipped. From that moment till King Farouk lost his throne 3000 years later, Egypt was governed only by foreigners.

Sheshonq's Libyan dynasty was followed by black Pharaohs from Nubia south of the equator and then came, 500 years before the birth of Christ, Cambyses, the Persian king. Alexander the Great, in his turn, was proclaimed a god as was the custom in Egypt and left a line of Macedonian successors, the Ptolemies. Then the Byzantine Empire ruled for another 700 years until the winter of AD 639 when Amr ibn al-As led an Arab army into Egypt from the east and set up an encampment, which in Arabic is called Fustat, not far from where the Nile divides into the two main branches that form the delta between Damietta and Rosetta. They were a somewhat chaotic, nomadic people and had no taste for building cities, so for a time they ran Egypt from their encampment.

The country was then ravaged by continuous battles between Arab armies attacking each other from east and west for yet another century while the Egyptian population looked after their irrigation canals and tilled their land with oxen much as they had done since the beginning of time. One Arab commander did build his own city outside Fustat and, since he had defeated the other Arabs, named it "The Victorious" or *al-Kahirah* which the Europeans pronounced Cairo. In 1171 a Kurdish soldier called Salah el-Din, the celebrated Saladin, incorporated Egypt into his own Empire and kept its people under tight control by means of a huge army of slaves. It was these slaves, referred to as the Mameluks who themselves eventually took over. They were a mixed bunch of Circassians, Turks, Greeks, Russians, Albanians and others. They established one of the most bizarre forms of government ever seen. They elected their own Sultan from among themselves and overthrew or murdered him at the drop of a hat. The Mameluks were succeeded, not by their sons who received their inheritance of land and property in the normal manner, but by more young slaves they bought in the markets outside the Moslem world. These boys were converted to Islam and trained for military service by their owners. They were freed and on becoming officers they, in their turn, became Mameluks and bought their own retinue of young slaves. After 300 years of this colourful regime the Ottoman Turks took over Egypt though they continued to bring in foreign slaves to rule the country. The Egyptians bent their backs to the soil as they had as far back as people could remember leaving the conquerors to come and go.

I was taught all this by Professor Hassanein who was a lecturer at the University. A young man with ideals and a great love of his country he came once a week to teach me Arabic as my parents had been shamed by our complete ignorance of the language of the country in which we lived. His own speciality, however, was eighteenth-century European literature, and he spoke with eloquence of the new Enlightenment about to shine on the Arab world this time round.

"Saint-Simon," he kept saying to me, "you should read Saint-Simon."

He admired Napoleon. Everyone did then, of course, as it was a time of war. We had feared Rommel and been grateful to

Montgomery. Our heroes were the great war leaders and Eisenhower, Churchill and Napoleon were judged in that context.

Beside Napoleon Professor Hassanein would place Mohamed Ali the Great, the founder of our ruling dynasty and great-great-great-grandfather of our own King Farouk. "An Albanian soldier," he would repeat each time the subject came up, "an astute politician, a wise administrator who took over from the Turks, and a great general. His misfortune is that he ended up with us Egyptians. What could he do with a people like us? The Corsican had France! Think of that! If Mohamed Ali the Great had had France instead of Egypt he could have conquered the world!"

I never had the heart to point out that Mohamed Ali Pasha had not conquered much so it would be difficult to judge his military skills, much less to compare him with Bonaparte. He had been, after all, only the commander of a disenchanted Albanian regiment stationed in Egypt when, in 1805, his rule was legitimised by the Turkish Sultan. True, he had consolidated his position by inviting his political enemies to talks and then murdering them. Although this ruthless act was much admired by the Egyptians, in my youthful idealism I could see it only as treachery, and not, like Professor Hassanein, as heroism.

When stamps were printed commemorating the victories of Saladin over the crusaders Professor Hassanein found it too difficult to bear. He told me that he was filled with embarrassment.

"Do you realise," he had asked rhetorically, "that we have absolutely no heroes whatsoever? Since the time of Rameses, for more than 3000 years, we have not produced a single soldier or statesman of note. We are so pathetic that in our present fit of nationalism we have recourse to Saladin, a Kurd who conquered us and never spent much time in Egypt anyway. He despised us so much that he set up a government of slaves to rule over us, slaves bought in the markets, standing naked with chains round their necks. Albanian slaves, Turks, Circassians, anyone except Egyptians. And now we lick his feet. We pretend he was an Egyptian.

What next? Shall we pretend that Churchill was one of us? Or General Montgomery? After all he beat the Germans in Egypt and, when we have forgotten who all these people were, we can print stamps of Montgomery's victory as though it were ours. Anything will do when you have nothing."

When I left for school in England Professor Hassanein gave me, as a farewell gift, a book that he had written and which had just been published, entitled *Modern Egyptian History for British Pupils*. It had two pages of dedication. The first carried a photograph of a youthful King Farouk wearing a tarboosh, his head encircled by an oval wreath. Underneath, the caption read: "The August Sovereign King Farouk the First". The second page contained a single dedication: "To my dear pupil, Ellis Douek". The only book ever dedicated to me, it disappeared when we left, together with my swimming medals. I suspect that my mother thought they were not worth keeping. I was more upset about the medals at the time and forgot about the book. As the years have gone by, however, I cease to care about the medals though I would like to have that book now.

Everyone felt that the British grip was loosening, that they were putting on an elaborate show of morality and democracy claiming that they were leading Egypt towards independence, but we knew it was a sham. Instead of Sir Miles Lampson's iron grip confronting Farouk with tanks and taking responsibility for the country, all the talk now was of self-rule. This must have been irritating to the Egyptians who, after so many thousands of years of abject servility to anyone who happened to be around, desperately needed to fight a proper war of independence. No country was worth having unless you had won it in battle, Professor Hassanein had said, otherwise you would not be able to defend it. The British, it seemed, were too shifty and sly as they had not the slightest intention of fighting. All they wanted was to go home as soon as possible and the only delay was due to their obsession with leaving things in good order as they had convinced themselves that if chaos ensued the Suez Canal would break down and their trade routes would be obstructed.

Laws were passed by parliament, itself manipulated by a government that enacted decrees and regulations, while the whole system was dominated by King Farouk who had his own increasingly cynical agenda, and the idyllic life of the brief earthly paradise gave way to tension and anxiety. Conversation among the adults was a sort of dialogue between optimists and pessimists and I followed the patterns it produced carefully as my mother was firmly on the side of the latter. She was convinced that there was no future for the foreigners in Egypt, much less for the Jews, and her arguments were reasoned if somewhat continuous and ranting, adding an emotional element which was unacceptable to many. I was often told that my mother was a bird of ill omen spoiling dinner parties by her predictions of disaster since the passing of the Company Law of 1947 which decreed that 75% of employees had to be Egyptian nationals and 51% of capital be in joint stock companies.

"She is like a Cassandra," an angry cousin had said to my father. "You must stop her or no one will invite you any more."

"But Cassandra was right!" I intervened to his astonishment. "Troy was destroyed."

"So we have a little intellectual already?" he had scowled, as these matters were important to him. "It is a different situation, I am only speaking in metaphoric terms, and it is right that the country should be Egyptianised otherwise it will always be in thrall to foreigners. Those of us who live here should apply for Egyptian passports."

"Does England have laws like that?" I asked, still defending my mother, but my father had bundled me away. He had agreed with her entirely but felt we should be rather cool about it and make our plans carefully. The family would leave but we would do so step by step, sending the children away to schools first so that we, at any rate, would not only be safe but established in education and careers, and I, as the eldest, would leave before the others. He and my mother would carry on in Egypt and see how things turned out, but at least they would have peace of mind. As for the dinner parties, it was none of my mother's business and she should stop haranguing her fellow guests.

"Try to understand them, Nelly," he had said, in an effort to make her see reason. "They are frightened of losing their livelihood and their status in society more than of losing their lives, which seems only a remote possibility, even after what happened in Germany. Besides they just want to have a good evening while they are still here, play cards, laugh. No one gains anything by anticipating the worst every minute of the day."

On 14 May 1948, the day before the founding of the State of Israel, the government of Nokrashi Pasha proclaimed Martial Law and brought in measures directed against Zionists, communists and, paradoxically, the Moslem Brotherhood. Both men and women were arrested but the definitions were very vague as Nokrashi himself said on a number of occasions that Zionists were communists and all Jews were potential Zionists. This meant that Jews could now be classified as enemies of the state and lose their Egyptian citizenship, and therefore their job, on a whim or a denunciation. Many began to leave quietly, deprived of their Egyptian passports and carrying only travel documents called *laisser passer* or *feuille de route*. As my mother's predictions were actually happening she stopped expressing them and began making plans to send me to Bradford where her sister Giselle was living with the English airman she had married during the war.

Nokrashi Pasha was assassinated by the Moslem Brotherhood and in retaliation the government secret services killed their leader Sheikh Hassan el-Bana. Life in the streets of Cairo became more unpleasant for Europeans who were subjected to hostile remarks and though there was no physical violence at first there was the fear that it might happen. Farouk's ministers were believed to be fomenting anger against the British. However, once they had demonstrators in the streets there was the risk that the volatile crowd might get out of control and turn against their own rulers. A word was found to describe these outbreaks which were slightly more than demonstrations and not quite riots as they were not totally out of control. We began to refer to them as *les manifestations*.

These *manifestations* became more frequent, lasted longer and occasionally turned sinister when Europeans were pushed and beaten and the streets became dangerous. When that happened they were known as *événements*. We began to miss school and stay at home during these *événements* and were given all sorts of advice as to what to do if we were caught in the street. The most common suggestion was to claim to be Greek as somehow that nation seemed to have escaped the general resentment for a while longer.

On one occasion I found myself caught up in a *manifestation*. The crowd began to push and shove me somewhat half-heartedly as though they were only doing their duty or perhaps what they had been paid for. I shouted: "I am a Rumi! I am a Rumi!" – the word everyone used for the Greeks. Those around me seemed relieved at not having to persecute me further and the shoves and pushes became friendly slaps on the back.

"Ah, Rumi! *Ma'alesh, ma'alesh*, never mind!"

As businesses foundered, however, even the Greeks began to slip away from Egypt. It was only decades later that I found out that "Greegi" is the Arabic word for Greek and that, shades of the Byzantine Empire, "Rumi" meant Roman, the word used colloquially for almost two thousand years. It seems that I may have escaped injury in 1949 by claiming to be a Roman citizen.

Europeans left gradually as a result of what was known as "loss of confidence". Those who had the means sent their children to schools or universities abroad while those without such good fortune tried to convince whoever was willing to listen that everything would soon settle down and Egypt would again become the earthly paradise we had known. Although each person could do what they wanted, people argued vociferously, anxious to convince others that theirs was the right decision, as a way of reassuring themselves.

Non-Europeans left in groups but none more dramatically than some Armenians. In fact they were among the first to go, following an agreement with Stalin. Many left for Erevan in the Soviet Republic of Armenia. Russian ships had come to collect them in Alexandria and as we had friends among them we went to see them off.

Huge banners had been unfurled with portraits of Stalin and King Farouk – an incongruous pair my father commented, though my mother was a little carried away by the enthusiasm. Bands were playing, Armenians wept as they sang the songs of the Caucasus. Everyone cried, including the Egyptians who had come to bid farewell, and we all waved. I heard later that this emotional group had not done very well in Stalin's Armenia.

Then events took a turn for the worse. Central Cairo was set on fire. The Turf Club was burnt down, an Englishman died, and everyone's preparations became more urgent. The main subject of conversation had finally become where to go? Now everyone was agreeing with my mother.

Europe seemed cold and unfriendly, damaged by the war and still subject to rationing so some would not consider the Northern Hemisphere at all and aimed for Brazil, South Africa, Rhodesia or the Belgian Congo. Among the Jews only a minority were Zionists planning to go to the new State of Israel, but there were many others who had little money and had somehow escaped the blessing of a European nationality so they were left with no other option. As it turned out most of them did very well in Israel.

America was another destination that had to be explored as my Aunt Yvette with most of her family had migrated to the United States from Colombia and now lived in Beverly Hills. It had become possible to talk to them on the telephone after the war but it was necessary to book the call three weeks in advance and you would be given a time at short notice. This had to be negotiated as there was a ten-hour time lag between Egypt and California.

The whole family, including the children, gathered in my grandfather's sitting room. We understood it was an historic event. True, Churchill had spoken to Roosevelt years ago but this was different, real people speaking not emperors. An ordinary family brought together by miraculous technology. At last the telephone rang when the connection was made.

"Hello! Hello! Can you hear me?"

"Yes, Yvette!"

Hand over mouthpiece: "It's Yvette!"

"Hello! Can you hear?"

Hand over mouthpiece: "She can hear!"

"What time is it over there?"

"It's morning over there!" Amazement.

"Are you all right?"

"Yes we are all right too!"

"Hello! Can you hear?"

Each took his turn to say hello and that they were well, even some of the older children were allowed to speak. My grandfather was later criticised for saying that we were all well when Aunt Léla had been sick but he insisted that there was no point in worrying them in Beverly Hills. Though not much was said much was felt, however, and the world was never the same again.

By and large the news from America was also not too good. There were no servants. As a child I could not quite get the measure of this as it was the smaller things that loomed largest. If one needed a glass of water, I wondered, who would go and fetch it? Life without servants seemed impossible. And yet most adults envisaged it courageously, even with excitement. My mother, for instance, claimed that she was fully prepared to face a world devoid of servants. It would make her independent, she had said.

The actual details, however, were more worrying. Someone who had returned from a visit to New York had a daunting story to tell. He had been visiting friends, people like us, he explained, and as the guests arrived the black woman whom he took to be the servant had said, "I am leaving now Debbie, goodbye all!" Everyone was amazed at the maid who had addressed the lady of the house with such familiarity but my mother insisted she liked the idea. It was high time, she said, to move forward. But worse was still to come. At the end of the meal, our friend had said, the men did the washing-up, even the guests, even he! Everyone was stunned. They had nothing to say. My mother, too, was silent. The future did not bode well.

Manifestations and *événements* now took place so frequently that it created continuous anxiety. The fact that neighbours and friends tended to leave without advertising their plans or warning anyone in advance was even more unsettling. I had been with a group from school when we were stopped by a *manifestation*. The street was blocked and Mr Beard, the English master, asked the police to let us through the crowd. They wanted to be helpful and certainly the rules of courtesy came first so they began to push people aside. One of the leaders, said to be an Old Boy of the school, exploded with mortification and contempt when he saw us. "Seldom!" he said bitterly to Mr Beard, shaking his head, "Seldom!"

"Seldom what, Habashi? You can't use the word like that, it has to be qualified."

"Seldom does Britain show her dirty hand so openly! Collaborating with the police, giving instructions to the oppressors! We know now where tyranny stems from!"

We were ushered through, however, while Mr Beard kept trying to improve Habashi's grammar for which he clearly felt responsible.

There were graffiti everywhere, written accusations against the British, threats to the Jews, insults to every nationality in turn. Across the road from the school someone had written in bold if dripping letters the ultimate insult: "Dirty British, your king is a woman!"

*

In July 1952, Claudia, Zaki and I were in Paris with our mother for a holiday. At the same time a group of officers led by General Mohamed Naguib overthrew King Farouk and we shared in the jubilation, feeling at one with the Egyptians.

I knew nobody, from the Egyptian servants to all our friends who did not see this as a good omen as Naguib was a reassuring leader, his kindly face lifted a burden off everyone's shoulders. Welcomed by general goodwill the officers could do no wrong in anyone's eyes. Even the realisation that one had communist contacts, another was in the Moslem Brotherhood and a third had been in favour of a German victory during the war only added different flavours to the novelty and confirmed a sense of unity.

At the end of my first year as a medical student in London I returned to Cairo in 1954 and was there on the Day of Atonement. A wave of anticipation spread through *Le Grand Temple* in the Rue Adly as the sirens of motorcycle outriders suddenly pierced the sound of mumbled prayers and the worshippers nudged each other questioningly. Then he walked through the door in an unassuming manner and the congregation rose, clapping in relief, calling out: "Mohamed Naguib! Mohamed Naguib!"

"Things will turn out well," people said to each other. "This is a fine gesture, coming here on Yom Kippur; no leader has done that since King Fouad. You see, I told you things will settle down again."

Encouraged by it all a group of leading businessmen arranged to see this approachable, if unelected, ruler to make some suggestions regarding the ailing economy, among them my Great-Uncle Musa. News of the meeting spread quickly. It had been friendly if unexpected as Naguib had not given them a chance to speak but had thanked them profusely for their offer to help the country and particularly for the donations he expected them to make. An officer then read out the names of those present, with their compulsory financial contributions. As Musa had a tendency towards depression it was in commiseration that we went to his house in Koubbeh Gardens only to find him serenely smiling to himself as he sipped a whisky and soda in the shade of a tamarisk tree.

"Governments," he said in explanation, "are like the weather as there is nothing you can do about them. If I make a mistake I get upset, as you know, but when you are dealing with things that you can do nothing about you just take them as they come."

That was an early sign of what was later called Arab Socialism. Businessmen, manufacturers and entrepreneurs took the hint and made arrangements to shift their money out of the country though, like everyone else, they believed socialism, whether of the Arab variety or not, might be a good thing even if not for them.

Communism was another matter. It was not a question of its economic theory which was no less acceptable than socialism, the problem was that it had been made illegal. The officers, it seemed, had no objection to Marxism or indeed even Leninism or for that matter the peasant philosophy of Mao Zedong and they had nothing but approval for Tito. It was just that they did not trust the party members to take orders only from themselves as was now required of everyone. Besides, they had a suspicion that there was, as yet, no Arab Communism and the individuals concerned were mostly Christians or Jews.

Great-Uncle Jacques had explained all that to my cousin when the latter had been suspected of communist proclivities and the party was banned.

"I only ask you to be fair," my great-uncle had said. "Some for the rich, some for the poor. Equality is all I ask, not everything for the poor, it is not fair to the rich!"

In any case, he pointed out, it was obvious that the poor were more content than the rich. You could tell that by their happy-go-lucky approach to life and their cheerful banter with no cares in the world while the rich were beset with responsibilities, worries and concerns. My cousin's defiant silence pleased

A Middle Eastern Affair

Great-Uncle Jacques. At least he was listening and letting him
speak.

"What I really want to tell you is this. We are a liberal family.
We accept everyone's beliefs but if you wish to practise communism, practise it freely in England or France or in Italy, not in Egypt
where it is forbidden and not very practical. What can you do? Go
to start revolutions in the villages? You cannot even speak Arabic
properly. I am sure they want to carry out their own revolution
without Jews and foreigners interfering, it gives them a bad name
in the eyes of the peasants."

"Why not Russia?" interrupted Great-Uncle Musa. "If you
wish to practise communism go to Russia. There it is respected
and you could do well. You could advance in life and become a
Commissar. I understand they live in very good conditions with
houses in the countryside – dachas, they are called, I am told."

As my cousin's expression became pained rather than defiant
Jacques objected to Musa's suggestion.

"Nonsense, Musa!" he said. "Life in Russia is grim and boring
even for commissars. Except for the opera and ballet. Do you like
that sort of thing? And how could your mother visit you? No, no,
it is best that he goes to Europe to practise communism. It is
respected there especially among the intellectuals."

Great-Uncle Jacques thought for a moment, then went on: "I
think you might meet film stars like Simone Signoret," he said.
"You could have a good life, eat well in France or Italy and make
a good living. The son of my friend Henri who is a communist in
Italy does very well in trade with Hong Kong. During the winter
he goes skiing in Cervinia with his communist friends."

The great-uncles were so pleased with their reasoning that they
repeated it to me just in case, like so many young people, I too
might develop an interest in communism. They had nothing
fundamentally against it, they stressed, on the contrary they could
see that it could well be the thing of the future and that it may not
be a bad idea to place oneself in a good position from the

beginning: the only problem was that it was against the law, as so many things had become, in Egypt.

Indeed, the Coup's grip had gradually tightened, constitutions were repealed, political parties suspended and, finally on 14 November 1954, Naguib himself was deposed and placed under house arrest. Under the new leader, Gamal Abdel Nasser, another era began. He was definitely an Egyptian and he was much loved by the people but I still wonder why it was necessary for him to seize power in such a blatant and intolerant manner as he would have won an election by a huge majority anyway. Many said it made no difference, but it did make a difference. He had signalled to his people that they had no choice. They had never had any choice and now they never would.

As a result any opposition had to be suppressed and the officer class entrusted with the new authority became the new aristocracy with all the nepotism and corruption it entailed. On the other hand they were Egyptians, and not foreigners as before, so no doubt most people still thought it was a good thing.

In that year of 1954 the atmosphere in Cairo was very tense. So many of our friends had left for ever that we were well aware that this was to be our last summer in the city of our birth. Hostility and suspicion towards Jews and foreigners had mounted to such a degree that I became anxious when I was told in London that I had to apply for a special exit visa simply to leave the country and that its granting was not a foregone conclusion.

I had to go to a government office called the 'Alam Makhsous which translated means the Special Pencil (though this is just the way translations go as it may also mean "office") in the Ministry of the Interior in Tahrir Square. The ground floor of the building was crowded, with a huge number of people milling around in chaos as there were no formal queues or organisation while the only seating was on the floor. Those who had come from the countryside to obtain some permit or other often had to wait hours, if not days, so many were lying asleep, stretched out in corners, their faces covered with a shawl, to protect them from the numerous flies infesting the place. Clustered near the doors, both inside and outside the Ministry, scribes sat cross-legged, holding wooden rests on their laps as they wrote statements for the less articulate or for the illiterate with pen and ink in calligraphic script. I noticed that some of the scribes had battered old typewriters which they struck violently to obtain an impression through worn-out ribbons, but those were more expensive and the poorest had to rely on handwriting to make their supplications.

The Special Pencil was at the top of the building and as the previous week an overloaded lift had become stuck for some hours, despite efforts to free it, resulting in many deaths from suffocation, I decided to climb the stairs. The sound of voices rose to a roar in the central atrium as I gradually made my way up but the crowds petered out the higher I got and the heat became less stifling. Suddenly I saw Maria. She explained that as an exploiting foreigner, an imperialist, she had been refused permission to take her savings out of the country. I insisted on going with her to the office in question but at first she refused.

"Maybe it is better this way," she said. "It is God's punishment."

I could not convince her that she did not deserve God's punishment, but she accepted my argument that her nieces and nephews in post-war Yugoslavia could do with the money. I could not convince the responsible official either that she was not a capitalist but a poor serving woman entitled to her savings. When I pointed out that Gamal Abdel Nasser was a friend of Tito's, however, and that he might end up in trouble he thought again and changed his mind. Fear of the military dictatorship was strong, fortunately in this case, but Maria was not sure that she should keep the money as it might diminish her chances of entry into heaven. I bundled her away quickly before she changed her mind and carried on up the stairs to the top floor.

The Special Pencil was quite different from the rest of the

building. There were comfortable though worn seats along the walls, and open windows let in a cooling breeze as we looked out over the Nile from high up, well away from the noise and chaos.

This office had a sinister reputation but my own case was a straightforward one since I was only a student leaving the country and taking no money with me. I had brought a certificate signed by my puzzled Dean but I had, fortunately, been warned by a fellow student that it would not be enough as he had been prevented from leaving the country until all the formalities had been followed in the proper order. On his advice I had taken the letter to the Egyptian Education Office in Chesterfield Gardens in London to be countersigned as genuine and then translated by an official Arabic translator accredited to the Egyptian Consulate in London. On my arrival in Cairo I took all this to the Ministry of Education to be countersigned yet again and authenticated as it had to be done in person.

As I waited my turn a bald middle-aged man with a familiar face caught my attention. He was short and fat so that he gave the impression of a little Humpty-Dumpty wobbling on its base. He had taken off his linen jacket which he waved in front of him as though he was attempting to dry the large wet areas under the sleeves. His tie had been loosened and left hanging below his open collar while at the same time he was mopping his brow with the handkerchief in his other hand. When he saw me he gave a big smile and waddled towards me like a penguin.

"Mitchnick," he said. "I know who you are. I know your parents. You are a doctor in London aren't you?"

"A medical student only, Mr Mitchnick," I said.

"It's the same, but I have something to show you, look!"

Suddenly his hand went to his left eye and to my horror he began to pull it out with a twisting motion.

"Duke-Elder," he said handing me his glass eye to inspect.

"What?" I asked, refusing to pick it up though he kept thrusting it into my hand.

"Sir Stewart Duke-Elder, the eye man in London, do you know him?"

I pulled myself together and tried to show enthusiasm for the glass eye.

"Are you leaving Mr Mitchnick? Are you here for your exit visa?"

"No, no," he said, "I have a court case. There has been an accusation against me. Quite unjust. No, my case is downstairs and I only come up here because it is the coolest place. You get a wonderful view of the Nile, don't you?"

It turned out that Mr Mitchnick's employers had transferred all their money to Switzerland and had run off, leaving him to look after the office. He had been charged as an accomplice though he claimed that he had known nothing about it. He said that his documents moved very slowly from one office to another and that he hung around the Ministry so that he could transport them himself otherwise they might get lost or some of the papers might fall out of the folder.

"All the time?" I asked. "You wait here every day?"

"Good Lord, no!" Mr Mitchnick replied. "Life would not be liveable like that. I only come on alternate days, my lawyer comes tomorrow. We take it in turns."

When my number was called the officials did not say a word other than to ask for one document after the other, but they were obviously disappointed when they saw I had them all ready.

At that point I thought I was leaving for ever the following morning. I had no idea that I would return one day for a visit with my wife. My grandparents had come only a little more than fifty years before. They had claimed that they had brought trade and development and contributed to the growth of the country, while others saw them as exploiters of the wealth of the cotton crop and the facilities of the Suez Canal. It is just a matter of opinion but at any rate we got the impression that the Egyptians were glad to be rid of us.

As I left the Special Pencil I suddenly felt an intense desire for the sweets I had coveted as far back as I could remember. I had no idea that it was only a matter of time before Lebanese immigrants would follow me and bring them and better ones to London. I walked to Issaievitch Frères, the bakery not far from the Rue Soliman Pasha, now renamed Talaat Harb, and ordered everything I could, starting with the mastic ice-cream they called *dandurma* and then *baklava* and *kounafa*. When the waiter tried to clear my plate I said I also wanted the honey bread, the *esh el-seraye*. And that was the moment Professor Hassanein walked in.

"Is it you?" he said embracing me, tears filling his eyes, "You have become a man! I got your letter, are you a doctor now?"

"Only a medical student."

"It's the same, have you come back?"

"No, I am leaving tomorrow. It is not likely that I will ever come back."

We talked for hours. Professor Hassanein was married now and had two sons. He had transferred his admiration from Mohamed Ali the Great to Gamal Abdel Nasser.

"He is a great man, you know," he said. "At last we have a leader who makes us really hold our heads high. He gives me hope for my sons."

My parents took me as far as passport control at Cairo Airport and I was asked to hand in the Egyptian passport I had obtained in an effort to conform with the Egyptianisation programme. *ANNULÉ* was stamped on it in thick black letters and I knew that that was the end of that. I kept it as a souvenir.

Two years later, at the conclusion of the Suez War, the last British soldier, the last foreign soldier after 3000 years, left Egyptian soil on 19 June 1956 and three days later a referendum made Nasser president and gave him supreme powers. There was no opposing candidate and no doubt everyone was very pleased.

15

A Toe in New Waters

We left Egypt for Europe but it was neither a desperate quest for asylum nor the result of a sudden and irrevocable expulsion. For many years I discouraged any suggestion that we were refugees at all. When I look back now, fifty years on, it is difficult for me to say what exactly were my motives in such a denial, but I think there were a number of reasons, and I suspect all are significant.

I did not like to see ourselves presented as victims, perhaps simply out of pride. Ultimately, my father had had the means to buy a house in London and a car, maintain his family, and set up a new business. He never saw himself as an impoverished exile. Then there was my own notion that I had left a failing, backward-looking country for an exciting mission as a doctor and a scientist in a world of progress, freedom and intellectual pretensions, something I had aimed for anyway, regardless of the Egyptians' role in my departure. Although I thrived in my new environment, finding my natural place there at once, I remained uncertain, as to whether I had been thrown out or whether it was I who had expelled Egypt.

Such a perception left me with a vague sense of guilt which quickly became associated with the anti-colonial and anti-imperialist atmosphere prevailing among those who fancied themselves progressive thinkers, a label very attractive to an idealistic youth. The exotic element in being Egyptian as long as one was successful, endowed with French culture and well-provided for, may also have been of some subtle advantage to me. It was only in time that I came to realise how much more comfortable it is to present oneself as a part of powerful forces and to benefit socially by participating in their apparent self-criticism than it is to be one of the victims. But it made me realise, also, that in striking that attitude, though I may have acquired approbation from the intelligentsias of Europe, I had disengaged myself from the tens of thousands of Jews and foreigners who had had a quite different time. By stressing only my own happy fate, I had diminished the suffering of the others, as well as my parents' courage and fortitude in pulling us through without complaint.

I am aware that, while I enjoyed the good opinion of those who overlooked the intolerance of an Egyptian tyranny by blaming, instead, a long-gone British imperialism, many less advantaged Jews were being deprived of passports, of their homes, of the means to earn a living, and were dumped in refugee camps around Marseilles, in Israel and even in Britain.

Because we had the means to travel to England, Italy and France as often as we wished after the Second World War, we could plan our departure as though it was our own decision rather than a pitiless expulsion and it was easier, at least for me, to think of it in that way. Our journey was thus not a single event to which I can give a date, but in the decade between 1949 and 1958 it was as though we were dipping a toe in the waters of Europe.

We had visited France which usually meant Paris, time and again, while my grandmother Eugénie, now widowed, returned to her tour of spas at Vichy, Evian or Uriages. She made it quite clear that she travelled only because her health demanded it and from what she told us it seemed that the whole Middle East, our Middle East that is, populated those invigorating watering places. They met at the clinics and then had coffee together exchanging information and thoughts about their ailments as well as the impending changes in their home countries, while in the evenings they went to concerts.

They had frequented the spas regularly before the war and had been relieved to find that the hotels, if a little the worse for wear, were still there, often with the odd surviving member of staff. They missed, however, the other regular visitors who had come from Vienna or Budapest or Berlin or the exotic friends they had made from Bucharest and even Bulgaria. These had not returned.

The English, too, had failed to materialise though the hotels had counted on the patronage of the victors, and the staff were only too anxious to offer the deference they deserved. They would whisper to my grandmother, pointing out the spies of the Inland Revenue who lurked in the meaner of the little hotels, waiting to pounce on any English person who had more than £25 to spend.

My grandmother was aware that before her own time, before the First World War that is, the spas had been full of Russians and the older concierges and *maîtres-d'hôtels* had been full of stories of Archdukes maddened with love and also of well-known revolutionaries and anarchists who relied on regularly taking the waters to preserve the purity of their minds and bodies.

"New people come," Eugénie had said. "Who will it be when it ceases to be our turn? Where will they come from then? Or does it turn full circle? Will it be Russia again? Is it the commissars who will take the place of the princes and the counts? Could it be," she added slyly, "that commissar will become a hereditary title as I am told that duke and count were originally only ranks in the Roman army, which powerful families hung on to."

My parents preferred the excitement of Paris to the spas and at first we stayed in the hotels along the Champs Élysées so that they could walk to Fouquet's for an aperitif and have tea at the Marignan. Invariably compatriots and relatives would join them as the crowded tables amalgamated, confusing the waiters who brought the *café liégeois* or the cassata ice-creams as well as the *thé citron*. It was a good time for us, it was our turn.

When we stayed for longer periods we rented apartments near the Parc Monceau and during the day Claudia and Zaki, who was still only nine or ten, and I visited one museum or art gallery after another so that we became autodidacts, acquiring an enormous quantity of information in a higgledy-piggledy manner which took many more years to sort out in our minds so that it made sense.

Apart from Paris my parents loved Italy where we roamed for weeks on end mixing business with pleasure. My father traded with Prato and so we stayed in Florence at a time when its streets were empty of traffic and of tourists, pestered only by the buzzing of the young men riding Vespas or Lambrettas. My father would always ask his clients for suggestions of nice places to go and that led us to Forte dei Marmi where the *pineta*, a thickly wooded band of maritime pines stretched uninterrupted from Marina di Pietra-santa to Viareggio, while Forte itself only peeped out among the trees, and also, to rest from our trip to Venice, to Pocol in the Dolomites with its two hotels which stood on the plateau over-looking Cortina d'Ampezzo. In September we stayed at the Villa d'Este on Lake Como where once the only other guests were Orson Welles and his party, and every day we took the boat to Bellagio or Menagio. A month at the Villa d'Este when today I could hardly afford a day there, what did it mean? How rich were we?

This question left me perplexed for a long time as my parents always referred to us as *bourgeois* until that became a term of abuse and they then insisted we were ordinary middle class. And yet how do you explain the grand hotels, the first-class restaurants and, most of all, how do you explain a whole month at the Villa d'Este?

Recently I was forced to recall this time with a person who finds the concept of wealth slightly distasteful and who likes to think, looking back, that we were all rather poor. That seemed to me too much of a distortion to satisfy her modesty, however endearing.

"How do you explain then," I said triumphantly, "a whole month at the Villa d'Este? We must have been rich. I was worried at having a single meal there last month and yet we had *demi-pension* for the whole time as well as breakfast."

"Oh," she dismissed me airily, "everyone stayed at the Villa d'Este!"

What she said was not entirely ridiculous as wealth is a comparative commodity. The man with millions in a devalued currency is suddenly poor while the one who holds a stable currency can buy what he wants. Egypt had kept out of the war while Europe was economically destroyed. My parents had been right to disclaim great wealth and yet compared with the citizens of France and Italy we were indeed very rich.

The meaning of true poverty struck me by chance in Rome early one morning in the summer of 1949. I had got up before the others and gone for a walk by some ancient ruins, hoping no doubt to be inspired, as one does when young and eager to learn. Parts of the ruins were arches, the remnants of an aqueduct. Such structures are so common throughout the Roman world that we don't give them a second thought other than when seeking a source of shade, but what were invariably present in the days just after the war were blankets strung across the arches forming shelters for homeless families. A middle-aged man drew a blanket aside and emerged dressed in a pin-striped suit with a white shirt and tie. He wore a black *Borsalino* hat and, carrying a document case, strode towards the bus stop as a little boy followed to wave goodbye.

I had seen much squalor in South America and Egypt and had accepted the dirt and poverty, the child beggars, the maimed and the sick lying in the dusty streets as a normal part of life. I had certainly felt compassion in Egypt as I had dropped a *piastre* into an emaciated hand, taking care not to touch it for fear of germs as I had been taught.

"Al-Allah!" I had said, commending the individual to God.

"Allah grant you protection," would be the reply in feigned gratitude.

But I knew that, however sad, such poverty had nothing to do with me. At first I had thought it was the way of the world and in time that it was the result of socio-economic forces. The difference with that homeless man was that with his decent suit, his shirt and tie and especially his black *Borsalino*, he looked like my father. It could have been us. No one, I suddenly realised, was safe.

I began to wonder at the calm way, even the amusement with which my father faced the business world of post-war Europe. Was he not worried, I had asked, that things might go wrong and that we might be destitute?

"No," he had replied. "There is rebuilding everywhere, every-thing must get better. Trade will start again. That is how things go and we will just travel to wherever makes us welcome. Wait till we go to Milan – that will raise your spirits and give you confidence."

Milan was certainly a city on the move and the hotels were crowded with businessmen from all over the world. Not many had set themselves up in offices yet and they clustered together in cafés and bars to do their deals as people and politicians had been doing for centuries.

Those from the Middle East favoured the Salotto in the Galleria Vittorio Emanuele II, near the Duomo. I suppose the Galleria must have been one of the modern world's first shopping malls protecting its patrons from the elements at a time when there was neither air conditioning nor adequate heating. In 1949 it was 70 years old but the Milanese, aware of its likely importance to the revival of business, had restored it to its original beauty before they had done anything else. Although the Galleria represented the beginning of modern times, a remarkably ancient sacrificial ritual had occurred at its foundation, although this time through a singular accident: the architect had fallen off the scaffolding and died just before the opening. The café Salotto itself, where I sat with my father who introduced me to a Campari-soda for the first time, made it into the twenty-first century though it is now facing closure, to be replaced, no doubt, by one of the more expensive designer shops. In 1949, of course, there was no thought of that when a man approached my father and asked him in a Syrian dialect of Arabic to read a telegram for him.

"It is about the nails and screws you ordered," my father translated for him. "They want $10,000 for the consignment."

The man grunted his thanks and walked on.

"Watch him," my father said. "He will ask someone else to make sure that what I told him was true. He can't even read and he has amassed a fortune. This is what happens after wars, some are toppled from their places while others find opportunities denied them before and we must not mock them."

My father's cousin Heschel had joined us when the Syrian came back. He wanted to take us to his apartment to show us something and although my father tried to get out of it, Heschel insisted we go. I got the impression he was looking forward to mocking the Syrian a little.

"So what national passport did you buy in the end?" Heschel asked him as we walked through Piazza della Scala.

"Panama," he replied. "But I had to buy the Consulate as well, they went together, cost a fortune!"

"So now you are the Consul of Panama," Heschel pressed him. "But what do you have to do apart from selling passports? Go to meetings and things?"

"Oh yes, I have to go to things. Last night I was sitting between the British and French Ambassadors and they asked me what we were going to do about the Canal."

"Did you know?" asked Heschel.

"No, of course not, how would I know? I just said that we were reflecting and they nodded."

When we reached his apartment in Via Manzoni he introduced me to his son, an adenoidal teenager younger than me who avoided my gaze and whose wet nose and permanently open mouth gave him a distressed if not actually defective look.

"This is Yohanan, he also will go to Ofzord and Cambage."

"Oxford and Cambridge you mean," said Heschel stifling his laughter. "It is either or, not both at the same time."

"Why not?" the Syrian was defiant. "I can pay for both!"

What he wanted to show us was the large painting he had bought of some nineteenth-century battle and he told us he had paid a hundred million lire for it.

"Isn't that rather a lot," my father asked, "considering it is not signed?"

"Who cares who painted it?" the man said. "I am really not interested in the artist, it's the picture I like."

"But then how do you know the value?" my father was genuinely interested. "Surely you don't take a figure from the air? And a canny man like you is not just going to accept any sum that the dealer asks."

"Look," said the man patiently. "If you count the figures in the picture you find that there are 30 people, that is if you include the dead and wounded which must take even more skill to paint, and the three women who are giving them water. See how pretty they look, especially that one there holding the towel? Then there are 20 horses, some prancing about, others standing still while some have been killed, lying there all tangled up. Could you reasonably ask someone to paint one of these figures for less than a million lire? Fifty figures makes 50 million. Then there are the trees, not so much for the bushes as they are smaller, but the clouds! You have to paint those too. Believe me I got a bargain."

Heschel was now anxious to go. An inveterate gossip and mocker, he was desperate to tell everyone he knew what he had seen and heard. But the man called out after me.

"Hey! Perhaps you can see my son when he is at Ofzord and Cambage?"

My father was more thoughtful than Heschel and as we left, he said that he had a feeling that Michelangelo may well have negotiated his fee according to the number of figures he was commissioned to paint by the Pope. I never saw the boy again nor did I try to find out what happened to him or his father, but recently I went to one of those rather esoteric lectures that we only get a chance to attend as our working careers begin to wane. It was entitled "Eighteenth-Century Italian History as Represented in Painting".

There was something familiar about the lecturer though I could not quite place him at first. Perhaps the dripping nose and obvious difficulty in breathing, perhaps the tendency to avoid others' gaze but the name meant nothing to me after all these years though his first name was Jonathan. The description of his achievements and publications in the booklet, however, included an Oxford degree followed by a fellowship at Cambridge. But I cannot be sure it was him, of course.

The 1940s, stretched out as far as they could go by the war and its aftermath, were finally petering out and the moment had at last come for me to be sent to England to study for my A-levels. What was left of the Orient Express started in Zagreb, already in the communist world though a less rigid Iron Curtain country, then it stopped in Trieste, then Venice and I was put on it at Milan by my parents.

"Go for it! We trust you," they had said. "Remember we depend on you for our future." I kissed my brother and sister with a tightened heart, found my carriage and tipped the attendant of the wagons-lits as I had been told, and felt the total confidence of my age.

At supper my three table companions barely spoke. There was an Englishman, travelling from Zagreb to Paris. I asked what he had been doing, getting only a tired shrug in response. There was a bearded man with dark glasses of uncertain nationality. He smiled sadly when I stared at his travel document and with the impudence of youth I asked what nationality it was.

"A Nansen passport," he said. "What they give to stateless

people who need to cross frontiers." There was no more explanation.

And then the beautiful woman, silent and distant. At least 30,
twice my age, but evoking those strange, unaccountable emotions
which can be understood fully only later.

I was the one who spoke most, describing my parents, my
hopes and ambitions in detail. Perhaps inspired by the beauty of
the woman I showed off by elaborating my philosophy of life
which, at my age, must have made me the most bizarre member
of the group.

We reached Ventimiglia in the middle of the night. The
attendant had taken my passport so that I should not be troubled
by the Border Control but there was so much noise that I woke
up. Not that I had slept soundly, I was too excited for that, but the
shouts and angry curses brought me out into the corridor. The
beautiful woman stood there, her dark hair loose around her
shoulders, her scent ever more intense as her belongings were
being strewn all over the corridor.

I had been well brought up. I had been taught rules of
behaviour which could, of course, be overlooked but which could
also be followed when at a loss as to what to do. I stood in front of
her and accused the French and Italian customs officers of unacceptable behaviour towards a lady. For a moment they stared at
me surprised but then I was pushed back into my compartment
with a warning to mind my own affairs. The beautiful woman
remained expressionless but there was a slight gesture of the head,
which suggested I should do what I was told.

The following morning she joined me at breakfast. She wanted
to thank me, she said, for having stood up for her. I said I was
appalled at what I had seen and I would get my father to make a
formal complaint but she shrugged her shoulders.

"They know me you see," she said speaking French in an
accent I could not quite place, "I am a currency trafficker and
they are furious that they have never caught me."

"But did you have the money?" I asked.

"Oh yes," she said, "I had it all right." She took me back to my own compartment and pointed to the space underneath my bunk.

I had shed my companions by the time I found myself on the cross-channel ferry and I had no concerns other than to find a place where I could vomit in privacy. I was so sea-sick and had never imagined it would be as bad. I asked a sailor if it was always like that.

"Oh God no!" he replied. "We are really lucky today with the sea like a mill pond, usually it gets pretty rough here."

I thought that I may well never be able to get off this island, but though somewhat dazed, I went on to London. The train, for some mysterious reason, had changed its name from the Orient Express to the Golden Arrow. In time I was to realise that this sort of thing often happened when one reached England. Unexplainable differences like driving on the left.

I made my way to Bradford, my destination, where my Aunt Giselle lived. She had ended up in Yorkshire with the airman she had married during the war and although we knew nothing about her life my mother had sent me there perhaps with the same lack of information or planning as when she had taken us to South America. I realised on arrival that no arrangements had been made for my schooling but it was late and I was tired. I could not quite orientate myself as of all the places in the world where I had been this seemed the strangest.

My aunt lived in a semi-detached house with no heating other than a bright coal fire in the living room. I later realised that this was how the majority of the English lived but despite all my reading and preparation I had never imagined such cold, or indeed such a place at all. It was not what I had imagined. As she had a small child still in nappies, which in those days had to be washed as there was nothing disposable, these cloth towels were hung out, imperfectly rinsed, on folding wooden frames referred to as "clothes horses" in front of the fire, to be dried by that sole source of heat. This meant that a faint smell of urine pervaded the room, but I was too sleepy to take it all in and went up to bed. I later realised that this aunt had gone native.

When I woke up in the morning and pushed my head above the bed clothes I had never in my life experienced such cold. It was only September and yet there was a thin coating of condensation that had frozen into ice on the inside of the window pane. I managed to switch on the single bar electric fire, an appliance that I had never even known existed and scraped some of the ice from the window so that I could look out.

The house was on a hill overlooking the city of Bradford which resembled a dark pit because all the buildings were jet black as they were covered with soot. Around the city centre the tall chimneys of the mills emitted so much black smoke that it completely obscured the sky. But the most depressing sight were the rows and rows of terraced houses, all black as if originally they had been built with black stones and all belching out the same dark smoke from countless chimneys.

There was a sink in my room with two taps, one freezing cold and the other scalding. No one had explained in any book that the English washed with little square cloths splashing in the sink and I did not know what to do. I cried a little to myself and wanted to go back to Egypt but my aunt was a kind woman and I did not want to hurt her feelings. I also did not want to give up.

She had been told that the best school was Bradford Grammar School and suggested I go there. She put me on the bus and told me to ask for a ha'penny half which worked as I was given a ticket but I was surprised when the conductress called me "love". She called all the passengers "love" and they too seemed to call her "love".

The secretary was puzzled when I explained that I had come alone.

"But you don't live alone?"

"No, no! I live with an aunt, but she could not come."

She thought I had better see the headmaster who said that he had never had a boy come by himself before but all my certificates and testimonials were in order so he was not sure what to do. I think he must have been somewhat intrigued by me as he thought a little, shrugged his shoulders and gave me a place.

"We must move with the times," he said gloomily. "Who knows what will come next."

After thinking again for a moment he called me back.

"Tell me," he asked "how do you see your future? Where do you think you will end ultimately?"

"I think I want to be a doctor."

"Ah," he said visibly relieved. "At least that is a straightforward ambition. We can handle that!"

In fact it turned out to be more difficult than I expected.

16

Paris

"And tell me," the man had asked, pausing for a moment as he leaned towards me with a contemptuous smile. "Are you planning to return to Egypt, if you do actually qualify that is, to look after the *fellaheen?*"

Although I had set off early enough for my interview at Guy's Hospital Medical School in London, there had been some delay on the Northern Line of the Underground and as I ran, anxious not to be late, I stepped slithering into a pile of dog excrement. I was breathless, tears came to my eyes and I held back a sob as I sat on the corner of the pavement to clean my shoe, scraping off the mess with a twig. The smell was particularly pungent and I thought it hung around throughout the interview though it may have been only a sign of my insecurity. I felt this was the end of my ambitions as every other medical school had turned me down and Guy's was the last one to agree to see me. I dusted my tweed suit as I got up aware of how inappropriate it looked, an older man's outfit. It was a time of shortages and recycling and no one had thick wool suits in Egypt. An uncle had given me this one and my father had taken me to Wanis Salama, his tailor in the Musky in Cairo to have it refashioned. I was a slight, somewhat weedy boy and between them they had agreed to leave it slightly large as I would surely grow into it and fill it out. I did not and it always hung helplessly on me, a ridiculous hand-me-down.

"I am sorry, I did not catch your answer," the man had continued, anxious to show off his knowledge of Egypt to his companions. "There are two sorts, those who want to go to the villages to help the peasants, *fellaheen* they call them, and those who plan a lucrative private practice among the Jews and Europeans in Soliman Pasha Street. Now which one are you?"

The thin smile never left his lips.

"I just want to be a doctor," I said lamely and, as they continued to stare at me I felt I had to add something.

"I want to help people."

There were other candidates waiting and they did not take too long in their deliberation. I could hear the man's words before I had even left the room.

"Not our sort of material, is he?"

I returned to Guy's Hospital 20 years later and even then it was with apprehension though it had been by invitation. Why subject myself to this again, I thought as I sat waiting? But this time the chairman himself came out and I was offered the post of Consultant Surgeon in the Ear, Nose and Throat Department. It was unanimous, they had said and they hoped I would accept as it was people like me that they needed. I was to be the new Chief.

In the summer of 1951, however, I was relieved when my parents told me to go to Paris to collect my brother and sister as the school holidays had arrived. Claudia was at the *Lycée de Jeunes Filles Hélène Boucher* at Vincennes and Zaki, now twelve, was at the *Lycée Michelet* near the Porte Maillot. It was a comfort to be told what to do. My parents had rented a large apartment in the Boulevard St Germain near the Solferino-Belechasse bus stop and had invited our grandmother Eugénie to stay with us as an adult presence. She was not, of course, expected to look after us as we were quite capable of doing that ourselves and, in any case, she had never looked after anyone in the whole of her life. She occupied a self-contained set of rooms at the far end of our apartment where she set herself up independently. She would only appear around lunchtime, perfectly made up and elegantly dressed to enquire what the menu was that day. On the other hand she was good humoured, of considerable intellect and with strong opinions, and there is no doubt that we enjoyed her company.

We also had a maid, a woman aged around 40, and I suppose that despite our familiarity with the French language and our sense of belonging in France she must have been the first French person with whom we had come into close contact. She stuck very closely to her contract which required her to cook lunch but not to do the shopping. That was to be for us and we went, all three, down the Rue de Seine where the food stalls were laid out. We got on reasonably well with our maid though she resisted our attempts at friendship and finally exploded with rage when one day we handed her the daily bottle of wine that her contract had stipulated. She was so furious that it was difficult to understand what we had done wrong, but eventually we gathered that the wine we had bought contained only 10 degrees of alcohol whereas her contract stipulated 11 degrees. We had known nothing about degrees till that moment but as soon as I understood I ran downstairs to buy two other bottles in compensation for the trauma while Claudia and Zaki tried to pacify her and stop her from leaving at once. She never trusted us again as I think she was convinced that we had tried to cheat her.

My grandmother left in due course, though as she had kept so much to herself, I cannot remember the precise moment nor where she went. Our lives as three very young people living by ourselves in Paris, and later in London, were to continue until our parents finally joined us in 1958. We brought each other up and remained more closely attached than siblings usually are but I think that we were considered an oddity by those around us.

Soon Claudia and Zaki went back to school. The lease on the apartment was ending and I was not sure what to do with myself. My parents, naturally anxious at leaving me unoccupied, telegrammed from Khartoum – where my father's business was expanding – suggesting I try to join the Medical Faculty in Rue de l'École de Médicine.

The system in France was quite different. In a fit of populism the revolutionary government from Napoleonic times had decreed that everyone with the academic qualifications required by the Republic was entitled to register at the university and faculty of his choice. There was to be no nepotism, no selection committee, no interviews. Of course the professionals then took over and failed 90% of the candidates at the end of their first year. The Republic offered equality of opportunity but not to the lowest common denominator, indeed it favoured the smartest.

I was accepted without question, an exhilarating sensation after the intrusive probing of my motives to which I had been subjected in England only to be found inadequate. In Paris no one wanted to know why I had chosen to be a doctor, that was my business and it might change or not over the years, they cared only if I passed. I was told to buy a white coat, get a stethoscope at Maloine's across the road and I was handed a detailed timetable. Suddenly it had all become so simple and I was a real medical student.

The first session was a lecture on the thorax at the Faraboeuf Amphitheatre, a large circular lecture hall in the old style with oak benches round the room and desktops that could be banged in moments of extreme tension. I had got there early but the hall quickly filled. The French students were rowdy and sang rude songs. The last student to enter was the usual attention-seeker, a shapely 18-year-old tossing her long dark hair about her shoulders.

"*Toute nue!*" the students shouted as they clapped their hands, "*Toute nue!*" "You can take your clothes off now!"

Embarrassed as I felt for her in my innocence, the look of radiant triumph on her face gave me a first glimpse of the quirks of human nature and I realised that the more worldly-wise students were actually playing to her tune. My life as a medical student had begun. The professor entered and, subdued by the sudden realisation that this was the very first moment of our lives as doctors, we fell silent as he started without ceremony.

"*Le thorax*. Let us pick up our scalpels," he began, brandishing his stick of chalk as slides had not yet invaded the lecture rooms. "As we cut through the skin we part a layer of fat – *le tissu adipeux*." He went on, his vocal inflections not dissimilar to those of the Comédie Française nearby. "*Ah! Mais le sternum!* This hard protective bone impedes us. What shall we do?" He gestured questioningly to the bemused audience. "*Que faut-il que nous fassions?*" he asked again, relying on the subjunctive tense to heighten the atmosphere, as he looked questioningly around the circular hall and up and down the tiers crowded with students on their first day. "The saw, of course*, Messieurs et Mesdames*, the electric saw!"

He scratched vigorously up and down on the blackboard with the chalk, setting our teeth on edge, then indicating with his hands the forceful separation of the two halves of the chest wall, he glanced briefly to the left then to the right and went on in a conspiratorial voice. "As we enter the thoracic cavity, temporarily obstructed by this fatty organ," his gesture was one of disdain, as he simulated the ripping out and discarding of the thymus followed by a dramatic moment of silence, and then his voice dropped to a whisper, "veiled on either side by the delicate drapes of the pleura, which we pull aside, gently, delicately, to expose . . ." now he pulled himself up, facing the audience, and with a flourish of his right arm, ". . . to expose*, au centre du thorax, Mesdames et Messieurs* – the heart."

Open-mouthed, we burst into applause as the professor took his bow.

That seemed to me for a long time afterwards to have been the defining year of my life. I felt I had become someone who was now able to understand all the workings of the world, from the way the valves of the heart opened and closed, to the exploitation of the masses by the military-industrial complex. I had become confident in my certainty and knew which books to read; I had become myself at last.

As the years have passed, and perhaps as I have shed one certainty after another, reducing any confidence I have left to the medical knowledge so painfully accumulated over the decades and the technical skills which inevitably must soon diminish, I have come to regard it as a time of some delusion even though the nostalgia and excitement remain when I think about it. With hindsight I see that two things were happening in my life, simultaneously and yet separately. On the one hand there was my life as a medical student. The contact with patients, with their sickness and their fear and the awareness of my own impotence and how little I understood or could do to help them was humbling. I craved the guidance of real doctors and desperately hoped that the skills of my professors would achieve what I could not. I had wanted to help people at once, immediately, and yet I could see that it would take me years of work and study before I would have anything to offer at all. I was taught to feel the enlarged cirrhotic liver before it had shrunk into a gnarled and hardened remnant, by passing my hand gently over the abdomen. I learned to recognise with dread, as I listened with my brand new stethoscope, to the *whoosh-boom*, *whoosh-boom* of the diastolic murmur, the sound which signalled the inevitability of the impending failure of the heart and the path to the end of life. I marvelled at the trust with which anxious patients uncovered themselves to me, whose opinion was hardly worth having, when they guided my hand to their breast, that so private area, as they willed me to feel the lump which might be the first announcement of their death.

In the afternoons we attended the dissecting rooms, large halls with glass roofs and the pervading smell of formaldehyde where we took apart, layer by layer, the rows of preserved cadavers stretched out on zinc tables, naked bodies that had been men and women. We joked, of course, to relieve the tension and we smoked to mask the smell as we separated the tissues of the body with our scalpels and our forceps, identifying with pride the tiny nerves or shrunken arteries, but underlying it all we learned respect and most of all humility as, young as we were, the first thing we had to face was that all lives, even our own, were finite.

I am told that medical students do not now have to dissect human bodies as there are plastic models which look even more real with all the right colours. I am sure that it is all to the good and that we must move with the times but I wonder if some essence, a sort of understanding, is lost when we avoid that early intimacy with death.

On the other hand there was another life in Paris, an exhilarating one, that of ideas. A life of discussion and politics and of philosophy, of meeting people from different places and different beliefs. I shared a certain sense of community with other foreigners and we were conscious that this had happened so often in the past, particularly in Paris. We knew about Hemingway, of course, and Gertrude Stein, about James Joyce and Beckett, and about the artists who had come to enrich and be enriched by that city, Modigliani, Chagall, Soutine, Picasso, Zadkine and Man Ray. This had led to a certain unspoken understanding that we, in our turn, would take our place in the pantheon of the famous. Men and women from elsewhere, freed from the supervision and constraints of their own cultures could allow their minds to wander, following uncharted paths or trailing after the forbidden ones of others. We felt superior to the rest of the world as we were convinced that we understood everything from the meaning of art, the causes of wars, the reasons for poverty to the plots designed to keep the masses in thrall. Those were heady times as we thought that the words we spoke, the arguments we resolved mattered in some way and would, in time, change the world. Those of us who were medical students may have received some protection from the wilder excesses of such illusions as we had to return to the wards each morning to take the bloods and do the rounds of real people in need.

When I look back something else comes to mind and that is the absence of Parisians in our social lives. I wonder if it was just me in my time or whether foreigners had always been shunned to a degree unless, presumably, they had already achieved fame.

I looked at it the other way round. Did Sartre, de Beauvoir and Raymond Aron have foreign friends? What about Lacan? Or Althusser? It may simply be gaps in my knowledge but I have a suspicion that Parisian intellectuals always kept well away from us and that foreigners just used the facilities. As far as I am concerned I was only invited once to the home of a fellow student.

He was an only child. We sat uncomfortably at table, his father his mother and the two of us trying to find a subject of conversation that would suit us all. The cheese was exceptionally good and unusual so I made my compliments and asked what it was.

"Oh, it comes from Germany, Bavaria," the mother said. "During the war we had that charming German officer billeted on us. You remember Franz, Julien?"

They had become close friends and he always brought them some of the extra food the German occupying forces had access to, and they had stayed in touch, continuing to exchange gifts. As they remembered the Occupation they recalled the good times they had had with Franz and I was left in no doubt as to what a decent and charming fellow he was.

My foolishness was such that having been fed on films and stories of the brave French resistance I thought I might have found another suitable subject of conversation, but before I'd got very far they looked at me astonished, as though that was something that had never had anything to do with them, which, I suppose it had not. The *maquis*, that unruly brush-land far into the mountains had little to do with the city.

"*Ah oui, la résistance*," the mother had said. "*Dans le maquis, bien sûr!* Awful things happened, on both sides of course. Ours were hardly blameless."

*

In the Paris hospitals of the time, first-year medical students were expected to turn up in the wards every morning. I was allocated to Lariboisière, in the *service* of Professor Ménégaux, known as *Le Patron*.

We hung around in the corridor in our new white coats on our first day uncertain what to do as patients were wheeled to and from the operating theatres, intravenous drips swaying, oxygen masks tight on their faces. Occasionally someone shouted at us: "Hey you! Hold this oxygen mask here!" or "The bloody drip has come out! You there, do something! Stick it back into the vein, didn't you see it had slipped out?"

"Sorry, sir, I do not know how."

"*Mon dieu*, it's the first years again! Why always us?"

We were ushered into the operating theatres where the assistants were operating. We stood as far back as we could in terror but no one fainted. At last *Le Patron* came in accompanied by an extremely fat woman, the head nurse. Professor Ménégaux had his mask pulled to the side with a lighted cigarette in the corner of his mouth sticking out horizontally. The assistants explained what they were doing and he leaned over the patient mumbling praise and advice.

Every time he spoke the cigarette trembled and we worried that the ash lengthening on the tip might fall into the wound. He showed us an x-ray demonstrating a plastic hip replacement. The first ever, he said, made by Judet at the beginning of the war. The Germans were amazed when they saw it for the first time in an x-ray.

"But on the other hand, we too were amazed when we saw the first Kunschner nails in our returning prisoners of war."

The war was not long over and the surgeon spoke much of its traumas. Road traffic accidents were still uncommon as cars were rare. When the chief had gone, the fat lady, the head nurse who we were told to address as *Madame* lined us up to inspect our fingernails.

"Disgusting," she said and sent us off to scrub. Only one third-year student dared answer back. We were not touching anything sterile, he had said, and in any case she had allowed *Le Patron* to come in with a cigarette. *Madame* was nonplussed for a moment and stammered a little.

"But, he is *Le Patron*, and, in any case, burning ash is sterile!"

It was my turn to spend the night in the Emergency Room, and Barbes-Rochechouart was not the best district of Paris. Even the Métro was above ground as it had not been worth hiding it from the view of the impoverished inhabitants whose outlook did not matter. People came in screaming with stomach pains. Women who had never been to a clinic walked in to deliver a baby on the floor. Drunks with suspected head injuries lay unconscious on trolleys and stabbing and gunshot wounds were bleeding in the cubicles.

"Do us a favour my dear little chap," the doctor said to me. "Go and sew up that Corsican bandit with the cut through the eyebrow."

The fact that I had never seen it done did not seem to worry him as he was tired – it was two o'clock in the morning. He shrugged his shoulders and told me that the nurse would show me. Mademoiselle Rose had a pink uniform. Later I learned that her name was not Rose at all and the colour simply indicated that she was a probationer, as inexperienced as I was. She had just been told to lay out the needle, the needle-holder, the forceps, scissors and black silk thread. At least she knew which tools we needed and even though neither of us had seen it done before we did our best and I was left with a sense of satisfaction. It was, after all, my first surgical operation, minor though it might be.

I slept little in the tiny room I had been given. Partly we were busy and partly I could not tear myself away from the doctors and nurses as they sipped their coffee and commiserated about life and the human condition, shrugging their shoulders. They would all be off on Saturday night, that was the way the rota worked. They told each other where they would be going; out with their wives and husbands and lovers. Some would be visiting in-laws in the country, others would stay at home, yet others would be living it up, dancing perhaps. Everyone would have supper, then in the banality of life, they would go to bed and make love. That, they told me, was life.

"*Et puis on se couche et on fait l'amour.*" They all shrugged their shoulders, there really was not that much more to do or indeed to be said. I knew I was with the grown-ups now so I too shrugged my shoulders and nodded in the full knowledge of what lay ahead.

I was up early for the Grand Round though I still did not need to shave every day. At the head of the large retinue was the chief flanked by *Madame*, the fat lady in charge of theatres on one side and by *Madame*, the ward nurse on the other. This one was thin and anxious and did not get on with the fat one who again insisted on checking our fingernails. They made remarks attacking each other's team which the chief pretended not to notice. Behind them was *Le Chef-de-Clinique* who had just returned from America, then the assistants, followed by interns, the third-year students, us, the probationer nurses, the physiotherapists and the nutritionists – contributors to healing and recovery.

Le Patron made sure everyone had their say as we went from one patient to the next. The student would give the history, the intern would describe the examination, the assistants would justify their diagnosis and the treatment they had given. *Le Patron* would enquire of the nurse, the physiotherapist or whoever was appropriate and then with great deference would turn to *Le Chef-de-Clinique*.

"And what do the Anglo-Saxons think about this?"

When we came to my patient, the Corsican with the slash through the eyebrow the chief lifted my bulky bandage to peep underneath and then quickly slapped it back on.

"*Bon, bon,*" he said and walked off. At the end of the round he beckoned with his finger and took me to his office.

"You have seen your mother sewing, no?" I nodded.

"She threads the needle, makes a knot at one end does she not?"

He waited until I nodded again.

"Then she goes through, across the cut and over. Through again and over until the end when she makes another knot, yes?"

"*Oui monsieur.*"

"Well," he said pausing, "we don't do it like that in surgery. Stitch, tie, cut. Stitch, tie, cut. It is called interrupted sutures. *Ça va?* You see what I mean.*"

"*Je regrète, Monsieur,*" I said mortified. "Can we undo what I've done?"

"No, no," he replied. "It all heals, you know, whatever we do heals, that is our secret, the secret of surgery. It may not heal well, of course, but then your Corsican knife fighter is not a model from Dior, is he?"

It was not easy to find accommodation in Paris after the war. Students who were lucky lived in *"chambres de bonnes"*, maids' rooms at the top of blocks of flats as the former occupants were gone. Today these tiny spaces have been amalgamated into penthouse lofts and their origins have been largely forgotten. Others lived in the hotels of the Latin quarter which had not yet been upgraded. I was in a hotel in the Rue-Monsieur-le-Prince, just behind the Rue de l'École de Médecine. It has gone now, even the school of medicine has moved to the Rue des Saints-Pères on the other side of the Boulevard St Germain. Maybe it was too difficult to upgrade my hotel as the rooms were small and there were no bathrooms, just one toilet between floors; maybe it was the plumbing that could not be altered. I washed from the sink and peed in the bidet. From time to time I would go for a shower at the *Bains Racine*, the public baths in the Rue Racine off the Boulevard St Michel. This was more for pleasure and indulgence than for cleanliness as you can keep quite clean washing from a tap. The heating was poor as the radiators were rusty so we studied in cafés such as the *Petit Suisse* or at *Capoulade* where we were tolerated. I had been taught, when the cold was most severe, to stuff newspaper underneath my pyjamas and into my socks, and study from bed, a technique I fortunately no longer have to use but which I can recommend as it proved useful in my later life as a military doctor in Stirling Castle.

The main reason for the cold at the Hotel Monsieur-le-Prince was the meanness of the owner, Mme Baroin. She grasped in all directions, every little service was counted as an extra franc here, another there. But one day everything changed. She was waiting for me, calling out, *"Docteur! Docteur!"* with a big smile exposing her tobacco-stained teeth. I was shown into the little parlour where her husband and two fat sons were already sitting at the table, glasses in front of them. Only after I had been forced to sit down behind the extra glass did Mme Baroin unlock the cupboard and take out a bottle of port. Her menfolk were already whispering loudly if conspiratorially: *"Le porto! Le porto!"*

She offered me a deal. She had to have injections of vitamins, *"intramusculaires"* she insisted precisely, vitamin B, because of her failing liver. *"C'est l'alcool,"* her husband explained. *"Le foie,"* she elaborated pointing to her liver as she sipped her port. "A little from time to time that's all."

The deal was this. The district nurse charged 200 francs (or was it still 200,000 of the old ones?) for each injection. Would I do it for half that amount? They were ready to haggle but I said nothing, pretending to think it over, so they turned the conversation to the events of the day and expressed their support for the finance minister M. Antoine Pinay. He had the interests of *"les petits gens"* at heart. They assumed I, too, like everyone else they knew, was one of his admirers. I could not bear this assumption. At that age and full of ideals I could not understand M. Pinay's pettiness, both material and spiritual, nor did I want to be associated with his supporters, even temporarily while talking to the Baroin family. I simply said I would be happy to inject Mme Baroin with her vitamins but I would do it free. I realised at once that this was the wrong response, that somehow I was doing them harm which was not what I had intended. They insisted, lamely, that I should be paid something, hopefully a nominal sum, but the bottom line, the way they lived their lives was that everyone should look after his own beefsteak, as they liked to put it. No, I kept on with what I now realise bordered on cruelty, some of us believed in helping people because it is intrinsically good and unrelated to money.

Their way of life had no answer to the smugness of idealism, and I still wince at the thought of how unjust youth can be and at the humiliation I had inflicted. Barely to my credit I did accept the glass of port which was offered after each injection. This created a relationship, even after the course of treatment was over, necessitating the odd conversation which I tried to keep to a minimum while she insisted on informing me of the activities of the other residents.

That the maid was called Madeleine everyone could tell as Mme Baroin would call out incessant instructions to her from the bottom of the narrow stairwell. "Madeleine! Madeleine!" I am afraid that I added to her burdens by pulling all the bedclothes from the bed every day and placing them on the open window sill. I had been advised to do this by a third-year student called Philip Philip. He was a little bitter at his parents' lack of imagination in naming him but he was always full of advice and information. He told us all, for instance, that the *Chef-de-Clinic* at La Riboisière owed his advancement and even his trip to America to the fact that he had married the daughter of a *Grand Patron* at La Pitié Hospital.

"In France," he said, shrugging his shoulders and making a despondent grimace, "you must have family connections, that's what it's all about."

Most of Philip Philip's information was of a more practical

nature and he directed it towards me, taking me under his wing because of my youth and obvious innocence. He had pointed out that the maids in the hotels rarely made the beds properly, barely pulling the covers over, and told me what to do. I still feel sorry when I remember Madeleine's cries of distress as she saw what I had done. "*O là là!*"

Philip Philip also warned me against personal relationships of an intimate nature with women living in the same house. He had put it much more crudely, but the risks, he claimed, were too great to be worth any possible convenience resulting from proximity.

"You can never get rid of them," he said ruefully. "They are always hanging around pestering you. Take my advice, look elsewhere."

Embarrassed as I was by my innocence, I was grateful to be included in the group of those worthy of advice. The opportunity did present itself, however, when a girl rented the other room on the first floor. She always dressed in black trousers and a black roll-neck pullover, her thick untidy hair was windswept or rather she herself was windswept as, thin and dark, she was always running. Up the stairs, down the stairs, out of the door, in the door, barely nodding acknowledgement. She was pretty in a crass sort of way and I tried to work out some excuse to speak to her or at least interrupt her rapid passage. I was ready, indeed desperate, to disregard Philip Philip's advice but my inexperience restrained me and I never got further than "*Bonjour!*" and fantasy.

On the second floor was an extremely thin elderly Chinese man. Whenever the door to his room was open I could see it was dark and the heavy wooden shutters were never open. The most significant thing about his room was the number of clocks he kept. All of them struck the hour, some the half and a few the quarter, all night and all day. Although they struck more or less together there was always a little difference, perhaps a split second between the timing of the clocks so that we could hear the separate tones quite distinctly. Some were high-pitched pings, others deep sad strokes, while others were little tinkles. Everybody grumbled to Mme Baroin who did nothing but hinted that she charged him a higher rent for the disturbance. No one spoke to the Chinaman himself. He grew thinner and the sound of vomiting was added to the noise of his clocks. Mme Baroin insisted I inspect the common toilet on the mezzanine after he had been there as specks of fresh blood had spattered the bowl. She wanted to know if it was infectious, but I could not tell her. One day an ambulance came to take him away and he died in hospital.

The man who moved into the vacated room was much closer to the Baroin family. Excitedly Mme Baroin told me he had canvassed for M. Antoine Pinay in his time and had actually shaken his hand. He had haggled for the rent with Mme Baroin giving in only at the last minute, affording her the exhilaration and the satisfaction of winning. He merited a glass of port and as it was my injection day I was invited join them. M. Grosjean was in his mid-fifties, bald and with a paunch. He had a little moustache like Hitler's and I wondered what made men grow such things, what sort of image were they trying to present, what fantasies did they elaborate about themselves? We made polite conversation and he told me that he was an employee of *l'Electricité de France* dealing with payment arrears. He confirmed his admiration of M. Antoine Pinay, his suspicion of intellectuals, his contempt of glamour and his hatred of the rich and powerful. He explained in detail his own affection for the ordinary in a strange panegyric of pettiness.

Mme Baroin's attachment to him was swiftly brought to an end after he entertained the dark young girl from the first floor. Madeleine had complained about the state of the sheets. Mme Baroin insisted on dragging me upstairs to inspect them. This time I refused. Soiled sheets were not a medical matter.

"But she was a virgin!" Mme Baroin expostulated. "There are blood stains."

"That is physiological not pathological," I insisted. But I saw she was upset, maybe she had developed some affection for the man. I too was upset. Perhaps I should have made the first move. Surely it would have been a better experience with me than with the middle-aged, paunchy M. Grosjean. But then I consoled myself with Philip Philip's admonishment. She would have pestered me would she not, I reflected wistfully?

In time I found a lovely friend. She was fresh-faced and pretty and she was English. She reminded me of the girls at the English School in Cairo with slightly protruding teeth. Everyone called her *l'Anglaise*, I remember her happy and interested face. She was on her way to Oxford. Though it is difficult for me to imagine, she is an old lady now.

17

The Intellectuals

I reached the old seventeenth-century house in the Marais where people were spilling over on to the street smoking *Gitanes* and balancing their glasses of champagne together with *petits fours*. A few had managed to bring down whole bottles with them.

The district had not then been gentrified and the buildings were rickety and covered with peeling plaster. As none of the inhabitants owned the properties they would not rectify their neglected state. The houses had been divided into semi-separate apartments. This meant that there were no real front doors and that toilets, which were always situated on the mezzanines were shared with all the disputes that that entailed. Bathrooms were rare and showers did not exist. This gave the whole area a Bohemian atmosphere.

The party was on the fifth floor of the narrow building so I climbed the spiral staircase which was crowded with people sitting on the steps, arguing about the turn the Korean War was taking or leaning dangerously over the banisters expressing some important opinion or other. We had been invited to celebrate the birth of a baby girl, the first child of an already well-known foreign communist writer, a refugee from persecution in his own country. There were many reasons to celebrate; the new life of course, symbolic of the victories we could look forward to and also the fact that we were all there, the artists, writers, composers and scientists of the future. We represented, we told each other, everything that was best and which would be the most successful in our time, and as we all agreed on that we could not possibly be wrong. It was a self-sustaining prophecy and a little intoxicating.

We were also honouring the mother who was holding court right up on the fifth floor, for the successful delivery, a traditional gesture that we had not discarded with other bourgeois conventions of family values, but there was also another reason for honouring her. She had made an important political statement, set an example, even, to other left-wing women as she had experienced a painless childbirth.

Stung by the British discovery of penicillin, the eradication of tuberculosis through streptomycine, and countless other new discoveries emerging from the United States as well as rumours of an American polio vaccine, the left needed something from Russia. True, we could easily dismiss fancy cars as an indulgence for the rich and nuclear power was a monstrosity which the Soviets had been compelled to emulate only to preserve the existence of the worker state, but health was another matter. Everyone demanded it as a human right particularly if they were not prepared to accept the will of God; no one was willing to die especially if there was no after-life.

There had, of course, been Trofim Denisovich Lysenko, the Soviet biologist whose experiment had continued through the 1920s, '30s and '40s, and who had been awarded the Lenin prize in 1949. He had shown that wheat could turn into rye if it were bred north of its natural latitude. The implications for humanity were immense, we were told, as it demonstrated that men themselves could be moulded into different, communitarian beings under proper conditions. One of our lecturers, a great admirer and propagator of Lysenko's ideas had gone to see the living proof itself, a plant which carried both an ear of wheat and one of rye on the same stem, a sort of transitional being. At first he would not talk about it but he had always had a propensity for drink and this had got progressively worse since his return. After a particularly lengthy lunch alone where he was seen to consume three bottles of red wine he had joined us in the classroom. He was weeping, and blew his nose loudly.

"What shall we do?" he said wringing his hands. "The world is finished. There is nothing left now, there is no future for humanity." He told us that he was sure the ear of wheat had simply been crudely glued on to the stem of rye. No one had wanted to talk about it in Moscow. "I could see the glue!" he cried as we helped him into a taxi. "I swear it was glue. The future of humanity was stuck with glue!" He did not come back to teach us. It was the liver that had gone, they said.

Not everyone had been so pessimistic, however, and Marcel Prenant, the leading biologist of the left had written the very popular *Biology and Marxism*, explaining that even though the results of some of Lysenko's experiments had not been confirmed, Lysenkoism as a way of approaching science would inevitably win through and mankind would flourish. This was not actually borne out as the following year, 1954, Lysenko's Lenin Prize was withdrawn, possibly because the twin ears had literally come unstuck. However, we were still in 1953 when I re-read Marcel Prenant's book so as to be able to refute the right-wing accusations against Lysenko and strengthen my status as an intellectual.

That was the time when painless childbirth had been proclaimed in Russia. Soviet women simply did not experience pain at all. The technique was not explained very clearly and in medical circles we wondered whether it was some sort of hypnosis though this was not favoured in Russia. Perhaps, we thought, it had something to do with an extension of Pavlovian methods of conditioning? One suggestion that I never heard anyone make was that it was simply not true. Everyone had given them the benefit of the doubt, and Professor Lamaze had established a similar method at a clinic which I think belonged to a CGT (Confédération Générale du Travail) steel workers' union in Paris.

The results reported from that clinic were simply amazing as woman after woman emerged without trauma following the new

Soviet methods of childbirth, and there was no doubt that it gave a tremendous boost to the confidence of the left. The clinic was so popular that it was very difficult to get a place there and even connections to the CGT were of little help.

"You have to go higher up," the exultant new father had explained when I congratulated him on the birth of his daughter.

"You know," he whispered in my ear "someone in the *Comité Central*; as for the cost, it was an arm and a leg."

"Have you just come up?" someone else asked "Did you see Sartre? He's just left, he was here a minute ago!"

I heard a voice I knew reciting loudly in English so I pushed through the crowd and recognised my friend, the English poet. He had a small following listening attentively.

> I lived, then at the heart
> of a painful love: I was, then
> a tiny fragment of quartz
> my eyes clutching at life.

"Quite imaginative, don't you think?" I said to someone next to me.

"Oh, he plagiarises," was the reply. "He takes from poets in different languages who no one reads in English. It's usually Garcia Lorca or Pablo Neruda, someone like that. We all admire them and no one reads them. Did you hear Mikis Theodorakis, by the way? Wonderful. He was playing that little Greek banjo or balalaika, whatever it is, and he sang one of his fantastic ballads."

"Where? Where?" I asked excited.

"On the third floor," he replied. "But he's gone now, you're too late."

"I thought their flat was on the fifth floor?" I queried.

"That's where they live, of course, but every time one of the old people dies they put in a bid for their flat. They pay peanuts as the flats are in such a poor condition. Little by little they have bought up the whole lot and own the building now. Can you imagine what it will be worth when the area cleans up?"

"But where do they get the money from?" I kept on.

"Oh, Lily's father gives it to her. He thinks it is a good idea, a roof over his daughter's head, so to speak."

In some way I was relieved that it was the provident father who had been so canny, and also that the father was hers so that the communist writer himself was at once or twice removed, remaining at a safe distance from all that necessary commerce, though why I felt that uneasiness I was not sure.

"Did you see Simone Signoret?" the English poet asked me. "She must have gone right past you. Didn't you stop her? I think I can get her to read one of my poems, in French of course."

He was very thin and small with uncombed black hair and a dark stubble that he never shaved. He was also invariably dressed in black and I suspected that this was because such clothes would not show the dirt and he could avoid washing them altogether. He always seemed involved in something, a happening in the Boulevard St Michel with Xenakis, or a poetry recital while gypsies danced, or a poetic film in mime projected on floating gauze strips which had been approved by Jean-Louis Barrault, but somehow nothing ever seemed to get done and, as far as I know nothing ever has. Still I was grateful to him as in a moment of penury he had recruited me to a writing factory. For a small fee we were expected to write a novel a week. I think I wrote two in all if I remember correctly. They had been almost identical, though I had changed the names of the characters at least. It is very difficult to write quickly if you have to study anatomy at the same time. The large warehouse in the Rue de Vaugirard was managed by a very fat, sweaty man who spoke with an American accent. There were long ink-stained wooden tables lined up in rows which reminded me of the dissecting rooms with dozens of people writing novels on old typewriters.

"Look," the fat man said, breathing heavily between puffs on his cheap French cigarettes. "There is a huge American army in

Europe. In France, in England, everywhere. In Germany there are millions. Millions!" he paused and looked at us. "Just think. Millions of American soldiers and we have to give them books to read."

He rubbed his hands together and smiled at the thought, then frowned and raised his index finger disapprovingly. "Not big books mind you! Not thick difficult books! They want easy books, simple words, soft stories that end well!"

I had stopped at the fourth floor to catch my breath and to check that Mikis Theodorakis had indeed gone, as I loved his music and was hoping to see him in the flesh, when I came across a round bald man who had not removed his khaki raincoat. He looked so different from the other guests that I suspected he might be an intruder come for the champagne and the *petits fours* as there were always those around.

"Mickey who?" he replied to my question. "I haven't seen any Mickey Mouse around."

Then suddenly he grabbed hold of the arm of a passing girl and said: "Do you want to come home and sleep with me tonight?"

"Let go of me, you pervert!" she said shaking herself free, but before I could say anything he had approached another woman.

"Piss off!" she hissed.

"Why do you do this?" I asked. "Don't you see it's disgusting?"

"What is disgusting about it?" he replied. "I only want someone to sleep with tonight. I am only asking."

"But don't you mind the rejection? It can't be nice to be spat at like that."

"I don't care," he said. "I don't know them anyway. How many women do you think I need? I only want to sleep with one and if I ask all of them here, and there must be dozens, one will come!"

I continued my climb up the spiral staircase and was finally received with real affection by Lily, the new mother.

"Where have you been?" She said Costas Gavras, the film director, had been there, "I am sure you would have loved to meet him. He has only just gone! You must know Barty Slipman, of course, another medical student?"

I had seen Barty from a distance but he was already in the third year and we had never spoken. We had barely shaken hands when Lily picked up her baby and made for the bedroom.

"I have to feed the baby," she said, "and I want to talk to you medical students, so come with me."

While she fed the baby she told us she had to be given pain-killers during an agonising labour. In the end the doctors had had no option but to carry out a Caesarian section. It had been a bad day altogether at the clinic and women were screaming with pain in all the cubicles which was not encouraging for the new admissions, as the midwives were running round with syringes of pethidine and gases of some sort or other.

"But why," I asked, uncomprehending, "why did you say you had a painless childbirth?"

"What?" now Lily was quite outraged. "While General Ridgeway is poisoning the poor Koreans with bacteriological warfare do you want me to let our side down?"

Barty and I walked down the staircase without saying a word as we pushed past the throng. Everyone who mattered in Parisian intellectual life had been there but somehow I had not quite met them; I never did.

As I walked into the street I saw the round man in the raincoat arm in arm with a tired looking but not unattractive woman. He waved at me and as I waved back he called out: "Hey! Remember, just don't be too choosey, it really doesn't matter that much."

I was also befriended by a group of Egyptian intellectuals most of whom were Jews though there were a few Copts and the odd Francophonic Moslem. It was actually my mother who had arranged for me to meet them as she knew their families, good families she had said, people like us. They were older than me and already had jobs. Like all parents she had feared that alone in Paris I might fall in with bad company.

I wrote to tell her that I had got in contact and they had been extremely kind and helpful. She had been very pleased that I was so well surrounded by friends of a decent backround. What she did not know was that they were all active members of the Communist Party.

I spent many weekends with them as they were such interesting company and although I was already familiar with Marxist discussion it was of a broader nature than theirs. I had retained a soft spot for Trotsky, for instance, and it had upset me that Stalin's agent had smashed his head in with an ice pick. He had been so far away in Mexico, surrounded by such friends as Diego Rivera, Siqueiros and Frieda Kahlo, why not leave him alone? They had winced at the name of Trotsky but explained patiently to me how his disruptive and hysterical activities had been such a danger to the future of mankind. He might well have been a paid agent of the British Secret Service for all we knew and, besides, they said there was no proof that the murderer had been sent by Stalin. It could have been to do with a jealous husband as Trotsky was a known womaniser. Not, they insisted, that they had anything against free love, indeed they were strongly in favour, but such ridiculous jealousies did occur among the *petite bourgeoisie*. I soon learnt not to mention the well-known communist writer and his wife Lily. I had at first hoped that their warm friendship might enhance my standing with my new friends, but it seemed that they did not consider him that highly. "*Il n'est pas sérieux*," they said with slight bitterness as they knew that despite the superficiality of his position, his celebrity value kept him in good stead with the Party.

At weekends they often took me with them to a sort of rest home which belonged to a union and to which they had access. It was in l'Isle-Adam, a lovely place on the river Oise. I learned to play chess and although I had secretly been attracted by the thought of free love and the fact that the girls who sold the French Communist Party weekly *L'Humanité Dimanche*, in the street were granted free weekends there in lieu of payment, they all proved so singularly unattractive that I confined myself to intellectual discussion. Though it may have been simply that I was frightened of them as my older friends were not so choosey.

If there was any event in the world too difficult for them to handle they would wait for Roger Garaudy, the columnist in *L'Humanité Dimanche* who was sure to explain it away with ease. If Tito had suddenly become bad after being a hero or a treaty had been signed by the Soviet Union with some previously hostile people they would wait for Sunday before discussing it. "Let us wait to see what Roger Garaudy says in *L'Huma*." They would all nod and put the matter aside.

I, too, found Garaudy very convincing as he was always able to add an extra piece of information, inaccessible to others, which explained everything and clinched the matter so I was happy to go along with them. It was only much later that I suspected that none of them wanted to commit to any thoughts in front of the others before they knew what the party line was. Whoever made the decisions, it seemed, it was not them but I had been witness to a particularly ugly scene when they expelled a long-standing member of their group as an "objective fascist".

He had inherited a small sugar refinery in Lower Egypt and intended to hand over the ownership and control entirely to the workers. That, his erstwhile friends had decided, was counter-revolutionary as the opportunity to run the factory would pacify the workers, reducing the rage and anger which should fuel the overthrow of capitalism. This made him, objectively of course, a fascist whatever his intentions had been. He had accepted their analysis, he said, and would close down the factory considerably adding to the rage in the village which depended on it. The group took this amiss and, saying that he was *pas sérieux*, expelled him anyway.

He refused to leave it at that and spat out at them, "How do you know that Stalin was not a Czarist secret agent?"

They were so stunned they had nothing to say, it was like questioning the Virgin Birth in a church sermon so he went on, "Just imagine if Stalin had been an informer planted by the police among the Bolsheviks and they won. What was he to do? He had to seize power or they would find him out, and then he had to kill them all one by one, Zinoviev, Bukharin, Kirov, Trotsky. I would not be surprised if he poisoned Lenin!"

They shook their heads wearily as he left, they had always known that he was *pas sérieux*.

At the beginning of the year the group had their greatest need for Roger Garaudy. On 14 January 1953 all the newspapers, including *L'Humanité*, reported that the previous day all the Soviet papers had published an announcement that the top Jewish doctors had been part of a cosmopolitan plot to poison the Soviet leaders and that 38 of them had been arrested. A few days later a Dr Lydia Timashuk was awarded the Order of Lenin for having, at great risk to her own safety, exposed the criminal plot.

Everyone was stunned, not just the communists but doctors everywhere. As far as the left-wing intellectuals were concerned the proof seemed to be absolute as no one could possibly arrest all the senior doctors in Moscow without being certain. Most of them thought Zionism was at the root of the problem as it was a distortion of the way progressive things should be, harking back to antiquity and nationalism rather than looking forward to a common and international future for mankind. Only those on the left who admired the kibbutzim were dubious but Roger Garaudy was very eloquent and convincing and dismissed those collective farms in the new Israeli state as even more subtly dangerous than the evidence of capitalist enterprise.

The matter may have rested there as people soon forget were it not for a letter addressed to *Pravda*. This letter had been circulated shortly after the doctors' arrest among the 50 most famous Russian artists, film directors, actors, writers, doctors and scientists and, sadly, almost all of them had signed it. It stated that all Soviet Jews must atone for their collective guilt regarding this crime, or attempted crime, by being deported to Siberia. Although it was never published it was difficult to keep the letter secret and the details were corroborated by so many sources that it was generally accepted as true, while many Moscow Jews of senior standing reported that friends had warned them to start packing. Anastas Mikoyan, then a member of the Politburo, later wrote in his *Memoirs* that the trains were ready, and after all it was less than ten years since the Nazis had shown how it could be done relatively quickly using cattle trucks. Roger Garaudy was already explaining the need for isolating the Jews partly for their own protection in anticipation of the letter's publication in *L'Humanité Dimanche*.

On 3 March 1953 Stalin's valet came into his room disturbed by the sound of unusual breathing and found him salivating and impossible to rouse. Soon the adjoining room was filled with doctors and members of the politburo. Every now and again someone peeped into the room but no one went inside other than the valet and no one touched the dictator. Would he suddenly wake up and have them killed? They knew he was capable of anything.

On 5 March 1953 he died and as Russia mourned and the leftist intellectuals held commemorative meetings in Paris, the Jewish doctors were quietly released and told to return to their homes and jobs and not to mention the matter to anyone. In time a small item in Soviet newspapers announced that a mistake had been made and the Order of Lenin was withdrawn from Dr Lydia Timashuk.

Not much was said about the Jewish doctors though it was pointed out how effective the Party was at correcting its mistakes. I think that it was the first time the Party had admitted to a mistake and I suspect that once this was done there was no turning back and from that moment everything began to unravel. I missed going to l'Isle-Adam for weekends but I did not miss the turgid discussions nor the girls who sold *L'Humanité*. I was working hard and I had made new friends; the Americans in Paris.

They were like a breath of fresh air, as though a window had been opened in a musty old room. Paid for by the GI Bill of Rights, they were studying in Paris partly out of choice and partly, at least as far as the medical students were concerned, because of a shortage of places in American medical schools. As I spoke both French and English I was frequently asked for my help as an interpreter. It is very comforting to feel wanted, whatever the reason, and if one enjoys popularity it is wise to acquire a skill needed by many.

Like all intellectuals in Paris they tended to be left wing and were opposed to the Korean War so they were admired for their independence and looked upon as heroes by the rest of the students. Their consular assistant in Paris was a woman called Mrs Schneider and they were sure that she was there to spy on them on behalf of Senator McCarthy or the FBI. They called her Spider Schneider.

Barty Slipman and his wife Judy had a central role and I was grateful to Lily for having introduced us. They were wonderful and everyone around them saw them as a model couple. My parents had had a happy marriage but somehow that did not count as I took their relationship for granted. Barty and Judy were of my generation and when I found the right wife my marriage would be like theirs. I imagined my future wife to be like Judy who worked hard as a secretary to see Barty through medical school and their plan was that when he was qualified they would return to New York and he would support her to do whatever degree she wished.

The Slipmans also acted as a bridge between the foreigners and the French intellectuals as everybody respected them for their integrity. Their modest apartment became a meeting place of the most exciting thinkers of the left in Paris. Even our professors treated Barty as an equal, and were often seen there eating a simple meal prepared by Judy. They seemed like the still, calm centre of the incomprehensible storm whirling around us.

On 17 June 1953 Barty was waiting for me outside the dissecting rooms. There was to be a demonstration the following day to try to persuade President Eisenhower not to execute the Rosenbergs who had been found guilty of espionage. He hoped that I would join in this protest against a monstrous act to be committed on an innocent couple, the father and mother of two boys. Julius and Ethel Rosenberg had been accused of passing information about nuclear weapons to the Russians. The evidence was based on accusations by Ethel's brother who had turned state witness to save his own skin when he was caught red handed. Julius and Ethel denied it totally.

A telephone with a direct line to Eisenhower had been placed next to both Julius and Ethel who were held in separate cells. Barty explained that the President had offered to pardon either or both if they confessed. All they had to do was lift up the telephone and he would cancel the execution.

"How can you place parents in such a predicament?" Barty had asked the little crowd of students, lecturers and anatomy demonstrators. "How can you ask two innocent people to confess to a crime they have not committed? They would either leave orphans convinced of their parents' innocence or survive to brand them with the stigma of treason."

The demonstration was the largest I had ever seen. The streets were so crowded no one could move from the Place de la République to the Place de la Bastille. There were people of every age and class and many were weeping while others were angry. Youth veers more towards anger than tears so with other students I began to pick up chairs from a café and throw them at the heavily armed security police. With their long batons, shields and helmets we were no match for them and we were beaten and dragged into the black police vans.

"Whatever you do," a fellow student told me, "don't give the *flics* your name or you will be recorded in their books for ever."

"*Nom?*" the policeman asked.

"Dupont," I replied.

"Oh come on!" he said exasperated. "And I suppose you live in the Sologne and have left your papers behind?"

The police were lenient and some said they were sympathetic to our cause. "These poor innocent people," said one officer shaking his head. "Who would lie in this way when their life is at stake? These Americans are monstrous!"

We spent the night in a large hall with nothing to sit on but iron benches and it was too crowded to sleep but I had never felt so much at one with society. We spent the night singing. We sang the *Marseillaise*, we sang the *Ça Ira*, we shouted when we came to "*tyrants descendez au cerceuil!*", and in the morning they let us go. I felt I was a changed person because I had participated with the rest of humanity in the cause of innocence and justice.

Over the years I continued to read about the affair. I felt with emotion the Rosenbergs' sons' attachment to their parents' innocence. And then one day, so many decades later, when that tale was almost forgotten, when the Soviet Union collapsed and the KGB archives were finally opened, I winced with pain when I read that Julius and Ethel had been lying all the time. They really had been traitors and spies. These two stupid or perhaps wicked people had left their children orphaned. What was in their minds as they died; electrocuted to protect the name of the Soviet Union as Stalin was preparing to deport the Jews to Siberia?

My mother came to fetch me. There was too much nonsense in Paris, a bit of growing up was all right but enough was enough. Her plan was that we should all end up in London. I protested that

I had been rejected by every medical school. She knew people, she said, and they would take me. There was no nepotism in Britain I insisted but we flew to London, had dinner with Professor Alan Morgan, the Professor of Pathology, and the following day I was accepted at Westminster Medical School. It had been a pleasant interview and no one had asked me about the *fellaheen*.

It had truly been a defining year for me in Paris but what it defined I still don't know. I gradually lost touch with the dwindling group of Egyptian communists. The last I heard of those who had returned to Egypt was that they had immediately been arrested and had written to President Nasser from prison approving his decision to jail them which, objectively, they felt had been correct. I am sure he must have been puzzled by their letter.

My friend, the famous foreign writer, went from success to success and became part of the French establishment and is also frequently invited to the United States where his criticism is much appreciated but Lily, driven by jealousy of his success, left him to set up on her own. She died young.

The Slipmans ended up in California and Barty became a psychiatrist. He was a great success and was much courted by the rich and famous but he and Judy divorced almost as soon as they returned home. Barty happily soon found another wife.

Finally there was communism which had loomed so large for us. I think my father gave me the answer in 1992 when he was ninety-four. I had entered my parents' house with my own key as they could not hear the door bell. He was haranguing my mother and he turned to me when he saw me come in.

"I told him it wouldn't last," he said. "He was like a mule!"

"Don't upset yourself," my mother said. "It was a long time ago."

"What didn't last?" I asked. "And who did you tell?"

"Jacques Antebi, do you remember him?"

"Papa," I said, "he was dead before I was born!"

"But you remember who he was?" he insisted. "My brother-in-law. I told him, 'Jacques, it won't last you'll see', and I was right. 'No, no', he kept on saying, 'it is the future of mankind.'"

"What was it that didn't last?" I asked frustrated as he was following his own train of thought.

"When he stood on that tank in Petrograd."

"You mean Lenin! You mean communism wouldn't last!" I shouted.

"Yes," he said, "communism. I told him it wouldn't last and it didn't!"

I had kept an eye on Roger Garaudy, the columnist in *L'Humanité Dimanche*. Applying a Marxist approach he had explained so well all the events of the time and I was anxious to see how he had handled the end of the Soviet Union. His views had once been too important to me for me now simply to ignore him. Apparently he had, immediately after the fall of communism, converted to an extreme form of Catholicism that made the Church, initially welcoming, very uneasy. They need not have worried, however, as the virulent anti-Semitism which had unnerved the bishops later found a more appropriate home among the followers of Islamic Jihad and he became a Moslem. The last I heard was that he was fined by a French court for Holocaust denial.

18

England at Last

When I first left England it was with a sense of failure. Though I have retained school friends from that time I had not been wanted by any medical school. I had been glad to leave but most of all, I wished to forget all about it, and in large part I suspect I did so. Although I was very fond of my aunt in Yorkshire I could not sympathise with what seemed to me the chaos of her life. Hers was a mismatch and I think that it was pride which had forced her to stick it out. Her parents had been opposed to her marriage and had not attended the wedding which had taken place immediately before their repatriation to Britain, and although my grandfather had left the same inheritance to her as to his other daughters I am not sure whether he ever spoke to her again.

I was too young to follow precisely the tribulations in the family but I always tried to listen surreptitiously. I can remember that my grandfather had asked his prospective son-in-law's commander for information and that the reply had been, "He is not for your daughter, Mr Sassoon." This had naturally only served to strengthen my aunt's resolve to marry her soldier lover and follow him to Yorkshire where she lived in circumstances vastly different from what she had known before. The plainest of all her sisters, she never uttered a word either of complaint or regret but I suspect that she was embarrassed by the outcome of her great love affair as she had cut herself off totally from every friend from her past life. I was out of my depth as far as understanding her but I had a certain insight into her feelings and I knew that it was best if

I said nothing, not that I would have any idea what to say. I did report to her that one old friend had complained that she had not given any sign of life but that he and his wife would be visiting London shortly. He had given me the name of the hotel where they would be staying and had said very delicately, perhaps too delicately for me to follow the direction of his thoughts, that if she would call them they would love to travel to Bradford to see her. That was the only time I heard her make any comment about herself or her life. She decided not to call them and said: "I have made my bed and I must lie in it."

Her mother, Eugénie, when widowed, had gone to see her, but as she eyed all her daughters with a slight contempt, she did not seem to care particularly for this one's condition and found her husband's fecklessness faintly amusing. His tendency to drink, sometimes to the point of making a fool of himself, usually by repeating phrases that for some reason he admired, like referring to the publican as "Mine Host" with a silly look on his face, would make my grandmother laugh.

"These Nordics," she would say. "They need to drink, you know. It's because of the cold!"

My aunt's life was one for which I had no affinity, even respect, and my only wish was to get away as quickly as possible from an England I had not even imagined existed and was at best distasteful.

Now I was coming back to England as a different person altogether. After all I had been welcomed at the rather superior Westminster Medical School and was to start pre-clinical at King's College in the Strand. More than that, I had lived in Paris, where I had little doubt that I had become a French intellectual.

There was, however, one essential thing to do on my return to England as my father had had a thought that shocked everyone around him. He realised that the number of people who held a British passport in parts of the Empire such as Africa and Asia ran into many millions. If the occasional few decided to live in

England it would be of no consequence. On the other hand if Britain were to get rid of those distant lands, having lost the taste for administration, or the zeal to maintain order, such countries would, in his view, revert sooner or later to an original lawlessness and all those people with a claim to British nationality would be obliged to leave and have nowhere to go but Britain.

"What would the British do then?" my father had asked. "They would renege on their pledge," he answered as he looked at the disbelieving faces around him, a harbinger of bad news. "They will simply cease to recognise their British passports!"

This meant that I had strict instructions to make an appointment at Somerset House, I think it was, in order to regularise my status, and that was how I found myself ushered in to a tiny room full of papers and bound documents piled up everywhere, especially on the floor.

"So," the elderly white-haired man sitting behind a book of huge proportions had said. "The children of the Consul have finally come home to roost!"

"I beg your pardon, sir," I said. "It's just that my father wanted me to regularise my status."

"Ah! I see you don't know about the Consul!"

He was a tiny man with a bird-like face and with his mass of white hair and the enormous book on his desk he looked like a clerk out of a Dickensian law firm. He was very excited about what he had to tell me as though he had made an interesting discovery of his own.

"It all started with the Levant Company."

He told me that during the reign of King James I a group of English merchants had formed the Levant Company to trade with the Ottoman Turks and with Persia. There was much to import, from valuable textiles to spices, and in return they exported highly prized English wool. The Company thrived so well that in due course it extended its business much further and became the East India Company. That powerful organisation was still to come, however, and in the meantime the Levant Company struggled to compete with Genoese and Venetian merchants. These city states had managed a successful coup in getting permission from the Sultan to establish consulates in the cities of the Ottoman Empire where they were allowed to trade. The advantage of this was quite substantial as it gave the Consuls access to the local pasha and therefore the possibility to bribe him, so the Levant Company had found itself out-flanked by its competitors and begged King James to appoint a Consul to represent them before the Grand Turk, as they called the Sultan. The parsimonious King agreed but on the condition that any expense should be borne by the company.

"That is where your ancestor comes in," the white haired official told me. "The original Mr Douek was the agent for the company in Aleppo, their main centre. What could be cheaper than to appoint their own agent as Consul as they would not have to pay him a salary nor provide premises?"

The official was particularly excited at the thought that my ancestor may well have been the very first United Kingdom rather than English Consul as King James had only just united England with Scotland.

"Just think!" he kept repeating, rubbing his hands. "Your family could well be the first people outside the Kingdom itself to be British subjects! Just think!"

He gave me the impression that I should look different in some way but he was talking beyond me. Various persons with the name of Douek, though using innumerable different spellings, would present themselves over the centuries at various British embassies and consulates reaffirming themselves as British subjects if it suited them. The family would disappear again for a few generations from the records of the British authorities only to pop up unexpectedly a century or so later. The last time had been in Aleppo in 1922 where the Consul, a Mr James Morgan, was in correspondence with Constantinople and referred to a group of men, claiming to be brothers and the sons of Abraham ben Ezra Douek, the Chief Rabbi.

As the book was too unwieldy to turn the official at Somerset House made me come round to his side of the desk so that I could read what had been in the records myself: "It is indeed suggested that they are not Doueks at all but imposters."

Another comment, though accepting that they were who they had said they were, concluded:

This is a very prolific family and their origin is doubtful . . . much less ground for adopting these numerous descendants . . . it will be well to shed them unless there are good and sufficient reasons shown for accepting them.

I have the honour to be,
With the highest respect,
My Lord,
Your Lordship's most obedient,
Humble servant,

James Morgan,
Consul.

I recognised the names of all these men as they were my great-uncles, some of whom I had got to know before they died.

The official told me that those descendants who had found themselves in British controlled territories, such as Egypt, were simply called up by the British Army in 1940 and, indeed, I remember all my older cousins in uniform so the matter was resolved for them.

"Presumably," he said, "that was deemed 'good and sufficient reasons for accepting them'. The problem for you is that you were too young and your father too old to be drafted to the Army and even though you have a passport who is to say what will happen?"

I was left confused with information but uncertain as to what I should do.

"Why don't you just let us naturalise you and be finished, rather than rake over your obscure connection with a seventeenth-century Consul?"

And that is how I became, finally and properly, a British citizen, Consul or no Consul, though the matter arose once more in an unexpected manner. While I was doing my national service in 1960 in Scotland and talking to an officer from a border regiment, I had asked him what nationality he was.

"Pakistani!" he had replied bitterly, but quickly added that he was not being facetious. His father had been the general in command of an area of what had then been India so that he himself had been born in Lahore. He had never thought anything of it until he joined the Army as his father and grandfather had done, and that was when he was informed that according to regulations he was not a British citizen at all but Pakistani. He was reassured, however, that he would be granted the right of abode in the United Kingdom. He had become quite distraught as every move he or his father had made was dismissed by one official or another. I told him not to waste any further effort but just to apply for naturalisation and be finished with it however much it might infuriate his father.

For my part I could start as a completely new person. Unquestionably a British citizen, my accent seemed to be accounted for by my being a Parisian intellectual as well, while my Egyptian childhood could only add a much-appreciated exoticism. England, I found, was now open to me from top to bottom. Every door ajar and every welcoming finger beckoning, for I had discovered the key. That England, the England of the 1950s, remains my territory. I discovered it as an observer from another planet might as soon as I was mature enough to embed myself into its substance and the key that I had found was its complex class system which was different from anywhere else in the world.

In colonial Egypt the differences were between the rulers, be they of European or Ottoman origin, and the Egyptians, but within our own little world my mother also referred to "Good Families". I was not clear as to what she meant as she never mentioned "Bad Families" so I had nothing to compare the Good ones with. Even after she had long left Egypt she would talk about people she had known there as being of "Good Family" though she rarely, and then only tentatively as though she doubted her own competence to judge, spoke in that way of English people. From what I could piece together "Good Families" were those whose members had managed to maintain a good reputation for a generation or two, within living memory more or less. This reputation appeared to involve probity in business and what is now known as family values but had nothing to do with wealth, though money acquired honestly and used charitably certainly did not detract. It demanded a degree of cohesion if not mutual control, as a dishonest member might drag the reputation of the rest down with him, though if the black sheep was quickly packed off to another country it was more than acceptable. I suppose it represented a self-cleansing capacity which could only be admired and to which was added the hope that the less well-controlled individual might actually do well in a different environment, out of sight of the conventions he could not handle, perhaps to the advantage of the family as a whole. Women had the leading role in deciding which were the "Good Families" and which were not and they lay considerable stress on the behaviour of other women. Those who were flirtatious, for instance, and who posed a threat to other women's husbands and the general marital harmony of the community definitely deprived theirs of the title of "Good Family". The men as a whole remained rather out of it and I never heard my father mention the term at all. Although he held strong views on individual behaviour he did not accept that it could stain the innocents whereas my mother, together with the other women, was instinctively aware of those families whose members could be trusted without the need for further proof.

I realised that none of this existed in the English class system of the 1950s as behaviour did not change status in any way, whether good or bad. Flagrant adultery did not mean dismissal from the aristocracy, for instance, and even wealth, unless extreme, also seemed irrelevant.

Unlike the Indian caste system to which it had been compared, it was not openly acknowledged but lay hidden, indicated by what seemed to me to be extremely faint allusions such as to schools or to where the parents lived. These divisions were criss-crossed by others which involved the books they read, and even more importantly the magazines or newspapers, the type of clothes they wore, the films they saw in particular cinemas and the music they listened to and where, if they did so at all.

At first I could distinguish no conjunction between these innumerable guidelines and it seemed to me like a sort of game though one thing was a very clear and obvious sign of status and that was the way people spoke. I saw this at its most extreme in a young solicitor called Ronnie who was doing very well and a great future was predicted for him. His father had kept a stall in the East End of London and the whole family spoke with a strong cockney accent as did Ronnie. It mattered considerably as far as girls were concerned as although he was quite attractive those he hankered after thought him "common". In fact he married an Italian girl, Sylvana, the daughter of a doctor whom he had met on holiday and who did not speak a word of English so she was unable to judge him on that basis and saw him only as a handsome and successful young lawyer. As he did not speak a word of Italian either I wondered whether anything about her had escaped him.

Having discovered the English class system and how I could relate to it, I realised that if you were a foreigner you were a threat to no one and if you were pleasant enough or if they found you interesting they would have no hesitation in welcoming you everywhere providing you did not attempt to be one of them. I put away my British passport and passed as a foreigner, causing little anxiety to anyone.

19

Doctors to be

On my first day the talk among those students in the year ahead was about the Lyceum and they promised to take the new intake there at lunchtime. Lunch itself, they claimed, as students do, was inedible in the college, so they took us to the staff canteen on the top floor of India House in the Aldwych. No one stopped us as we walked past the elephantine carvings on the sides of the entrance and we were warmly greeted upstairs where you could get an excellent and ample curry meal for one shilling and ninepence. I felt uncertain as everyone else in the canteen seemed to work in the building and the meals were probably subsidised, but those in the year ahead who always knew everything insisted that Indians are very kind people and did not mind us.

After that we all went to the Lyceum, which, despite the academic allusion in its name, was then as it is now, a theatre. I have never been to any performance there in my life but as a student at King's College, across the Strand, I went almost every day for the dancing during the lunch hour.

For a sixpence entrance fee there was naturally no live band, and the equivalent of today's disc jockey was employed only to put on one record after the other without making any enlivening comments. Jiving was popular and vigorous. The girls were there to dance and as far as I could see no one tried to pick anyone up so that conversation was very limited. You could ask what they did as you paused to get your breath, but the answers were always brief. "Shop" or "secretary" though my mentor in the year ahead advised me against confessing that I was a medical student.

"For some reason they don't like us," he had explained, "so if they ask you just say 'sales', they seem to respect that."

No names or addresses were ever exchanged and after energetic dancing they all went off to their shops or offices and we went back to the Medical School where I had had to start the pre-clinical course all over again. The English medical establishment had no faith in what I might have learned in Paris and as far as they were concerned I was starting medicine at the beginning and, for my part, I did not mind repeating anatomy and physiology. It was easier the second time round and I rather enjoyed myself, especially as no matter how many times one repeats these subjects one always sees the human body from a different angle.

We all wore old clothes as rationing had only just ended and few people had had anything new for a decade. It was a world where elbows were patched, while cuffs and collars had been "turned". The process of turning was a relatively successful one if done carefully as it involved placing the worn edge on the inside after detaching the collar by undoing the stitching, but patches were visible despite a cult of "invisible" mending, and even socks had to be darned. Hand-me-downs were standard for students. There was no youth style so young men wore only faded tweed jackets and worsteds inherited from fathers or uncles and adjusted for size more or less adequately. These modifications were always crude and everyone was shapeless, classless and ageless.

Out on the street, things were beginning to change with the emergence of a new phenomenon, the precursor of what was to become in time the high fashion of the youth culture of the sixties and probably eventually the trendy boutiques of today. This was the appearance of the Mods and the Rockers. The former had begun to add colours, as well as textures such as velour and silk with imaginative if outlandish designs, to their clothes and the Rockers were the beginning of the motorcycle culture with leather and metal studs. Others attempting to extricate themselves from the drabness of rationing were the "Teds". They were young men in elaborate suits based on Edwardian styles and hence their designation as "Edwardians" or, when London slang took over, as "Teddy Boys". An added feature of the Teds was the habit of always carrying a comb and frequently grooming their long and greasy hair in public. All that was only part of the background as far as we were concerned as class distinctions were a great deal more obvious and the Mods, Rockers and Teds were a particular outcrop from the working class and to some degree were associated with violence, or at least with some sort of sectarianism, and there was no attempt yet by middle-class young people to copy working-class trends and language.

Our teachers at King's were exotic. In a direct line from the past our physiology teacher, Professor McDowal had known Pavlov. Dr Brownlee, the reader in pharmacology, told us that he had been sent to Brazil during the war to obtain Indian arrow poison. This was called curare and eventually became the anaesthetic drug we use to temporarily paralyse the muscles during surgery. He told us that he had thought he would buy it in a shop but found he had to go to the Amazon and order it from shady traders who, in turn, had obtained it from the forest Indians. He said it was delivered in two forms: the first was in a calabash, and the second was packed into tubes formed from the stems of bamboo. The curare from the tubes was more potent and our present drug, evolved from that product, is therefore called d-tubo-curarine.

There was a very elderly distinguished professor who had come as a refugee and who, although 80, taught us as an anatomy demonstrator as there was still a shortage of qualified people. His English was very poor and he used a Latin nomenclature long abandoned but he was good humoured and fascinated by the way joints functioned. "You see here, ya? Ze astragalus articulatio mit ze talus und heere iss connected mit ze peroneus, nein?" I now wish I had talked to him more, but the lined face and the white hair of the old is forbidding to the young despite the kindly smile. When, later, I was told that he had died, I had felt I had let him slip by, and that I had let a little more of life escape me than I might have.

The students, too, were a unique mixture. They were divided into three distinct groups. There were those just out of school, but in a state of near infantilism – it seemed to us. At the other extreme were those who had fought in the Second World War. They were already in the final class, looked tired, tended not to talk much, worked hard, and were anxious to get it over with as little fuss as possible. They seemed less ambitious in their ultimate aims as though awed simply at the thought of qualifying at all and some were even married, anxious to provide for families. In-between were those who had chosen to do their national service before university, foreigners and people like myself who had spent some time elsewhere. I think that we showed each other remarkable tolerance and friendship. Certainly I gained much from such mature students and after five years together the differences had been smoothed out as we all became junior doctors; there was more to bind us together than to separate us.

In our first year at King's we had our lectures in the morning while the afternoons were reserved for dissection. I remember those sessions as it got late, in the autumn penumbra, when there was not quite enough daylight but the electric lights had not yet been switched on. Those intermediate minutes were longer then, as the habits of wartime penury and the fear of nightly bombers had not yet been put aside. We had covered the cadavers with plastic sheets, strong sweet tea had been brewed and conversation turned philosophical as we lit our ubiquitous cigarettes.

The discussions on the uncertainties of life were led by the technician Len, a thin man, already cadaveric himself, who tidied up, prepared the bodies for dissection and poured out the pervasive formaldehyde. He "held the spittoon" as the French graphically say of one who monopolises the conversation, telling us in the modified cockney accent of one who had left the East End of London and been in the wider world about his army experience; the landings in Sicily, the unending, unexpected battle of Montecassino, the wounds he had to tend as a medical orderly and his conclusions, while his assistant wiped the instruments and nodded confirmation when required, hoping it would not be too long before he could get away. Len had an inverted way of looking at life.

"The future cannot be changed," he would repeat more than once, "no matter how much you try. It is written, as the wogs would say." Then he would smile cunningly and continue, "But you can change the past. Oh yes you can! The past alters each time you obtain more information, or when you understand differently what you had thought was going on, so it even changes by itself as time goes by. Changing the past can then alter the course of your life."

Those among us who had not understood the tortuous path his thinking had taken would argue that we could directly influence the future through exertion of the will but then Len had his views on what people could make of their lives. We had whatever qualities we had come with and flaws as well, but the most decisive factor was the circumstances into which we were born. Those were the facts that would shape our lives though he would always add that by altering the past we could reinvent ourselves and become someone else with a better chance.

When all his thoughts and beliefs had been tidied up as well as the dissected cadavers and the instruments, the signal that we could leave was when Len uttered the words.

"I dunno . . . at the end of the day, all I want . . ."

Then he would stop a while to think again, to make sure he was not misleading us or himself. "At the end of the day all I want is a cuppa tea an' a ma'aroon."

He would sigh and only then could we make our way home.

*

I also had had to find somewhere to stay. Although nowadays students live either in halls of residence or share flats, in the 1950s not enough halls had been built and wartime destruction had left a shortage of available flats. We lived in freezing rented rooms, sharing inadequate bathrooms, and we were often dominated by landladies. My first digs were at the end of a row of houses in Pimlico most of which had been badly damaged by the bombing and when the time came for redevelopment I was sorry to leave my room above "E. Crouch, Electrician", with its gas fire and the pile of shillings needed to feed it. I had a gas ring, too, where I would reheat my food repeatedly, day after day, until the solidifying mess was finished. There was also a chip shop at one end of the crumbling row where the steaming batter-coated fish and soggy chips were wrapped in newspaper. I still remember the special flavour and wondered once out loud why this seemed to have disappeared.

"Don't you know?" my listener had said. "It was the ink. The print from the newspaper gave it something extra. Later on when they wrapped it in greaseproof paper it lost that added tang, it was a taste we had all acquired."

It did not prove easy to find new accommodation. I visited room after room but I suppose my requirements had grown with maturity and I could find nothing suitable until I rang the bell at 10 Platts Lane in Hampstead and an old lady suspiciously half-opened the door. The room she showed me was beautifully furnished, over-furnished perhaps, in the central European style, with lots of little *bibelots* and lace but it was better than anything else I had seen. Though expensive at fifty shillings (£2.50) a week with breakfast, I took it at once.

"But please," the old lady said, alarmed at my haste, "we must first ask my husband!"

She spoke in the lightly musical Viennese accent common in Hampstead at that time and, rather put out, I followed her to the sitting room.

"You must excuse him, doctor," she warned me. "He is tired as he took the bus from Baker Strasse and had to change again at Schwitz Cottage."

Then she threw open the door and said: "My husband, Mr Mahler, the great-nephew of Gustav Mahler!"

I had no idea who that was and I saw only a tiny old man sitting on the settee but he came straight to the point.

"Do you like music?" he asked in the same soft accent.

Taken aback by the question and fearing that there would be more, my experience of frequent oral examinations had taught me to come clean at once rather than struggle with stupid mistakes so I admitted my ignorance.

"I was brought up in Egypt," I said. "We did not have much Western music."

"How old are you?" he asked and when I said I was nineteen he thought for a little and then nodded firmly.

"You will learn."

After that there was a little note on my desk every evening: "Concert. BBC Home Service. Eight o'clock." If I forgot to turn the radio on there would be a knock on the door.

"Doctor Douek! Concert!"

I kept pointing out to Mrs Mahler that I was not a doctor yet but she persisted.

"Oh, you know us Viennese, how we are!"

"But what will you call me when I become a real doctor?"

"Professor, of course!"

Sir Malcolm Sergeant, the conductor, used to send them tickets to concerts but as Mr Mahler was not well and unable to go, his wife took me to the Albert Hall and the new Festival Hall and that was how I learned to enjoy classical music. In return I would act as a sort of surrogate young relative "to lighten the atmosphere" as she called it for their old Viennese friends. They used to go to the Cosmo Restaurant in Swiss Cottage which survived to the end of the century and they had tea at the Dorice in Finchley Road where there was a piano player. The Mahlers also held afternoon teas where ageing actresses would give readings from Schiller in German or recitals of Kurt Weill songs in somewhat fading voices to an audience of Viennese refugees.

"She used to sing so well in Vienna, she was famous you know," Mrs Mahler would whisper to me as she pressed another sweet cake from Lindy's on to me.

I was expected to stay only a few minutes, just enough to remind them that youth still existed but when the Mahlers' niece, Lisl, announced she was coming it was obvious they counted on my presence for much longer periods. To my dismay I found myself trapped into a bigger commitment as the excitement of her impending arrival rose and conversation veered incessantly towards Lisl who I pictured as yet another Viennese lady with the lilting accent. Lisl, it turned out when she came, was a cheerful blonde Canadian air hostess.

It was not all classical music and though there was no "pop" world, there was a constant stream of silly songs with catchy tunes on the radio. There was "Two-Way Family Favourites" which was supposed to be experienced by all ages clustered around the only set in the house. Men were still serving in Germany and elsewhere so requests were made for loved ones away from home. When I look back I think the most bizarre was "Workers' Playtime" which provided backround music for factories. Medical students also enjoyed the final days of the music halls. Our favourite was Collins Music Hall in Hackney. It was literally falling apart and if anyone removed one of the seats and took it home no one would have noticed as the audience was so small that most seats were not needed. Indeed quite a few rows of the faded and worn red plush seats had found their way into the pub next door, itself too disused to warrant renovation. In many parts of London where swathes of the city were still derelict, entire communities seemed to have gone, abandoning disintegrating buildings, and I continued to see little groups of three or four seats still screwed together from Collins Music Hall in various student digs over the coming years.

The bar was at the back of the hall where it remained permanently open as the doors had been removed from their hinges, probably to be sold off, as good wood was at a premium. On the other hand, there was a white line painted on the floor across the opening with a notice saying: "London County Council. It is forbidden to take drinks into the auditorium". This explained why so many men watched the show standing in the hall and holding their beer at arm's length just inside the line marking the permitted area.

The show itself consisted of *Tableaux Vivants* with vaguely erotic pretensions in that they included naked women taking up poses of a classical nature. My own favourite was "Rule Britannia" where a rather plump Britannia, naked except for her helmet and shield with the cross of St George protecting her private parts, sat on an armchair. The performers remained in their poses for five minutes before the curtain came down and had to keep perfectly still as even a slight movement was illegal. Nudity was within the law only if immobile. The students, with cruel irresponsibility, would shout out in an attempt to disturb the women as the inspector from the London County Council often came secretly to the hall in the hope of catching the performers moving and the slightest scratch might have led to a fine.

Once, when we were behaving worse than usual, the manager came out. He was a small, bald, very stocky man wearing his vest; it was a hot summer's evening.

"Look," he said, in a hoarse voice, "you fucking know this is a fucking rotten show, I fucking know it, the fucking performers fucking know it but the fucking audience doesn't fucking know it so you fucking well shut up."

Time passed quickly, too quickly as we faced the examinations that would allow us to start our clinical studies at Westminster

Hospital in Horseferry Road. Our introduction to clinical medicine was given by Sir Adolph Abrahams, a long-retired physician who wore a winged collar with a black frock coat. He was the last one who still dressed like that and I suppose it associates me with another era simply to have been his contemporary, even briefly. To us his main claim to fame was that his brother Harold had won a gold medal in the 1924 Olympics. A film of the event, *Chariots of Fire*, made many decades later, won four Oscars.

I remember Sir Adolph vividly as he stood thin and stooped, in his antiquated costume and addressed us in an archaic form of speech on medical ethics. He had been charged with informing us that it was strictly forbidden to have a sexual relationship with our patients. This was the main, perhaps the only problem in medical ethics at that time and gave rise to many questions. For instance, how should one handle a situation if one fell in love with a willing patient and wished to marry them? It was difficult, apparently, but possible if handled discreetly and delicately. An affair not leading to marriage? No, no never! What about female doctors? We looked brazenly at the small group of girls in our year and they responded with stony stares. Sir Adolph, ahead of his time, was quite certain that women doctors, having joined us, would have to behave with exactly the same propriety.

Often in the autumn and winter the fog was so bad that we could not get home and were put to work in the wards. People died by the dozen during those dreadful nights. Today we get an impression of what these fogs were like in old black and white films such as *Waterloo Bridge* or Sherlock Holmes' stories, though the reality was worse as the films do not catch the yellowish tinge that gave the name "pea-souper". Nor do they suggest the acrid smell.

It was the odorous particles that killed – the sulphurous evidence of the smoke that emerged from the million chimneys of the city forming what we had begun to call smog. We tried to make ourselves useful as the patients crowded the wards and corridors, their expanded chests barely moving. We placed them in oxygen tents and saw their blue bloated faces quickly go pink only to watch them gradually slip away, their exhausted attempts to breathe given up altogether as their tired eyes closed.

We struggled to keep them awake, begging them to go on breathing knowing that if they lost consciousness we would lose them altogether. We gave them black coffee and injections of nikethamide and lobeline, magic potions no longer known to the pharmacopoeia. When, too often, they died we took it as a personal failure, a fault, although we knew that even if they got well enough to go home they would be brought back by the next fog. The battle was fought on every level, our own efforts were dependent on instructions from our seniors and we took part in their own struggle to understand why our patients gave up, why they died even though the life-giving oxygen kept their colour pink and normal. We joined the discussions as to what could be done. Should we pump oxygen into them whether they wanted to breathe or not? Could we do this with large tubes down patients' throats? Should we cut a hole in their neck, perform a tracheotomy? It worked, but at considerable risk.

The answer was elusive but little by little as the facts added up, as analysis of blood gases became possible, more or less in real time, bit by bit, the incredible truth dawned on us. We were killing them with the oxygen itself, the source of all life was at the same time its destroyer. It was part of the paradox of the human condition. It was the balance that our patients required to live. The oxygen given in profusion washed away completely the carbon dioxide, the useless waste product of breathing and of living. It was this gas, now looked on even more suspiciously by a humanity concerned with its environment, that kept us breathing. It was carbon dioxide that stimulated the brain into giving the first impulse of life, the need to take a breath.

And then, suddenly, it was time for renewal. Now we were sent to obstetrics, a seamless passage, midwifery as it was called then where the patients were healthy girls and the outcome a victory as you picked up a baby by the feet to exult in its first cry, the first breath of its perfect lungs as yet untouched by the filthy smog. The social mix of the patients was varied and we looked after every level of society indiscriminately. The pampered daughters of grand families shared the labour wards with those of the housing estates of Pimlico. Husbands were excluded in those days and each girl who came in labour had a student assigned to her. We chatted, kept them company, held their hand, told them to push and sometimes became friends of the family.

Following her successful delivery of a boy at St Stephen's in Fulham Road, a young artist invited those of us who had attended her for tea at her studio. It was the first time I had seen sculptures outside museums or public places and it was a new experience when she urged me to touch her pieces, even the unfinished ones. As I wandered around the large room I was jealous of the untidiness, of the way tools and implements could be left lying around in her profession as opposed to mine. I wondered what would happen to those sculptures I stroked, would anyone ever buy them? How does one judge the value of such work? I shut my eyes to feel them without looking and I knew that I would always be given the opportunity to enjoy wonderful things in exchange for my own skills. From time to time I go and find her sculptures again though I cannot risk touching them now as the young woman's pieces have since found their place in the museums of the world and I can hardly tell the attendants that it is all right for me to stroke them as she had encouraged me to do so all those decades ago.

For two weeks we did deliveries on the district. We had the use of an old bicycle and waited by the telephone for instructions from the district midwife. We were called to the local homes of what was then a very working-class area and the procedure followed a constantly repeated pattern. The women, grandmothers, sisters, neighbours and even daughters were in the bedroom encouraging the parturient mother. The men all sat in the living room with a crate of beer which remained untouched until the child was born. It was then ceremoniously offered first to me and often they would ask my first name. Usually they were baffled when I told them I was Ellis. They would shrug their shoulders and say they would call him John. I despaired of having my name called out around Pimlico though one baby girl was called Alice as a result of my participation.

I had already learnt that by claiming to be a foreigner I could roam among the social groups of England with greater ease than those still rooted in their own class, who would always pose a threat to someone. Now I discovered that this freedom also applied to the doctor who could come and go, doing what he had to, without disturbing the social order which was what mattered most. Our surgical chief had pressed the point as he finished gently palpating the abdomen of a vagrant admitted from casualty.

"And this afternoon," he had sighed, "I will put my hand on the tummy of a king. Which of you lads wants to come with me?"

I learnt too that there were all sorts of doctors but that there was room for all. I had had to suppress my distaste when I heard a gynaecologist call out: "Come in dear, take your knickers off and lie on the couch!"

The assistant had caught my expression and asked me: "You wouldn't refer your mother to him, would you?"

"No," I replied. "I would send her to the other consultant who is gentle and courteous."

"Ah yes but they both have large, devoted clienteles. You see, for every crude, vulgar doctor there are crude, vulgar women who feel more comfortable with banter and familiarity."

We came to the end at last and suddenly, with little ceremony, we were doctors.

20

Residual Ideology

"I will never appoint a married man as an assistant," Professor Ian Aird had said to me when I had gone to seek his advice at the Hammersmith Hospital. I was approaching the end of my medical studies and the distinguished professor was also an advisor, on behalf of the Royal College, to young doctors who wished to become surgeons. Like many young men I had fallen in love more than once but I knew, in a sort of parallel consciousness, that these relationships were not to be. My plans, or perhaps ambitions, stretched far into the future and I could not yet see a place for marriage, not to speak of a family. That was the general outlook of most medical students at that time so there was nothing unusual in mine and I suspect that that was the reason why girls with matrimonial intentions would eye us with suspicion, often dismissing our attentions altogether.

"If a surgeon who is single contracts tuberculosis I can get rid of him and replace him at once so that the work of the department can go on," Professor Aird had continued. "If the man is married and his wife has TB there is nothing I can do as I cannot sack him and his work will lack total commitment."

Despite my lack of any particular female attachment I had thought he was mad. He was an outstanding and dedicated surgeon and I heard that many years later, when he had lost his own skills through the normal passage of time, he tragically took his own life. Although Professor Aird was exceptionally outspoken in expressing his views they were not out of the ordinary in the way we understood vocation to be tinged with a degree of monasticism, which lent itself very well to the new National Health Service.

As the years have passed its failures have became so numerous, so obvious and so frequently discussed that most of us have ceased to listen, but as I look back I think of the princess and the pea.

Perhaps I can now recognise the pea that we had not noticed in the fairy tale of the National Health Service, the trivial little flaw, the tiny fissure that in another metaphor was allowed to grow into an irreparable crack, for we can only talk about the Health Service in metaphors. It was, after all, a symbol for so many of our yearnings and beliefs about the better world that we would one day build that even to criticise any of its malfunctions was, for many, equivalent to pulling away the underpinning to their lives.

The pea which had been overlooked was that the NHS had been based on the expectation that each year it would cost less than the year before. The silliness of such a calculation is so great that today few could imagine that a premise of this type could ever have been taken seriously, and yet it lay there, hidden under the mattress and there was no princess to sense its presence.

The Health Minister Aneurin Bevan and the Founding Fathers had reckoned that once everyone had been issued with free spectacles and false teeth the requirements would drop to a much slower pace. Blinded by the magic of antibiotics they envisaged the end of infection and particularly of tuberculosis so that their accountants were urged to work out the savings resulting from the closure of the chest clinics and the like. They had failed to understand the nature of progress and had built reaction into a system which they could not imagine extending beyond their own outdated dreams, and yet, believing themselves to be the revolutionaries, were unable to see what they had done.

In fact the New National Health Service to which my life's work was destined, relied entirely on goodwill. The doctors and nurses accepted long hours as it was normal to remain on duty when needed, whatever the pay or the state of fatigue, and that gave the period the aura of a brave new world manned only by dedicated people who were happy to accept respect and gratitude as remuneration. In any case it was widely assumed that vocational work was recompense in itself.

It is perhaps the afterglow of that time among those old enough to remember it, as well as those who need to imagine golden ages, which suggests that what destroyed it was greed.

During the Suez War young doctors who had already done their military service were, to their horror, called up again under the name of Z-Reservists. Even though the number to leave was not great, so glaring a gap was left that the fragility of the National Health Service was exposed. Those who had not gone with the invading force were sent to camps in England, ready to be flown to war, but as the invasion petered out in response to Russian and American disapproval, they had gradually drifted back to their hospitals, claiming that they might just as well wait there.

When the call came to oppose the Suez War by joining my friends in the demonstration in Trafalgar Square I knew my place. After all, in Paris I had responded to the call of: *"Tous à la Bastille!"* on more than one occasion so I saw myself in a state of permanent opposition to the powers that be, whatever they were, having convinced myself of their innately malevolent intentions.

The second plank of Gamal Abdel Nasser's policy had in some respects been dictated by the first which was to get rid of the foreigners. He had, after all, to find a way of replacing the small businessmen, shopkeepers, artisans and functionaries that the foreigners had, by and large, represented as the multi-nationals, other than the *Compagnie du Canal de Suez* itself, had not yet emerged, and the really rich, as ever, were few if colourful. The military leaders had not initially considered it to be a problem as they had assumed that true Egyptians were standing ready to take the places which were theirs by natural right and from which they had been thwarted only by the presence of the foreigners. When Egyptianisation failed to live up to their expectations, with the encouragement of their new Soviet friends, they pulled out their ace card. It was to be Arab Socialism.

As a medical student in London, enamoured of the new National Health Service, I was delighted by this turn of events and especially by the introduction of the word "socialism" into the Egyptian political vocabulary. My father, who had come to see me, had proved sceptical, even derisive, and that had hurt my sensibilities.

"What does he mean by *Arab* Socialism?" he had sniffed contemptuously. "Is it to be like *National* Socialism?"

"Of course not!" I had retorted angrily. "They are not Nazis."

"Then why can't they simply be socialists like everyone else?"

"*Ça ne présage rien de bon!*" my grandmother Eugénie, who was also visiting at the time, threw in for good measure.

Although I could find no answer, I saw in this disagreement an opportunity to pursue a different path from that of my parents who had the disconcerting habit of claiming to endorse even the more far-fetched opinions that I expressed, though they had never yet insisted on attending any demonstration with me and my friends.

For us, the Suez War had major financial implications and the manager of my local Barclays Bank asked me to come and see him right away.

"A terrible mistake has been made," he had said, rather agitated. "You withdrew quite a lot of money last week and you must give it back at once!"

"Certainly not," I replied. "It was my money, sent by my father and anyway I have spent it."

What had happened was that the British Government had frozen Egyptian funds in order precisely to compensate British subjects like ourselves who had been dispossessed. Barclays Bank, like all the others, misunderstood the intention and it was our own remaining assets that they froze as they had come from Egypt. It took an extraordinarily long time before that situation was resolved. When my money began to run out I went to the bursar at Westminster Medical School to explain that I could no longer pay my fees. He assured me that there would be no problem and gave me a form to apply for a grant from the Middlesex County Council to which I was apparently entitled. As I left his office he called me back.

"I am truly sorry," he said. "You were the only one who still paid his own fees. You were our last contact with the way things were."

Those like me, whose childhood has escaped financial anxieties, are unable, in later life to worry about money for long, however dire the circumstances. I could not believe that I might be penniless. Somehow or other I just assumed that my parents, eternal providers, would as always see us right.

Friends whose lives had made them worldly wise were, however, more concerned than I was and kindly introduced me to the editor of a political weekly, the *New Statesman* in the hope that he might accept work about the Suez War. As he paid £12 for an article, a sum which could keep me for a week, I took a great deal of trouble preparing my first offering, making sure that my conclusions were unbiased by bringing in every possible point of view.

When his secretary telephoned to say that the editor was pleased with it but he wanted me to change the ending, I rather foolishly replied that I was no hack to be told what opinion I should express.

"I think you had better come and see him," she had said. "I don't think you quite understand."

The editor was Kingsley Martin. I remember his white hair and what seemed a lugubriously long lower jaw. He told me that he did not mind what opinion I expressed so long as I expressed my own and not everybody else's.

"But I am trying to be impartial."

"Let other people say what they think in their own articles," he had said, "journals like this are ephemeral, they give your opinion on the day. Tomorrow things change, you may change your mind. Remember that you are not writing the Bible."

He explained that his readers wanted to discuss the situation in the Middle East with their friends at dinner on Saturday night and wanted to know exactly what to say. They did not want diverse opinions where they would have to make up their own minds. He then suddenly changed the subject and began to talk about the Second World War, though it did not relate, as far as I could tell, to what he was trying to explain to me. He told me that he had been sitting on the second-floor lavatory reading proofs when a falling bomb blew off the wall of the building leaving him precariously exposed. He said that a small crowd had formed in the street calling out to him: "Don't move! Don't move!"

He was finally rescued by people who had brought ladders.

I did not understand why he told me this story but the thought of him on the lavatory, open to the street, obviously made an impact since I still remember it. With some trepidation, as I was uncertain of my own opinion, I did change the last paragraph as he had suggested but it made no difference to the conduct of the war.

I wrote under the name of "A Correspondent" as my parents were still at risk while someone else also wrote anonymously as "A National Serviceman" describing the actual war. I was told that he had subsequently made a career of journalism and later became an editor himself so I sometimes wonder whether I could have made a different life for myself if I had persisted.

Somehow we survived. My brother and sister were at boarding schools in Paris and my parents who were in Khartoum managed one way or another to send us enough to live on. The amount and the means they had to use to get it to us varied but they shielded us from any major anxiety about money, even though they must have suffered their own anguish in a situation so uncertain.

In my own case I suppose that this lack of awareness of the precariousness of our situation contributed to an interest in movements dedicated to the betterment of others as I felt that we were so secure that it was somehow demeaning for us even to consider our own advantage. I realise that I must have been irritating in my high-minded opinions and that explains the angry reaction I received from time to time when I expressed them.

I became peripherally involved in a publication called the *Universities and Left Review* which eventually grew into the *New Left Review*. I attended meetings as often as I could and it was with excitement that I thought I was participating in a great revival of left-wing intellectual concepts and contributing to a ferment of ideas. I saw it as my moment in history.

Those were heady days. I was barely aware that the various movements that I was involved in contained two separate groups who intermingled so thoroughly that their differences were not obvious. It was only in later years when they had made their own lives that this distinction became apparent. There were those who sought to improve the lot of others and were convinced that in achieving the general good they would find their own contentment while the second group sought only to better themselves and seemed to believe that somehow everyone else would benefit in the process.

The impulse to repair the condition of mankind, a youthful aspiration which had no doubt led me to become a doctor in the first place, was easily manipulated as it became confused in my mind with unrelated political stances such as the Suez War itself. If that war had been allowed to proceed to the removal of Nasser, my family and I would not have lost our home, our distinct culture and our livelihood, and yet I was unable to see it that way.

I found myself in the opposite camp, against my own side, in the belief that supporting those bent on destroying us and everything we represented expressed a higher morality. That is why I had gone to Trafalgar Square, shouting with the crowd: "Eden out! Troops out!" I cheered loudly as speaker after speaker rose to the rostrum beside one of Landseer's lions to defend the rights of those who had got rid of us and the superior justice of their motives. But perhaps I did feel a slight sense of remorse as I knew that mine were not such bad people while some of the actions of the military dictatorship that ruled Egypt were definitely questionable.

However, soon after he had finally come to settle in London, my father said: "Why can't you let them support their side and you help explain our case? Why do you, too, have to be on their side? What harm have we done to them? Why did they make our lives impossible? Why don't you ask them those questions?"

I was able to reply haughtily: "Because I am on the side of the greater good."

Another political movement with which I was involved was the Campaign for Nuclear Disarmament. Atomic weapons are probably more dangerous and easier to come by now than they were in the middle of the 1950s and yet it seems that we have learnt to live with them. There is even scepticism as to whether there is a threat at all and certainly none of the emotion that pervaded the atmosphere then. The Campaign had a permanent core of a few dedicated organisers and charismatic leaders. My contacts with these leaders were brief and disappointing as however meaningful they sounded in their public statements, in practice most seemed to me to be self-interested and regarded those who clustered around them as a sort of sycophantic court. When, in later years, I came across this behaviour again it was through occasionally having celebrities as patients, and I was struck by the similarity.

There was, however, one aspect of the Campaign which to me was extremely attractive. This was the Aldermaston March which acted as a focal point for so many young people until it grew into a huge demonstration which went on for days as it travelled from the demonised atomic research establishment and ended in Trafalgar Square. Some were there at the start, some at the end, while others camped during the night or were offered accommodation by delighted well-wishers.

There was something exhilarating about this event which must have resembled the companionship and fellow-feeling that young people enjoy today at music festivals but there were differences too. Although most of us were young there were people from every age group including some who were quite old. It was the presence of our seniors that gave us an illusion of direction despite the underlying chaos of the leadership while celebrities such as Bertrand Russell as well as a number of academics, literary personalities, actors and a few clergymen added the certainty that we were marching for right and justice and the general salvation of all mankind. Our demand was for unilateral disarmament by the West and whether or not the Soviets bombed us, again it meant that we were against our own side and that, as usual, that must be a good thing.

My sister was about to join me having been accepted at St Martin's School of Art in Charing Cross Road. Our brother Zaki would be arriving later so I had to leave the little Viennese enclave of the Mahlers' home and look for a flat. I was sorry to go as I had become fond of the elderly couple who had introduced me to the special world of pre-war Vienna and had initiated my love of music. I had been sent there entirely by chance and yet this was to decide where I was to live for the rest of my life. I had little time to look for somewhere for us to live as I was always studying but when I could not stand it any longer I would go out and walk the streets to clear my mind. I would go towards Swiss Cottage and have tea at the Dorice or get something to eat at the Cosmo. At other times I would walk north along the Finchley Road whose name I remembered from Dickens, most foreigners' first glimpse of London, as I think it was Mr Pickwick and his party who had travelled along that road to Finchley.

I would go as far as Golders Green, then devoid of shops, to have tea at Lindy's where Mrs Mahler bought cakes, and I realised at once that proximity to the bus and tube station would be a considerable advantage so I began to look for lettings in the windows of the few newsagents and the recently established launderettes.

There were hardly any available flats in the sense that we know them now, with their own separate entrance, as the ingenious conversion of houses on a large scale had not yet taken place and what was referred to as "second-floor flat" was no more than a couple of rooms thrown together with a kitchen sink and an oven with a hob placed, often illegally, against the wall. The owners would live downstairs where they had had a new bathroom put in, again usually against existing regulations, and most of them depended on the rent of the "flat" for their survival. As you made your way up the stairs you had to ignore the inhabitants of the other floors where you were regularly waylaid for company or complaints. It was in a flat of that type that we ended up just a little further along the Finchley Road from Golders Green in a stretch of nice, semi-detached houses that did not merit a specific name but was nevertheless known by everyone in the area as Temple Fortune. I was intrigued by the name especially when I found out that it was derived from Templars' Fortune, and that the land was believed to have been bought by the Knights Templar with money originating from their activities in the Middle East.

The owners who had held on to the ground floor were a middle-aged couple called Emil and Janey Trenner. They had no children and the wife who had come from the East End when it was almost entirely Jewish insisted, to our surprise, that we call her Auntie Janey, but we were happy to do so. Emil, who had not asked us to call him 'uncle' spoke little, perhaps because his English was hardly perfect having himself been quite a late immigrant from Eastern Europe. He was a diamond merchant and every day he took the underground to Hatton Gardens, carrying handfuls of diamonds wrapped in folded tissue paper which filled his pockets. In order not to attract the attention of thieves he wore a shabby old black coat, much the worse for wear, and a dusty, shapeless black hat. The down-at-heel effect was enhanced by his uncertain gait and stubbly grey beard. When he did speak, he tended to do so with an open scepticism of accepted beliefs and this attitude came to the fore during the excitement of the Russian launching of the Sputnik in 1957, the first satellite to orbit the earth. We were all aware of the momentous nature of the event as we heard on every radio the "Beep-beep-beep," the signal from man's first emissary into space.

It was difficult not to make some sort of momentous statement. Some were reminded of Christopher Columbus, some were already looking at other planets, and those who read science fiction came into their own with predictions and explanations. Emil, on the other hand sat in a corner sneering contemptuously as he read his paper because he did not believe it was true.

There was no proof, he had said, as the Russians could have been transmitting the "beep-beep" from anywhere but what we had found the most infuriating was that we were unable to refute his arguments. At first we laughed as though he had claimed that the earth was flat, but soon we all had to admit that we based our certainty simply on the assurance of the Americans.

"They also want you to believe," he had said, "it is in their interest too."

Auntie Janey baked a cake every day so there was always something to offer guests who seemed to turn up at any time. She usually made a second one for us to take upstairs, and who knows how many others she may have distributed. Having only just left the diffident, sophisticated German-speaking Viennese refugees I was plunged into a world of warm, welcoming Yiddish-speakers from Eastern Europe and London's East End with their emotions, and their interminable, loud telephone conversations. These were so expressive that even though I did not speak a word of Yiddish or even German I sensed that I could understand what was conveyed. Auntie Janey introduced us to the people she knew who appeared to be enormously fond of her. I do not think I have ever met such kindness and at a time when we too had suddenly been turned into refugees it was a great comfort.

The top floor contained a large, airy attic room where Joseph Jacobs lived. His relationship with the Trenners was different from ours as they treated him like the son they had not had. I suspected that he had lost most of his family though I knew that he had a brother who was a rabbi who had also survived. Joseph had only just finished his medical studies but he was older than me as he had completed both a degree and a doctorate in chemistry before he had taken up medicine. He was extremely intelligent and I got to admire his quiet reticence and the way he dismissed silently the activities of my politicised friends. I think that by saying little and refusing to be drawn into discussions he had a greater influence on me than he could have imagined.

In 1958 when Joseph had left to start his hospital work, my parents arrived from the Sudan finally to make their home in London, and we added his room to our "flat". I am sure that the comforting atmosphere created by the Trenners in Temple Fortune contributed to my parents' decision to buy a house in Golders Green.

Joseph went on to become a respected general practitioner in London. When Auntie Janey reached the age of eighty he gave a party for her in his house. This was so successful and so well attended he held it again for her ninetieth and then for her hundredth birthdays, and when she finally died at the age of a hundred and two it was at his house that prayers were said.

That time with my brother and sister was a happy one. My mother had told me that I was responsible for them though they were both very independent. I did not even dare tell them of my commitment as I was sure they would have taken offence and neither of them would have been prepared to accept my authority. We brought each other up and I suspect that I may have gained more from them than they did from me as I had a tendency both to extreme opinions and to expressing them often in an outlandish if not cranky way. My sister was always ready to put me in my place with a combination of scepticism and a need to express the other point of view and Zaki, though six years younger, was also able quietly to bring me back to a more realistic position.

When my parents arrived I nevertheless had a feeling of relief as though a burden had been lifted from my shoulders and since then I have been wary of responsibility without authority. I never knew what mandate my mother had given my brother and sister and they may well have been instructed to keep an eye on me but I have not asked, even now.

When I qualified in 1958 I went to my first job at St Helier in Carshalton. The hospital stood at a major crossroads that produced a constant stream of victims of road traffic accidents which had somehow to be fitted in amongst the heavy load of surgical cases.

I arrived on the ward very early on my first day so that I could see the patients who had been admitted the night before for operations that morning. I introduced myself, listened to their questions and tried to reassure them when I was told to report immediately to the operating theatre.

"What is the meaning of this?" an infuriated anaesthetist shouted at me. "What sort of doctor are you? You have not cross-matched any blood for this patient, what do you expect me to do, you incompetent nincompoop?"

I tried to explain that I had only just arrived that minute but he refused to listen and continued shouting. I thought he was going to hit me as he became livid with rage.

"I don't care when you came! The blood should have been ready for the operation!"

I managed to calm him down enough to persuade him to re-schedule the patient to the end of the morning to give me a chance to find some blood, and so it went on until nine o'clock at night when I was called to Casualty to see to a comatose motor-cyclist. I put up a drip with difficulty as his veins had collapsed and then I had to intubate him as he needed ventilation. The nurse brought me a cup of tea and a sandwich and then said that there was a telephone call for me. It was eleven o'clock and I felt I could not face any more. It was my old friend Raphael Samuel from the *Universities and Left Review* and he said he only called me so late as he had been dealing with an emergency.

"Me too," I said and he sounded surprised.

General de Gaulle was about to seize power in France, he said, and we had to be ready for a massive influx of refugees fleeing his dictatorship.

"I thought there was going to be a referendum or something," I said, but he seemed to think there would be a coup anyway, and sounded thrilled at the prospect. He was collecting names of people who would be willing to house the refugees. I was so tired that I was not sure I had heard him correctly.

"I rang your mother," he continued. "I was trying to get you but she came on the phone and I asked her. Speaking French, big house, you know."

"What did she say?"

"Well, that's just it," he continued. "She did not seem keen, so I thought you might reason with her."

"Why don't you call your mother?" I asked defensively.

"I have, I have, she is very happy to take three people."

"I will see what I can do," I said.

My mother had thought it was completely ridiculous, that there would be no dictatorship and no refugees. She was right as de Gaulle won the election by a huge majority and everyone seemed quite happy with that.

"What was all that about?" my colleague, the other House

Surgeon on call had asked, as I put down the telephone. "Is your mother all right?"

"Just old friends I don't get much time to see. Well-intentioned people."

"Ah," he sighed. "They don't leave us much space for a life of our own, do they?"

At that moment a confused, old man appeared in the corridor. He was barely covered by a hospital gown that had come undone and showed the catheter which led to a urine bottle he was carrying in his right hand. He stared at us in astonishment until the nurse got up to take him back to his bed.

"Come on granddad," she said kindly. "We'll find our way back together. At least you didn't pull the catheter out again. The poor doctor would have been so upset if he had to put it back in the middle of the night!"

"That is what the end of the road may be for us," my friend said. "Wandering about confused, carrying our urine bottle!"

"Not for a while yet I hope," I said. "Don't you believe in the Brave New World?"

"Up to a point," he replied thoughtfully, "up to a point."

We finished our tea and went to bed as we had to get up at six to take the bloods. It was midnight by then and I could see there would be no further place for ideology in my life.

In fact, everything would have to wait as I had been called up for military service.

21

Military Strategies

I doubt that I can have much in common with Yves St Laurent or Elvis Presley. I imagine that they are unlikely to have had much in common with each other either. We never met; we never exchanged notes about our experiences and even though I know quite a lot about them, I presume they would never have heard of me. Despite that, I have always had a fellow feeling for them and have defended them in conversation if ever the occasion arose, which it did from time to time.

This is because Yves, Elvis and I entered military service more or less at the same time and I kept an eye on them, as one does with contemporaries, checking whether they were doing better than me or had found a more suitable way of handling life. With this element of competition there is also the understanding, which borders on compassion, that we feel for those who are in the same boat.

Of course we were in different armies and the French would call up the relevant class using large posters stuck on to town hall walls with titles in thick black lettering announcing *APPEL AUX DRAPEAUX*, a call to the flags, in the tradition set up by Napoleon. A warrant was issued for the arrest of anyone who did not present himself to the authorities.

The American draft was a lottery but there were complex ways in which people could get out of it. Elvis did not attempt anything like that and he went with good humour even though it interfered with his singing career. It was after the Korean War and before

Vietnam so he was posted to Germany where he did very well and was universally liked. I read that it had been quite a good time for him.

I, too, showed goodwill and reported without complaint to the depot near Aldershot although some said doctors could avoid conscription, getting deferment by doing various jobs, as the call up was likely to end shortly. As it turned out I was inducted in the last week to be called but we were not sent home and I had to stay for the two years. I did not mind as I could see that the twentieth century would be fixed in history as a time of huge armies with tens of millions of men under arms and I felt that I should, like Elvis, be part of my century. To be one of the last contingent also added a certain touch; being present at the end of things is almost as emotive as being there at the beginning.

Yves St Laurent, however, was soon discharged on medical grounds and everyone agreed that he was much more useful designing dresses than wasting his talents killing people in North Africa or Indo-china.

My own call up was hardly dramatic as it came very discreetly in a brown envelope. In due course I was made a Captain, not because I had any military ability, but all doctors were promoted to give them some authority. I was sent a rolled-up document in a cardboard tube signed by the Queen in a facsimile of her hand-writing, which was addressed to me as: "Dearly beloved, Ellis Douek."

After being issued with uniforms, we were taken in charge by a sergeant major who gave us a general explanation of our situation in curt, almost shouted utterances. Much of it had to do with saluting and who had to initiate the process.

"You know the Krauts?" the sergeant major asked as though there may have been some uncertainty. "They click their heels!"

He showed us how it was done, and then took a low bow.

"The Nips," he said, "they bow, that's the Japs for you. But we, in the British Army, we stamp our feet!"

He gave us each a little stick which officers carried around as a badge of rank. It was called a "swagger stick" – I think it has gone out of fashion now and even then it seemed to be optional. We worked out all sorts of uses for it, like knocking off the heads of flowers if bored, though hitting people would obviously lead to court martial.

"Even enemies," one colleague pointed out. "It would be against the Geneva Convention."

"What do you mean?" said someone else. "You can kill them but not hit them?"

We found it useful for stirring the washing as it boiled in large cauldrons and also in lifting up a disgusting toilet seat without using our hands. We went on marching around for a little, stamping our feet until we had got the knack and then we went for a beer at the nearest pub.

"You blokes recruits?" a middle-aged man in a check suit and cloth cap asked. "I thought it was all over, National Service, I mean."

"Not yet," I replied. "There are still millions of us. Tens of millions if you count the Americans and the French, not to speak of the Russians." I was still awed by the thought that I was part of that immense brotherhood of young men in uniform all over the world, but the man looked at me with pity.

"It's a scam!" he said knowingly. "That's how they falsify the employment figures. That's all you are, men taken off the labour market, marched up and down on low pay rather than put on the dole. It's a saving really if you work it out. If they sent all the armies back home, unemployment would be so great there would be revolution, believe me."

Apart from stamping and marching, which was done in a desultory sort of manner, we were given firearms training. For some reason we all enjoyed this enormously, especially when handling the Stirling, which could fire individual rounds or be used as a machine-gun. The Stirling, I think in retrospect, was not a particularly successful weapon and did not go on to have the widespread use that made the Uzi and the Kalashnikov household names. Maybe that is why it was given to us, a group of doctors who were not supposed to shoot at people anyway. I never quite came to terms with the delight that such harmless, well-intentioned people experienced in letting off these deadly weapons.

It was arranged that we should have one lecture on atomic warfare and we were looking forward to gleaning something of the measures planned for such an eventuality. There was a large audience as a number of physicists, chemists and mathematicians had been added to the doctors and while we sat waiting we read the roneoed handouts which stressed the dangers of radiation. It turned out that it was our sergeant major himself who had been chosen to give the lecture and he was clearly not at all impressed by the qualifications of his listeners. He explained that we should understand the atom, the molecule and similar particles first so that we could master the bomb itself. He stressed that they were all very small. "Very, very small," he said looking at us dubiously, unsure of how much we understood regarding degrees of smallness as we sat open-mouthed and puzzled. He muttered "very, very small" as he thought how he could get us to accept these difficult concepts. His face brightened up finally.

"Look," he said, "this atom is small. Say it is like a football pitch . . . no, no," he interrupted himself, "as you were, as you were! No, the molecule is like the football pitch, the atom is the football!"

He looked round triumphantly and then he seemed troubled again.

"As you were, as you were! No, no!" he said, "the electron is the football."

He stopped suddenly then looked at us sideways, conspiratorially.

"It's like this," he said. "The molecule is small, very, very small. The atom here is bloody small and the electron, well that is fucking small!"

The physicist sitting next to me was amazed. He told me he thought the sergeant major had invented quite an acceptable system of dimensional classification.

We all wanted to go to Singapore, Hong Kong and other exotic places and those seeking greater excitement were opting for Cyprus where the military were active against EOKA, a movement demanding union with Greece and which also wanted to drive the British out.

To my astonishment I was sent to Scotland, which had not been an option. I knew nothing of that country which suddenly seemed as strange and exciting as any place in the Far East. I was to go to a military hospital called Cowglen in Glasgow, and was given a railway warrant to take me there. It was the first such warrant that I had seen though they were widely recognised by transport staff as they had been used by almost everyone during the war and by national servicemen afterwards. I did not realise at the time how important they would become to me in travelling free back and forth from London and that we could exchange them for favours, using them as a sort of currency.

When I look back, my experience in the British Army seems to have been the strangest part of my life. Not unpleasant but strange. From this point on I began to understand Britain, the country where I would now live my life, in a manner that I could never have done otherwise. It was as though I had been allowed backstage to observe and acquire hidden skills that would be of use to me one day, as indeed they were in handling organisations like the National Health Service, without getting too frustrated.

It took all day to get to Glasgow in a very shaky pre-war carriage though I tried to get some sleep by lying on the dusty luggage rack and that was when my grasp on reality faltered. Somewhere near Rugby the train stopped and after a time the passengers started climbing out on to the track to see what had happened. There was nothing to be seen, only fields and there was no engine either. We had seemingly been abandoned in the middle of England.

When an engine was eventually sent to fetch us, we all got back on to the train which carried on with no explanation or apology, as if nothing unusual had happened. I remained anxious as I was sure I would be in trouble with the military authorities in Glasgow for being late as I did not think anyone would believe my story. In fact they were not expecting me until the following week. The guard in the little gatehouse was very dubious as to whether he should let me in so he would not open his door completely and spoke to me through a crack. "You are not in the book, you can't come in."

He then shut the door and locked it and I found myself on a dark, cold night in a field on the outskirts of Glasgow and it was just beginning to rain. I was tired and angry and began to bang on the door, kicking it though to no avail.

"I am a Captain!" I yelled finally. "You should salute me, you are only a corporal, I saw your stripes!"

That brought a reply after a while and some whispering inside.

"You are not in uniform so I can't salute you." Then, as an afterthought, he added, "Sir."

"I know you have a woman inside!" I shouted desperately, "Open the door!"

That did it. He obviously did not want to get into trouble for having female company in the guardhouse while on duty and he opened the door though he would not let me in. I had understood how the *quid pro quo* worked in that establishment. I learned another thing right away, too, as he made me sign a form exonerating him from the responsibility of letting me enter. In the army it is wise to get people to sign for everything in order to pass on the blame, whether things go right or wrong, as blame is an omnipresent and integral part of the system. I have seen senior officers asked by their juniors to give their orders in writing so that they cannot wriggle out of it afterwards. This open show of distrust does not seem to cause offence and has since been taken up in hospitals as nurses now ask doctors to write every instruction down, however trivial. They say that it is to avoid mistakes but I know that it is to avoid blame.

I got to know the corporal quite well later on as I felt he could teach me a good deal, even protect me. I found that he carried on a discreet little clinic of his own to deal with venereal disease among the men and since it was really needed I turned a blind eye and we got on very well. I never asked him what he got in exchange.

I was eventually shown to a large bedroom by an old Glaswegian lady who said she was my "batwoman". I did not know what that was but assumed she was some sort of domestic servant so as it was late and I was tired I asked where I could have a bath.

The officers' bathroom was a huge area with perhaps a dozen baths, each in a cubicle for privacy. The partitions did not go up to the ceiling and I could hear another officer splashing and humming "itsy bitsy teeny weeny yellow polka dot bikini", then a popular tune. It was all so strange that it was only when I finally relaxed in the warm water that I began to realise what had happened to me. On the one hand I had somehow become a captain in the British Army, on the other I was far away, it was difficult to keep warm and I was afraid I might cry. A voice came over the partition. "You must be the new officer," he called out. "There is no one else here, everyone is gone."

His friendly tone set me off. I told him my name. I told him I did not know how I had ended up there. I said I was born so far away, in such a hot place, in Cairo, Egypt, overlooking the Nile. I wanted to explain that it was almost impossible for me to have got where I was but the only thing I could say was: "My earliest memory is watching the funeral of King Fouad from my grandmother's balcony."

There was a silence and I felt embarrassed at the irrelevance of what I had said. Then the voice came back: "Well," it said, "my name is Michael Sternberg and I was born in Vienna. My earliest memory is going out on to the street with my school. I remember I had white socks and waved a little Nazi flag with the swastika when the teacher sent me away. 'Not you Sternberg,' he had said, '*you* must go home.'"

The following morning when I went down for breakfast in the officers' mess everyone who introduced himself told me that they had not expected me and had nothing for me to do. They were all young doctors about my age except for two considerably older majors who were "admin" and had risen through the ranks. Michael Sternberg understood my predicament best; in time I heard that he had become a psychiatrist.

"You've worked so hard that you don't know how one stops, do you?" he asked. "Don't worry, it was the same for all of us and it goes on till the end. There are two things, though, which you must remember. Don't leave the base because if they can't find you there will be trouble. If you have nothing to do you can't visit a museum or gallery unless you are off duty when it's best to run away quickly. The second thing is that it is best to hide because if they see you they try to give you something to do and it is always useless and unpleasant. The best thing is to go to your room and read a book. Have you got a book? Would you like me to lend you one?"

Nobody told me to but I insisted on reporting to the colonel as I felt that I was in a sort of limbo and I needed to regularise my position if only for my own peace of mind. I could not just be nowhere. The orderly waved me into the colonel's room and he looked slightly taken aback as he was just serving himself a whisky. He offered me a glass but seemed relieved when I said it was too early. He too said he had not been expecting me and wondered if I wanted to go back to London and wait there till my orders arrived.

"How long will that be?" I asked, uncertain as I had left in some sort of glory to do my duty and I thought I might appear ridiculous if I returned the following day.

"Who knows?" he said. "It could be weeks. Once or twice it has been months, but you must not leave the country."

I said that on the whole, I thought it was better for me to stay, if he did not mind.

"Not at all, my boy," he said genially, waving again towards the whisky. "Stay as long as you like. Do you have a girlfriend? A fiancée? Something like that?"

When I said yes, he said that he thought I had better stay.

"They don't like it when you come back unexpectedly, they make other plans you know. Never turn up unexpectedly as it upsets everybody you see. No end of trouble. Sure you won't have a whisky?"

I saluted and stamped my feet as I had been taught and he waved vaguely at me but then he called me back from the door.

"I say, since you are here, would you mind being on call tonight? The chaps will be awfully grateful."

That evening I was eating by myself as all the other officers had disappeared, when the sergeant came in to remind me of the dance.

"What dance?"

He told me that there was a dance that night and that the duty officer was expected to make an appearance after it had got started and then leave again to let the men enjoy themselves.

"What about the girls?" I asked. "Who did they invite?"

I knew that the soldiers had come from all over the country and that there must be a great shortage of sisters and girlfriends. The sergeant had seemed rather shifty about that. He mumbled something about them being fetched in coaches.

The problems started quite early. I had looked into the hall which was part of the canteen hoping to make a sort of entrance only to find that the women had not arrived. The men, disconsolate, were already drinking. They knocked back double whiskies and then settled down to pints of beer which they drank slowly for the thirst. I was offered a whisky by a corporal who must have been at it already for half an hour or so. I could see that they were uneasy about the coaches as anything could have happened to them in the foggy northern night but they did arrive and out poured the passengers; all the prostitutes that could be found on the streets of Glasgow. Apparently the delay had to do with payment negotiations for the evening and it was explained to me in detail for approval by a corporal who was normally in charge of bookkeeping for the mess. He said that he had been prepared to pay something on account and offer more at intervals during the evening as the prostitutes could not be trusted.

"They could slip away as soon as we get them here," he said to convince me of his sensible approach. "Drink is free, of course," he added and I could only nod approvingly at his generosity.

"Any little tricks they can make out on the side, it's up to the lads to pay them individually, no?" He had looked at me questioningly but I could only agree.

"Yes, of course," I said with finality. But I felt it my duty to enquire a little more as after all I was the officer in charge, I was a doctor and at twenty-four I was quite senior.

"Where," I said. "I mean where?"

"Oh, in the bushes, sir," replied the corporal and with a sweeping gesture of his hand added, "around".

"You mean in the bushes? Isn't it cold?"

"The lads are very sturdy, sir," he replied firmly. "All the exercises in Fifeshire keep them fit."

"No, no," I insisted. "I mean, the women."

"Oh, no sir," he explained, "they are rough sir, very rough. From the street, you know, all we could find."

It was suggested that I should open the dance and I looked at the scantily-dressed women now that I had to make a choice. They looked dreadful. I asked one of them to dance, I think because she was the most motherly. She was certainly old enough to be my mother. I returned to my quarters and had gone to sleep when there was knocking at my door. Two sergeants, both only slightly drunk, had come to get my permission to fetch the dogs. The party had got out of hand. The lads had started fighting over the women who had themselves turned out to be difficult when drunk.

"Very rough, sir, very rough."

When both the men and the women had started smashing bottles and "gubbing" each other in the face with the broken glass, the sergeants had been unable to clear the hall. They had lost control and had to call for the dogs as they believed that that would clear the place quickly enough.

"Best if you came too, sir," they had advised. "You'll have to get up to casualty anyway, so you can see the cuts you'll have to stitch up. Terrible fighting, I think one chap has his eye gouged out. You'll have to get him to the eye doctor."

By the time I got to the hall the dogs were already there and the soldiers and the women were half-heartedly fighting outside. I was worried some of them might freeze to death as they rolled unconscious to the ground.

Then the dogs started to behave strangely. I thought they, too, were drunk as they had been licking up the vomit and spilled whisky from the floor. Soon they could not be controlled and we decided to lock them in the hall. The dog handlers would come in the morning and take them away.

I spent the rest of the night stitching up the wounds and removing broken glass. In the morning I went to the colonel. Kindly, he offered me a whisky and when I declined in view of the early hour he helped himself with a slightly questioning "d'you mind if I do?" look. I told my terrible story but he only nodded and had another drink and the new day started.

Leslie Ratner was a doctor from Leeds. His uniform was worn and his cap crumpled as he kept it forced into his back pocket. He was leaving the following week for Leeds and a good job at St James' Infirmary leading to a brilliant career. He was cocky as nothing could affect him now, but on the other hand he was not a destructive person and like many such individuals he liked to see things done properly, even if it would no longer make any difference to him. Although his perkiness might have irritated the regular army officers, he guided them when they were unsure what to do, and his warm goodwill had made him many friends.

I, in contrast, was worried and even a little frightened. I had two years in the army ahead of me and I had to replace Leslie.

I decorously did my round in the ward allotted to me, wearing a white coat over my uniform, the nurses of the Queen Alexandra's Royal Nursing Corps in their red and grey accompanying me. It went quite well though it was rather boring as all the patients seemed to be suffering from an advanced degree of alcoholic damage to their stomachs. We had them on milk diets and intravenous drips giving them glucose and saline solutions which, in those days were administered from glass bottles capped by rubber bungs, themselves perforated by red rubber tubes leading to the wrist where the needles were strapped into the veins.

I thought that I had handled the ward round rather well, suitably impressing both patients and nurses as I bid them goodbye. As I reached the door a voice from the back of the ward called out.

"Hey!" it said anxiously. "Hey! Captain, what about the whisky?"

"Are you mad," I said. "It would kill you chaps! If you drank whisky it would burn a hole right through to your peritoneum. You've no stomachs left to speak of!"

What I said seemed to make no difference as they started calling out.

"Captain Ratner always gives us whisky! He always lets us have whisky! Where's Captain Ratner?"

Somewhat shaken I fled to the officers' mess as the patients called out after me and breathlessly I told Leslie how they had tried to get whisky out of me.

"You mean you did not give them a whisky?" Leslie was horrified. "They'll go mad! They'll get DTs! They'll be crawling all over the walls. Let's go back right away."

He grabbed a bottle from the bar and started running towards the ward as I ran after him, just catching up. There were cheers as he waved the bottle triumphantly and he then did something I had not thought possible. He took down the glass flasks, removed the rubber bung and poured a tot of whisky into the intravenous fluid of each bottle.

"You can't do that," I said in horror. "Not directly into the vein."

"Why not?" Leslie replied. "It's pretty sterile, whisky. Kills any germs."

As the alcohol entered the bloodstream, the atmosphere in the ward lightened at once.

"Hurrah for Captain Ratner," they called out and began singing.

Leslie clutched his hands above his head like a victorious boxer as the soldiers cheered. I tried to give the impression I was part of the general success and as we left the ward we were followed by the strains of "Scotland the Brave". After the round there had been nothing for me to do so I went to hide in my bedroom as I had been advised. After a couple of hours my telephone rang.

"You are late for the clinic," a sergeant I had not yet met introduced himself.

"But I was told there was nothing for me!" I pleaded, panicking.

"Well there are 20 patients waiting."

I arrived breathless at the clinic to apologise profusely to the waiting men, explaining that I had not been informed that I was expected but the sergeant quickly pushed me into the consultation room. Later he told me that he was a pharmacist in civilian life.

"You don't have to apologise to them!" he said scornfully.

"They are patients, human beings."

"No they're not!" he insisted. "They are soldiers. In peacetime the army has nothing to do, it just hangs around waiting for war. They are much happier spending the afternoon sitting in this warm waiting room than returning quickly to their base and being made to run around in the cold."

One of the medical officers had seemed odd when he arrived and later became very strange indeed. He kept to himself, avoided conversation in the officers' mess, and was generally felt to be inadequate and unpleasant. Naturally every effort was made to post him somewhere else and finally he was sent to an army station near Kirkudbright to everyone's relief and in time we almost forgot about him, but we were aware of the odd rumour. The colonel did not want to hear anything and turned away if the matter was mentioned. We might have heard nothing more if it had not been for a devout soldier belonging to a small Scottish fundamentalist sect who made a formal complaint to the chaplain in Kirkudbright. The chaplain was a decent fellow and tried to dissuade him from taking the matter further as these things happened and it was better not to take them too seriously. The soldier on the other hand was in a difficult position and when he next had stomach ache he refused to go to the doctor on the grounds that he did not want to undress in front of the woman. The local commander had tried, with the help of the chaplain, to persuade him that it was quite proper to undress in front of the nurse.

"She be noo nurse," the soldier had said. "She be Julia!"

Eventually the military auditors questioned the cost of housing the doctor in the best double bedroom in the local hotel but were satisfied by the reply that the room also served as an army medical centre.

From increasing reports and rumours a picture emerged. The withdrawn doctor had changed into a lively individual overnight. Having taken the best room in the hotel and invited Julia to share it with him, he had ordered a regular consignment of champagne and caviar to be sent in at the army's expense. He carried out his medical consultations in his bedroom and most of the soldiers had not made any fuss about Julia's presence. After all many of them had slept with her for a small fee in the past as she had long provided a useful service to the army in that particular Scottish outpost.

We were jealous of the caviar, and of Julia, and did not think it was right that he should get away with it so the facts somehow got leaked to the ADMS and the DADMS. These men, who went by initials, were the Assistant Director of Medical Services and the Deputy Assistant Director. They in turn passed it back to the colonel who again nodded and poured himself a whisky. He was quite generous and always offered us one too; although he said little we could see how relieved he was that nothing disastrous had happened and that he did not have to do anything.

A few months later there was more serious trouble when this same doctor in Kirkudbright proclaimed an epidemic. The DADMS and the ADMS were informed of the gravity of the situation when he sealed off the town. The sheriff was alarmed, especially as he could not obtain any details about the nature of the epidemic. There was a sort of stand off between the army who stood by its doctor and the local health authority which was suspicious of the army's activities. I think that even the Procurator Fiscal was also somehow drawn into the argument. The colonel was forced to allow us to make an enquiry regarding the exact nature of the epidemic.

After some weeks we received a parcel from Kirkudbright; a cardboard box wrapped in thick brown paper. Inside was another box, again well wrapped and tied with string. Inside that was yet another box, like Russian dolls, and at the heart of the collection, in the tiniest box, there was a small hand-written note which said that this was the cause of the epidemic. Inside that, wrapped in toilet paper was a small piece of human faeces.

We told the colonel that we had to take the doctor away, the time had come, and, after reflecting on it for a while, he nodded. We dealt with the certification ourselves and drew lots as to who would take him to the mental hospital down south. To my disappointment I did not win as I had hoped to steal a few days in London though those who did had a hard time as he had run away on the train.

Another event happened soon after, and although it was minor by comparison and caused little excitement, it, too, left a lasting impression on me and affected the way I have understood life. I remember that it was a Wednesday at lunchtime as the older officers who had served in India prepared a curry lunch themselves once a week, much to the disgust of the cooks. Someone came in to the mess dining room asking what to do with the documents that had been discovered in Major Garelly's office.

I disliked Major Garelly who, though not a doctor himself, maliciously intervened in my life as often as he could, using every bureaucratic concept ever devised. His particular skill had been obstruction and I dreaded the moment his name was mentioned, as I always knew he would succeed in preventing any new proposal I might make. He had retired the day before, much to my relief, and it now appeared that in clearing out his office the workmen had ripped out the old linoleum floor covering and had found a large number of documents hidden underneath. It became obvious that whenever he could not cope with a problem he just hid the relevant papers under the linoleum, an offence against Army Regulations and possibly a crime, and I exulted in the thought that at last we had nailed him.

The colonel was speechless and when one of the medical officers quietly got up from the table and said he would deal with it, he gave him a look of intense gratitude. I could see that they were sharing something that escaped me. After a while the medical officer returned to the table and I asked him what he had done.

"Burnt them," he replied tersely.

It was my turn to be dumbfounded, he had destroyed all the evidence we had against Major Garelly, but he had said there was no point in pursuing the matter. No one would gain by it, the man had now retired and we should leave him alone. As I was not vindictive by nature I felt rebuked as though it had been my own silliness that had been uncovered but I continued to insist that people like him, who obstructed the march of progress, should be made an example of.

"You think of obstruction as invariably a bad thing," he replied, "but inertia is often a force for progress as it can prevent reaction. You should learn to make use of it instead of opposing it automatically."

22

Did your Mother Keep Servants?

It was generally believed that if you had survived a year in the army you had become an old hand. What was needed was the appreciation of a few basic principles, which should be achieved early, and everything else would evolve from there.

I certainly felt that my life was now to some extent under my own control, at least in so far as I could manipulate the army's lumbering bureaucracy, and this gave me a completely unwarranted impression of being at home. Although it was true in the sense that I could easily influence my own local environment, the micro situation as Michael Sternberg called it, I had not realised that I had no input at all on decisions made at a higher level or the macro situation.

This false sense of power led me to ask to be transferred to the surgical unit as I had already decided that I was eventually going to be a surgeon. I got as far as looking after the post-operative cases when the surgical team had gone off duty but I had no idea how incompetent the army surgeon was.

"By the way, there is a senior naval officer, admiral, commander or something. Gall bladder out, absolutely fine. Just pop in to say hello will you?"

That was the signal that my moment had finally arrived as early on a Friday morning the team were off for a long fishing weekend. Although we were the army hospital we also dealt with navy personnel in Scotland and I thought I would show zeal and go in to check right away. I saw at once that the officer was desperately sick and I ran out to catch the surgical team before they left. They were in the car and had already started the engine as I ran up to them.

"Stop, wait a minute," I cried, "he's got yellow stuff pouring out of his wound, I am sure it's bile!"

"Och, no," they said as they moved away with my hand still on the car. "It'll be the iodine."

"He's got a temperature," I shouted as they drove away.

"It'll settle down," their voices trailed.

By lunchtime he was shaking, the septicaemia was taking hold. I put him on intravenous antibiotics and rang the university hospital.

"Well done," Professor Illingworth's senior registrar said, when I told him I had started the therapy. "Yellow stuff you say? Pouring out? They must have cut the common bile duct. We had better take him over right away."

I felt I should go with him to hand him over properly.

"Professor Illingworth wants you in theatre," I was told.

I took it as a compliment. A recompense for my quick action, accepting me as part of the team, the Prof's team rather than the military. On the contrary, Professor Illingworth appeared to be holding me personally responsible.

"What is this?" he said as he searched inside the abdomen. "Cut flush with the liver! That's what they did to Anthony Eden down south. What do you expect me to do? What do I sew to what? What were you thinking of?"

I was silent. His team too were mute at the embarrassment, horrified at the incompetence.

"Go on," he goaded, "what do you want me to do? You brought him here, he's your patient, you tell me what I should do!"

So it went on while he sewed the small bowel to the capsule of the liver. I slipped away quietly, hoping they had not made a note of my name.

At half past eight on the Mondary morning I reported everything that had happened in all its embarrassing detail to the colonel. I elaborated on my story, describing the operation in detail, repeating Professor Illingworth's words and my own humiliation on behalf of the army. As usual he said nothing and no one else said anything either.

Things did change however, as our surgical team, if one could call it that, simply disappeared. We were informed that Mr Hutchinson, a well-known consultant surgeon from the Glasgow Royal Infirmary, had been persuaded to take over surgery for the army and I immediately saw my chance. I begged the colonel to let me assist Mr Hutchinson and although he was quite willing to do that he told me there was a snag as this consultant held the army in great contempt which included national servicemen such as myself. One false move, one unnecessary word and you were sacked.

Mr Hutchinson did not greet me. In fact he never said a word to me unless it was absolutely necessary, like "cut" or "tie" though mainly he just pointed. He was a very good surgeon and he hummed as he worked. Sometimes he sang the words and it was always the same song which he repeated again and again: "What do you want if you don't want money? What do you want if you don't want me?"

Occasionally one of the livelier Queen Alexandra nurses would join in but that made him stop. Once but only once he mumbled the words of another song. An even sillier one: "I see the moon, the moon sees me."

Somehow, perhaps because I kept very quiet, he did not sack me and eventually he let me do minor operations by myself. These were appendicectomies, hernias, piles, what the surgeons liked to call "bread and butter stuff" and circumcisions.

There was much army lore around circumcision. It was understood that erections would be very painful for at least a week afterwards, and even tear out the stitches, so the patients demanded bromide to prevent libidinous thoughts. We had other calming drugs then and bromide had long disappeared from the pharmacopoeia though not from the minds of the soldiers. Firm beliefs persisted of bromide secretly administered in their tea to prevent soldiers from making free with local women.

Circumcision led to an unforeseen phenomenon that affected not so much the army as the navy, as a growing number of naval ratings requested the operation. They described their symptoms so vividly that I felt obliged to offer it to them. Not that I would have refused as it gave me something to do and any surgery was better than none. I have to confess that I enjoyed it too but then no surgeon can perform properly unless he enjoys it.

Then a naval surgeon-lieutenant was ordered to find out what was going on. He was obviously depressed when he arrived in the misty darkness of the Glasgow afternoon. I asked him how it was that the sailors were not seasick. He looked even more miserable and his face took on a sallow, almost green tinge.

"We are all sick," he had said, "I am sick, everybody is sick. I give them pills, that's all I can do."

As he got up the surgeon-lieutenant looked out into the darkness and I commiserated. "Dreadful isn't it?" I said. "The cold, the wet, it gets in your joints in these northern cities."

He sighed unhappily and told me about the wildness of the North Sea near to the Arctic regions with the wind, the tossing of the ship, the vomiting sailors. He added that a surgical operation such as a circumcision timed carefully, just before the fleet left, meant a three-month shore posting, well worth a week's pain in the winter. The United Kingdom was involved at that time in a fisheries battle with Iceland, the so-called Cod Wars, and the Home Fleet was responsible for fisheries protection.

Out of the blue a random order arrived. I was to go to the Outer Hebrides to replace a medical officer who had been given leave to get married. All my plans and scheming to do surgery had been dashed by events which had nothing to do with me personally.

The army had a base on Benbecula, a tiny island between North and South Uist. The islands have other names which the local people are now trying to revive. Benbecula is Beinn na Gaoghla while the North and South Uists are Uibhist a Taath and Uibhist a Deas respectively. But as far as the army was concerned, Benbecula was Benbecula, at least at that time.

My predicament brought back memories of when, as a teenager, I had read the novel *Michel Strogoff* by Jules Verne. The hero had been posted somewhere far off and got involved in a Cossack rebellion against the Empress Catherine led by a peasant called Pugachev. I felt the same sense of despair as Michel when he left Moscow for the wild steppes and I remembered how he had been captured and blinded with a hot poker. I was not sure what the inhabitants of the Outer Hebrides were like but feared the worst. I tried to reassure myself because Michel had somehow regained his sight.

I took the ferry from Oban to South Uist where I was picked up and we drove along the beautiful if windswept country to Benbecula. The incumbent was packed and angry as he had expected to leave sooner. He was not unkind, however, when he guessed my misery and told me it was a good place and he was anxious to return so I would not be stranded there. He told me that during the Second World War a cargo ship laden with crates of whisky intended for America had foundered on the rocks and the people of the island had managed to unload most of it before the ship had sunk. As the excise men were quick to arrive the whisky had to be hidden very rapidly so that much was buried, hidden in cracks in the rocks and the sites had often been forgotten. The story had inspired a novel by Compton Mackenzie which was turned into the successful film *Whisky Galore*. My departing colleague assured me that it was still worth hunting around for hidden bottles and as he left he added that the girls were loose.

"Loose?"

"Very loose," he repeated. "There is a 'caelidh', a party that has been going on for ten days already. People come and go, night and day, the numbers present vary. Why don't you go along and meet them. I tell you the girls are very loose."

The officer in charge of the base was also helpful. He explained that I was not really needed as there was an excellent general practitioner, who was also a Fellow of the Royal College of Surgeons, on South Uist. I was given a car and encouraged to wander about, visit the little rock pools, the lakes and beaches, and hunt around for whisky as my attendance was required only when rockets were test fired in case there might be an explosion, and these took place rarely, lasting only an hour or so. Reassured, I asked when the next firing was but he refused to tell me saying that it had to be secret. The previous medical officer never had any trouble, he added. The following morning I was woken up with a cup of tea by a nice old lady. She had white hair and spoke in the beautiful lilt of those islands.

"They'll be firing the rocket this morning," she said, then added, "at ten o'clock."

"How do you know?"

"Oh, everybody knows!" she said.

I put on my uniform and went to the firing range. There was a row of ships on the horizon, also watching, and I was told that it was part of the Russian fishing fleet. Obviously they, too, had known the time as they had not been there the previous night.

The rocket was an early type of missile called the Sergeant and if it went off properly it would fly well past the horizon towards the north Atlantic. When I asked how the landing was observed there was an air of mystery.

"St Kilda."

I had never heard the cryptic name of that mysterious place before, indeed the existence of the saint herself seemed dubious to say the least. Some said it was near the arctic. Most thought it was uninhabited. Finally, the commanding officer said that I might as

245

well know now. St Kilda was an island and the military were truly on it. Not many but some. What did he mean by "know now", what had it got to do with me? It was all so ominous that I did not sleep that night. I dreamt of *Michel Strogoff* but this time he was captured by Cossacks on a snowbound island in the mid-Atlantic.

I was relaxed and happy on Benbecula. The days went by, balmy days, which I was told had something to do with the Gulf Stream which brought warm water to the shores of the Outer Hebrides. I had been taught at the English School in Cairo the importance of the temperate climate in the British Isles and that it was all due to the Gulf Stream swirling round them. The master had even explained the sequence of inevitable steps which had led to the eventual formation of our great Empire, as starting with the beneficial effects of the Gulf Stream.

Then I heard I was to be sent to St Kilda. I cried a little quietly and when the commanding officer noticed my puffy, tear-stained face he took pity. "You can wear the tie, you know."

"What do you mean?"

"There is a tie which people who have been to St Kilda are entitled to wear. You will be able to get one. You know, like a college tie."

Somehow I had become involved with these islands but I am not good at sea and the worst journey of my life was that to St Kilda. It was so stormy, that it was thought we might not be able to land at all and would have to go back to the Outer Hebrides. I prayed to be allowed on shore as I did not think I would survive a return journey. When finally I was set down on that inhospitable coast, together with supplies, I had the feeling that I could never be taken off again. In fact I thought I might actually prefer to stay there for the rest of my life rather than risk the turmoil of the elements again.

After I had recovered from the unsteadiness, the nausea and the vomiting I was able to look around. We had landed in a small bay where the boat had been secured to the ramshackle pier. The atmosphere was lonely and overpowering, exuding a sort of gloom, perhaps because there were no trees on the island or because the peaks and rocks were strangely jagged and dark which made them appear threatening. As I looked up at the mountain in front of me, I saw what seemed like scattered dwellings but they were all ruined, contributing to the desolation. Some were only collections of stones but there were also a few uninhabited black houses of more recent origin with no glass left in the windows. The base was close to where we had landed and consisted of the usual army structures which clashed with their surroundings as no attempt had been made to blend with the environment. Nevertheless the sight of such familiar, if tasteless, buildings made me feel much better and the soldiers seemed pleased to see me. They had set up a radar tracking station and, as I had been told, were keeping a check on what happened to the rockets fired from Benbecula.

The soldiers who appeared to like this isolated spot kindly tried to make me see the interest of the place. "There is the largest population of gannets in the world nesting on these rocks," one said. "And there are fulmars," another added enthusistically. "The people who lived here used to get their oil from them. They say they squeezed a couple of pints out of each of them and then ate them."

When it was evident that I was not too concerned with birds someone else said: "You know that St Kilda is the westernmost part of the British Isles. It escaped the Ice Age." There were no natives now, he told me. The few there had been had asked to be taken away in the 1930s, now there were only the soldiers.

When they saw that I had calmed down a little they came to the point and told me that there was a serious health problem which they expected me to deal with. The sheep were dying in a sort of epidemic. "I am not a vet, I know nothing about sheep diseases," I exploded.

"You were all they had available."

I had to do something, they insisted, as otherwise the sheep would become extinct. They were a unique species and if they all died I would be responsible for their extinction. I would be equivalent to the Dutch sailors who killed the last Dodo.

When I walked around the island and saw many carcasses of rotting sheep, I thought they might become a problem to humans so we dragged them into little piles, poured petrol over them and set them alight. The soldiers said that it looked like a pagan sacrifice to the Viking gods but I thought the isolation must have affected them as to me they were just dead sheep.

Somehow this worked and no more sheep died. When I was back in Glasgow a few weeks later I reported to the colonel, perhaps a little boastfully, that I was responsible for saving, single-handedly, a whole species and he put me down. He did not like excess, he did not like people to sink too deeply into misery, or to raise their heads too high above the parapet. He liked an even keel.

"It is only a small species. A sub-species really."

"It is my species. I saved it. Not many people save species however small."

"Very unlikely," he said. "These epidemics tend to peter out. They are self-limiting, like measles. Some die, some survive to form a stronger immune breed. You know, survival of the fittest and all that."

He had another job for me, quite different, and he implied that it was a sort of recompense. I was to join two Highland regiments at their headquarters in Stirling Castle, the Black Watch and the Argyle and Sutherland Highlanders.

"Very prestigious," he said, "a feather in your cap to have served with them. Balaclava and all that, Sebastopol, you know, the Crimea. And then there is the cook."

"The cook?"

"Yes," he said, "they have that cook."

He explained that one of the last national servicemen to be

called up was a young trainee cook from the Savoy Hotel, and that somehow the officers' mess in Stirling Castle had managed to acquire him. They had given him a free hand and, delighted by the opportunity to practise with the fresh produce of Perthshire, the results were now famous throughout the military establishment.

When the day came I drove up the steep, twisting slope through the first gate of the castle and its barrier. Somehow I felt ever smaller as I drove upwards. Perhaps the soldiers looked taller and the strength of the castle itself, the thickness of its walls, the raggedness of its stones was formidable. I reported to the colonel. I was awed by the size of the room, a hall really, with walls of raw stone, and the huge size of the man himself. He was wearing a kilt which exposed his thighs and I could see their diameter was larger than my own waist. At a loss as to how to handle the grandness of my surroundings and their overwhelming size I saluted and stamped my feet.

"Yes, yes," he said. "You don't have to do that all the time."

He was a very active senior officer and I could imagine him defending the beleaguered castle from multiple attack, ordering ladders, firing flaming arrows from the north side, pouring boiling oil down from the south. I got to like him in time and he came to see me as a patient not long before his death forty years later, his hearing weakened by gunfire. He told me then that he was working as a consultant on military matters for governments in Africa, but on that occasion when we first met he had asked me only one question.

"You are not English are you?"

Taken unawares I just said no, waiting for the next question but it never came.

"Thank God for that," he said. "They keep sending us these English medical officers and the men don't like it you know, they don't like it at all. By the way you don't have to, of course, but if you could wear a kilt from time to time it would be a courtesy."

As it turned out I got on well with the men and I enjoyed

going out on exercises with them in the beautiful Scottish countryside. Lying on the banks of Loch Earn, I thought about what had happened to me; everything in entirely logical steps along the road and yet so strange in its conclusion. I also liked when I was sent out to pick up paratroopers who had injured themselves when they had jumped over Fifeshire where the training took place. I took with me a small group of RAMC orderlies and stretcher bearers, driving an old ambulance with crash gears which I was obliged to double declutch with every alteration of speed. I had been warned that if I killed a sheep it would cost £9 and the army would not pay. A cow, the colonel had added as an afterthought, was £11.

One of my RAMC orderlies thought that the paratroopers were mad. "I just don't get it. They chuck them out of these aeroplanes while we wait down here and then we have to pick them up and stick them together again, and up they go again."

In the evenings Stirling Castle was mine. The senior officers had families and lived in flats in the city. This left me, as a captain, the senior officer in the castle. When, on my first evening the sergeant major brought the book for me to sign that all was in order, I refused on the grounds that I was the doctor and did not want to get involved in anything else. He, on the other hand, only wanted a signature and insisted that as I held the most senior rank it had to come from me. There was a deadlock until he realised how he could convince me.

"Mary Queen of Scots' captain signed the book," he said "and here, in this space after so many others there will be Captain Douek!" He had figured me out correctly and I signed.

There developed a style to which we all contributed. The officers wore their dress uniforms, the Argyll officers on one side of the long table and the Black Watch on the other. Along the middle the massive silver ornaments the regiments had brought from India, polished and shining, were placed in a line. These were intricate constructions with elephants and camels that turned out to be salt cellars or water receptacles, while high above our heads, arranged in rows, some tattered by gunshot others muddied or splattered, were the flags of the battles.

I must have stood out at this nightly dinner as on my national serviceman's salary I could not afford a dress uniform so I wore a dinner jacket and sitting at the head of the table I must have appeared as a sort of arbitrator between the two regiments. I had acquired a taste for the bagpipes and insisted on a piper piping us in, though the other officers put up with this only to humour me. One evening I was informed that an English general was staying the night and I invited him to join us in the Queen Anne Room for drinks. He was delighted by the Highland pomp and by the story of the ghost which the younger officers had invented for him. When the bagpipes began to play as we entered the dining room and I sat him on my right he was clearly overjoyed at the marvellous surroundings.

Mellowed by the claret, the bagpipes and the deference he showed me, as though I were the host, the laird at the head of his table, I began to wonder what I was doing there, aged twenty-five, in an environment so alien to my own background that I felt the need to explain myself. I told him that I was born in Cairo and that my childhood was spent in the sun, the heat and the brown dust of Egypt, far from these mountains and lakes.

He interrupted my story; his eyes looking into the distance. "Gezira," he said suddenly.

"I beg your pardon?" I thought I had not heard right.

"Gezira," he repeated.

Oh yes, I thought as I, too, recalled the island on the Nile, the Gezira Club, the Grotto, it was all so far away but the general was on his own, following his memories.

"Zamalek!"

"Yes, yes," I nodded. "Of course, Zamalek, that's where I lived."

"Abbasiya," he continued, "where the barracks were."

"Esbekieh Gardens!"

The general went on remembering. Sometimes he gave a sad smile remembering places visited long ago: Ismailia, Alexandria, Port Said, Midan Soliman Pasha. And then his eyes brightened at a name. Helmia, Heliopolis, Dokki, Giza. Pause and name, memory and name, no other word, no descriptions, no details. He kept those to himself.

As we got up he thanked me and I noticed that his eyes were moist. For my part I understood that it was neither here nor there that I was a Jew from Cairo and that what mattered was that it was I who sat at the head of the table with the Argylls on one side and the Black Watch on the other, with the flags of the victories as well as the defeats, as the British celebrate both. The food was exceptional that night, as the officers had all received fish and game from their relatives who owned land nearby and our young cook had surpassed himself.

The general, already emotional from the wine, the bagpipes, and perhaps also the memories, was flabbergasted and said that he could not believe what went on in these Scottish castles. At first I was worried that it would all be taken away, as one should not be seen to be too content in this world, but he kept repeating that it had been a privilege, and then added, as he wiped a tear: "Like in Wellington's mess! A privilege, a privilege, thank you. Another age."

National service ended gradually. As each man completed his two years and went home, the British army shrank. As the soldiers left, their doctors also disappeared one by one, leaving the diminishing few with a sense of loneliness as well as anxiety about what would happen to us in the real world. Would our girlfriends still be there? Would there be jobs for us?

As my colleagues departed and I found myself increasingly isolated I had to take on their jobs as well. Battalions and regiments added themselves to my responsibilities with little formality but as the numbers were so small there was little work. Eventually I took on the post of Acting Deputy Assistant Director of Medical Services but I was told that despite the fact that I was only making requests for medical equipment, and even that only to myself, I still had to do it in writing as a copy had to be filed in a special section of the Defence Ministry.

Boredom and time had to be filled and my letters to myself became longer and more elaborate. By and by they became detailed and explanatory.

Dear Captain Douek,

I realise the need for syringes diminishes but a certain bare minimum remains essential for us to carry out our duties adequately.

Yours truly,

(signed) Captain Douek, RAMC.

At times I become philosophical, sometimes even melancholy.

Dear Captain Douek,

Although it is not my responsibility to draw these matters to your attention I would beg you, as a human being, as a doctor who is also by force of circumstance in a position of authority, to consider them. Have you noticed that although we are already in 1962, a decade past the mid-point of the century, the world is still overrun by armies? When will this stop? Are we to wait until the 21st century, when wars will be fought at a distance by pressing buttons before this will end?

Yours truly,

(signed) Captain Douek, RAMC.

As I accumulated more and more senior posts of Assistant and

Deputy and Director I began to reply to my junior persona in a fatherly way.

Dear Captain Douek,

You are a young man. Do you not think that in just such a century, where hundreds of millions of people have been soldiers, you would not have wished to have missed one of the basic experiences of our time? After all you have served in an army and you have not had to kill anyone! Ponder on that. Ponder young Captain, ponder.

Yours truly,

(signed) E.E. Douek, Capt RAMC, Acting Deputy Assistant to the Acting Assistant Director Medical Services Scotland (Lowlands).

At times I wrote angrily. Sometimes making formal accusations about the Assistant Deputy (Captain Douek) to the Deputy Assistant Director (Captain Douek). Sometimes even threats. In my final loneliness and frustration I asked myself for permission to attend the anti-nuclear march from Aldermaston to Trafalgar Square. After considering this and setting out my reasons I granted myself permission. When I reached London I wondered whether I need go back at all or if my departure would even have been noticed but I did, to round it off, so to speak.

"What an army!" my French cousin had said. "They give permission to go on an anti-war demonstration."

He did not know the half of it. He did not know either that copies of my long correspondence with myself had gone regularly to the army establishment in Stanmore, Middlesex. Had anyone read it? Is it still there in some archive?

I went back to Loch Earn, a lake which was somewhat under-stated and had benefited as a result. As usual, I lay down on the bank and let my mind wander there for the last time. I could see clearly the old "Hydro" at Crieff, a grand hotel fashionable in the 1900s, as it stood on the hill overlooking the loch but I have not dared ask what has become of it as even then it was run down and I would prefer not to be told that it has gone. Down the road was the pub which had served us drinks at every hour of the day and most of the night, and when I had asked if the authorities ever checked, the landlord was most insistent that the local policeman always took his duties seriously.

"He lets us know, of course, when he is coming," he had added, and I could see the value of letting sleeping dogs lie rather than pushing people too far.

In the distance I could just make out the roofs of the Bridge of Earn Hospital where I had so often referred the soldiers who were sick or had broken a limb, and suddenly I felt uncertain. Would the doctor who settled for a job there not have something of value? Was I letting a different life pass me by? But this twinge of remorse did not persist and I left for London.

I was taken to the railway station in Glasgow by a retired general who had done medical boards with me. He was kind and said that I had shaped up very well despite everything, which left me uncertain as to whether this was a compliment or not. The fact that I had got on so well with the men, he added, and gained their confidence had probably helped. The army liked that. I said that this was because I felt such empathy with the working people and they had sensed that I was at one with them. The general looked surprised.

"No, no," he said, "don't you know the reason? Your mother kept servants, didn't she?"

"Yes, but she treated them very well," I said loyally.

"Exactly. It is because you treated them as though they were your own servants. That's why you got on so well with them. You knew how to support them, to feel responsible for their well-being." The general shook my hand and I walked into the station.

23

Happily Ever After

"What did he do after he retired?" my son had asked on the telephone from America.

"Don't you know?" I replied. "He worked till he was eighty. Didn't you ever ask him?"

Perhaps the young do not wonder what their grandparents do, or indeed have done, until it is too late to enquire directly. Dim recollections of family stories repeatedly heard but scarcely remembered suddenly become important; perhaps when we feel we need guidance as to how to manage our own lives.

My father had continued to take the underground to town every morning after he had ceased work, only now he visited museums. He had told me that in that way he had felt the excitement of being a tourist on holiday, until lack of mobility restrained him.

"I have a role model; I know what to do till I am ninety-four," I had said to my son. "After that I am on my own."

At the age of sixty-one, in a country with which he was not familiar, my father had set up again, one last time, the textile business that his family had favoured, from an office in Grand Buildings in Trafalgar Square, not five minutes from Somerset House where I had first been told of our British connections. He had done well enough for me to ask him why he did not retire when he was in his mid-seventies.

He never complained when crossed by misconduct in business or by devious transactions. He would simply tell the story with astonishment, the look on his face, almost disbelieving, suggesting amazement at the poor behaviour of certain individuals.

"Where do such people come from?" he would say, shaking his head sadly. "What sort of education has he had? And to think they made him a Lord!"

On the other hand he loved to complain about trivial matters. Aspects of parking at the supermarket, people cutting in front of him at the petrol station or things related to the dustbins would inspire great anger as he went on and on enlarging on these events, presenting them as serious examples of the way the world itself was declining, to my intense irritation particularly after a long session in outpatients.

"In Egypt," he would begin, as though about to attribute to that country the same exceptional qualities that his own parents must have projected on to their native Aleppo, city of their youth, but I would interrupt him.

"In Egypt," I would say mockingly, "they kicked you out!"

"No, I mean," he would stutter, embarrassed, "I meant under the British."

He was shocked when I had suggested that he should retire rather than grumble.

"I have to complain!" he had insisted, and I realised that it had become a need, but he claimed that the reason why he continued working was because his family was long lived and he feared that as the decades went by they would run out of money.

After all Great-Uncle Jacques had outlived the surgeons who had treated both his cancers and he had felt abandoned, uncertain where to turn for check ups and reassurance, while Great-Uncle Musa had arrived in Montreal at the age of ninety expecting to take over the textile business his sons had set up. Musa must have been over a hundred when he took to his bed. His numerous descendants had come one by one from all over the world to say goodbye. After his farewells Musa said a prayer and then died.

"You won't remember Mourad, of course," my father had said,

"but you may remember your Great-Uncle Saul as he had come all the way from Brazil to visit us in Cairo. He, too, must have been a hundred or so when he died and one of his sons sent us a book of sayings he had published in honour of his father."

I did remember the excitement generated by that visit just at the end of the war as Saul was the oldest surviving great-uncle at the time and the whole family, including the children, had gone to the airport to meet him only to be told that the aeroplane had been diverted to the old military airfield at Asmara where there were quarantine facilities. Smallpox had been found in Brazil so the passengers could only be greeted at a distance, separated from us by two rows of barbed wire with a gap in between. I could just pick out a little old man wearing a black skullcap to whom everyone was pointing, waving and blowing kisses. Scores of us went to the airport every day until the quarantine was over. Of course I had not forgotten; how could I?

My father had continued to take the tube every morning from Golders Green to the Strand. From time to time I wander through the long corridors between the Bakerloo and Northern Lines as they twist and turn beneath Trafalgar Square so as to emerge just in front of Grand Buildings.

The whole structure was pulled down some years ago, and when I saw the plans for replacing it I was sorry as Grand Buildings, competing as they did with the National Gallery in dominating Trafalgar Square, carried memories of my father. In fact the planners didn't have the heart for such a change either and an exact replica was rebuilt. It is the only time I have come across such a decision, and it happened so quietly and so smoothly behind huge screens that I do not think anyone realised that it was an entirely new edifice.

Despite his enjoyment of complaining my father had always seemed content with his lot and in particular he had never appeared to feel out of place wherever he happened to be, accepting his obligations and claiming his rights as any native born citizen. With my mother, however, it was a different story as I always sensed a vague disappointment despite all our efforts to please her, although it may simply have been that everything she had planned had actually been achieved, leaving nothing to soften the way the human condition inevitably leads us downhill. She was a very intelligent and able woman and in different circumstances she could have benefited from a career of her own, rather than have to rely on her children's progress so it may be, too, that it represented regret or frustration about herself. The impression with which I was left was that the only person who had never disappointed her was my father and in that she had been singularly lucky leading her, perhaps, to the point of misleading her children regarding what can be expected from marriage.

I became a surgeon but that of course is another story, though I am always asked what it was that guided me to the ears, nose and throat. My reply is often that I was good with my hands and that I proved skilful at doing fiddly little things, but although that was true it is not the whole answer. For a long time I was too embarrassed to say that what drew me in that direction was a quest for the human soul as this sounded grandiose if not ridiculous when put that way.

It started when I was still at medical school and both romantically and philanthropically inclined. I thought that in order to study the soul I should become a psychiatrist and looked forward to joining our chief in his clinic believing that would be the turning point in my life. Dr Garmany was a very good teacher specialising in neuroses. As I listened to patient after patient tell their stories I realised that I could not do that for the rest of my life. It was not that they were not deserving or interesting cases, but rather that each one seemed identical to one or other of my relatives and that I had enough of listening to them at home without making a profession of it.

I had then turned briefly to neurology and neurosurgery but I was again disappointed by the mechanical nature of both the diagnosis and the treatment and I finally decided that becoming an ear, nose and throat surgeon would give me access to hearing, smell, taste and balance; actually to all the senses except vision and through them I could peer into the inner man.

Indeed, when I was appointed a consultant at Guy's Hospital I was asked to give a farewell talk at King's College Hospital where I had been the senior registrar and I had chosen the title "The Senses, Windows of the Mind". I was gratified by the unexpectedly large audience, but although I received liberal applause, someone pointed out that that I had got many of them to come under false pretences. They were, he had said, psychiatrists from the Maudsley Hospital across the road who had been misled by my promise to talk about the mind whereas I had referred to the senses only in relation to the brain. I did not have the courage to mention the soul to him.

Although I did my best probing olfaction as well as hearing and language, with time I learned to accept the limitations of what I could achieve but I was comforted, too, by the fact that, intellectual considerations aside, I simply enjoyed doing operations. I must have chosen well, I think, as I have had a lot of fun.

My sister, known professionally as Claudia Roden, became a much esteemed, and indeed much loved, writer on food. Many believe that she has taken the subject beyond similar authors' contributions, in that she has placed the dishes of the Middle East, the Mediterranean and the Jewish people in the context of their history and their numerous migrations, and in that way she has also maintained our family's association with that part of the world. My wife and I continue to enjoy tasting the recipes as she decides which one to include and which to leave out of her books. She presents us with small portions of different variations so that we can select the one which will go in. This often leaves us feeling sorry for the other recipes as though they are living things which we have snuffed out, banning them for ever from a place at the table, and we try to persuade her to find some way of including them too, perhaps as exotic variations.

Our younger brother, Zaki, was named after his grandfather Isaac Sassoon who had himself been known as Zaki to intimates, in the Arabic style. While the latter was still alive our brother tended to be referred to as Zakito, or "Little Zaki" adding the Hispanic diminutive still favoured by Sephardic Jews five hundred years after our expulsion from Spain.

Because we had been alone together in Paris or London with our parents often inaccessible, somewhere in Egypt or the Sudan, we had grown particularly close, and the three of us never lost that relationship. My brother and I had begun to meet for lunch every few weeks when seniority had given us the privilege of absenting ourselves in the middle of the day with no one questioning our whereabouts. Our conversations now involved the more practical matters of how to conduct our lives and work rather than concerns about the condition of mankind in general which were our main worries in our youth. Nevertheless they sometimes took a surreal turn when I told him about the extraordinary behaviour of some patients while his own life, too, had taken unexpected paths. He had been a research chemist and then became a civil servant for a while until he had finally set up as an independent consultant. We were having lunch at his club, the Reform in Pall Mall, and he told me that he would be going on holiday and then to Nepal, a country that was having problems with India and which was paying for his advice. Suddenly he asked, "Do you think I should speak to the King or to the Prime Minister?"

Taken aback by such a question I asked who was the real ruler and he said it was definitely the King.

"Then don't waste your time," I said. "Just speak to the King."

We had thought for a moment in silence and then had burst out laughing, to the consternation of the adjoining tables. We could not easily come to terms with our own words which had suddenly seemed oddly absurd.

"How did we get to this?" I had asked. "What on earth are we doing here? Should we not have been textile merchants eating grilled pigeon while watching the *feloukas* gliding by as the Nile shimmered in the midday heat?"

That was the last time I spoke to him. Not long after that his wife telephoned at six in the morning from Corsica.

"Your brother is unconscious in hospital and I don't speak French. I don't understand what they are saying."

Zaki was flown to the neurosurgical unit in Marseilles and I joined them there. As I waited, day after day, in the hope that he might regain consciousness, I walked around the old port and along the *Corniche* where one café or restaurant after another spreads out on to the pavement. They were teeming with people of every colour and ethnic origin who seemed to be wandering about aimlessly, chattering in French, greeting each other in the friendly gestures of the south. In the warm Mediterranean evenings and preoccupied as I was, my mind of course elsewhere, there were moments when I thought I was in Alexandria.

I finally had to bring Zaki back to Guy's, my own hospital, but he never regained consciousness. Richard Hughes, the Professor of Neurology had said to me: "Bring him here, Ellis," when I explained the state he was in. "We will look after him." And, somehow, this made me feel as though I was taking him home. My sister and I had to tell my parents what had happened and I could see that they had lived too long as one should not have to outlive one's children.

When my mother died, she did so in my arms. My father, then ninety-four, was devastated but also astonished.

"Why?" he had asked "Why did this happen? We were living so quietly, we were no trouble to anyone."

His turn came shortly after hers and it seemed as though they had secretly believed that if they avoided attracting attention they might actually get away with it against all the odds, as they had with so many other things, and live together for ever. Only fiction has found a formula to deal with the inevitable conclusion of such longevity when it is accepted that, by and large, they had lived happily ever after.

My family's long affair with the Middle East had come to an end, at least for the moment, but my story cannot have an end as it has no beginning. It is the story of a family which had lived there for centuries, some of them having escaped the threats of the Inquisition in Spain more than five hundred years ago.

Our journey westwards, travelling from Syria to Egypt began only late in the nineteenth century and then moved on to England in the middle of the twentieth. It had always been in relative comfort so that we cannot boast of surmounting great hardships which might, perhaps, have improved our character. As the second millennium dawned my sons had already moved on to America suggesting that the impulse which drove my grandparents in that direction had not yet been exhausted, but whether that continent turns out to be the Promised Land or only another resting place in a perpetual cycle remains to be seen.

24

Never an Exile

"This child is always listening to gossip," my grandmother had said, suddenly noticing my presence as I sat wide-eyed, absorbing accounts of adult behaviour that I had not thought possible.

"Look at his ears," *Tante* Marcelle said teasing, as she always did. "They are growing all the time. Already they stick out of his head like two handles. If you don't stop we will soon be able to lift you up by hanging on to them!"

A book was placed into my lap and the striking red leather of the binding with the rectangular yellow, black and green indentations even now excites my imagination. I had seen many books as our house had been full of them and, often to my despair, my mother always seemed to be reading, but I had never seen anything like this one. Opening it proved disappointing, however, as it contained only densely printed text which was too hard for me to follow and I quickly returned to eavesdropping, my hands caressing the velvety calfskin surface of the book.

"You are not reading!" my grandmother had said accusingly.

"It is boring," I replied.

"*Balthazar*? By Anatole France?" She had said, visibly outraged. "How can it be boring?"

It was not easy to find something for me to read as during the Second World War there were no new books from Europe, and certainly nothing for children, but finally someone had discovered the old bound copies of a French girls' periodical called *Fillette* which had been collected by my grandmother and her daughters during their childhood and which must have dated from the early decades of the twentieth century.

At first I pushed them aside, offended at being offered something so obviously intended for girls, but it was illustrated, and soon my eye caught a picture which filled me with dread. There was no colour but the artfully crafted drawings, etchings or woodcuts with delicate shading and exaggerated curly lines were, I suspect, considerably more evocative than the solid boundaries and flat coloured surfaces of the books that are handed to my grandchildren today.

I have not seen them look with horror at a picture book where even wild lions are now given friendly smiles and they have to turn to television to experience that particular thrill, but I remember the frightening expression on the face of the dwarf as I deciphered the title: *Le Nain Jaune.* I can still sense the vivid yellow of the description with an intensity that no real pigment can suggest.

Throughout the war I had looked at these illustrations and read the books and periodicals designed for little French girls of the turn of the century and, one way or another, with their mixture of romance and terror they may have formed the basis of my outlook on life and especially on art.

As I began to learn the language I read English books and these, too, dated mainly from well before the Second World War. We read the tried and tested stories of Robert Louis Stevenson and James Fenimore Cooper. The US Army, when it came, brought illustrated comics with it. Superman and Batman were irresistible with the inevitable victory of the underdog implying the hidden inner strength of the hero selflessly dedicated to justice and to righting wrongs. Today, when I can find only criticism of American popular culture I hardly dare mention the comics which, together with cowboy films, emphasised those fine human qualities. They were almost entirely, I believe, the fantasies of the children of immigrants who were themselves influenced in their own writing by stories of overwhelming Tsarist oppression or only recently exposed to Nazi persecution.

It was Captain Marvel who had captured my own imagination most forcefully and it was to him that I was dedicated. I exchanged the rare copies boys had obtained from American soldiers for the most fabulous coloured marbles which were our major currency. It was not only the philosophical influence of these comics to which I am indebted but they also left me with a hankering after futuristic architecture which their illustrators imagined, so much so that I remained despondent throughout the grim years of post-war modernist concrete buildings, functional or cheap as they may have been, and my hopes were only rekindled when I saw the soaring sails of the Sydney Opera House. I am glad that I have lived to see the art gallery in Bilbao and the breathtaking towers of Hong Kong and Shanghai and the innovative museums in America. I still remember crying with mortification when a teacher confiscated the comic I had hidden inside my World Atlas as I dreamt of strangely-shaped glass buildings and my inability to explain the intensity of my reaction when he looked at me in disbelief.

"Don't be silly, boy," he had said. "This is rubbish."

I could not understand it, of course, but I was becoming part of Western culture and even though I was surrounded by Egypt with both its ancient and its Arab heritage it remained in a separate place.

Naturally it impinged on my life and when I returned to the beautiful leather-bound copy of *Balthazar* I could recognise the geometrical pattern on its surface as inspired by an Ancient Egyptian temple. *Le Secret du Sphinx* was still sold in the perfumeries of the *Khan el Khalil* in Old Cairo and reference to antiquity was everywhere but we saw it only as though we were in London or Paris.

It had all started in 1922 when Howard Carter, the British archaeologist, discovered the first stone step in the sand that led to

a tomb in the Valley of Kings in Luxor. Three weeks later he had
brought his sponsor, Lord Carnarvon, to witness the opening of
the sealed doorway as he made a small breach in the upper left
hand corner. By the light of a flickering candle he had seen the
contents of the funerary chamber of Tutankhamen as they had
called him then, but it was from the pages of the *Illustrated London
News* that had been kept by the Gezira Preparatory School that I
learned to recognise the ancient artefacts, much as anyone in
England would have done and not from my life in Egypt.

Arabic music and the beauties of the Arabic language had been
entirely alien despite the last minute efforts of Professor Hassanein
and it was always clear that my parents had wished that we should
remain exclusively a part of Western culture. Although my early
years had been spent in another world it is within Western society
that I always belonged and even though we touched on the Arab
world, we did so only from the outside.

The fine line which connects these memories to the present
does so only imperfectly and when I have tried to follow it
backwards as Theseus retraced his steps through the maze with
Ariadne's thread it could only be with hesitation. For many years I
liked to think that I stood astride two cultures, that of the Orient
as well as that of the West, and that this duality had given me a
superior understanding and, in these times of deep division,
perhaps even some sort of special role. Now I understand that the
Orient I knew was not one which I shared entirely with the
Egyptians even though to me it was no less real.

When, decades later, I did return to Egypt my circumstances
were different and I was greeted warmly but as a foreign professor
come to give his talk at the *Dar el-Hekma*, or "House of
Wisdom". I had insisted that the Dean should introduce me as
native born, from just across the Nile, but this drew little interest
and my audience was concerned only with the new surgical
advances that I practised in the West.

"Professor el-Barbary has come to listen to you," the Dean had told me. "It is a great honour as he has not attended a lecture here for years."

I went to thank the old professor who was well into his eighties and he drew me close to him so that he could whisper in my ear.

"I remember your family," he had said. "That is why I came to see you."

He reminded me that the Cairo of my school days had harboured three million inhabitants a considerable number of whom were Europeans whereas the homogenous city of today had eighteen million. My audience, he had explained, were the descendants of the new migrants, those who had poured in from Upper Egypt and from the small towns in the delta. They had been attracted by the hope of wealth, not least because they had watched on television the shining cities of "Dallas" and "Dynasty," and they had seen Cairo as the first step in that direction.

"Neither they nor their parents even know that you have been here," Professor el-Barbary had said.

As I heard the call to prayer electrically amplified from the minarets rising above the mosques I could see that our presence had no lasting effect at all. We had only been gone a few decades and yet there was nothing left of our presence, while tens of millions of Egyptians prostrated themselves in response to the muezzin's call, seeking their comfort in Islam.

The Egyptians had been unable or unwilling to make much use of us, eyeing with distrust the breathless impetus that took us into the race towards what we call progress. I had for so long pretended that I admired their world for its refusal to be coerced or shamed into participating in our enterprise that I had convinced myself that their failure to seek a future in the modern world deserved respect. I now see it as a tragedy.

I wish them well as they turn towards Islam and I watch with compassion their attempt to preserve its values and civilization and take refuge in its particular identity. I hope that they will find a way of sharing in the human project but I know that it is not for me.

We are people who do not stand still and when I look back to my great-grandfather in Aleppo, I see that in his probing of Talmudic texts, and in his written comments, books distant from the science that I know, he, too, was exploring and analysing complex ideas. I accept now that the impulse that has driven me may be the same one in a modern guise, and that my physical movement westward was impelled by the need to give free rein to the evolution of ideas.

It probably explains why, like my father, and perhaps my grandfather and maybe his father too, I have never felt displaced in a geographical sense and wherever I have found myself has seemed the proper place for me to be. I have never been an exile.

And now, destined to continue travelling along the unreliable Northern Line of the London Underground, I like to remember that during the mania that followed the discovery of the tomb of King Tut in 1923 the excitement was so great that it was suggested that that line should be called the Tutankamden Line as it stretched from Tooting Bec to Camden Town. After all the one which went from Baker Street to Waterloo had been called the Bakerloo, but that allusion to the British connection with Egypt was not to be.

On my last visit to Cairo, when I had finally accepted that our exciting affair with the Middle East was truly over and forgotten, I lay feverish in the hotel room, no doubt the result of careless eating at *Ain Shams* University Medical School. The shutters had been closed to let me sleep, but the sunlight is so intense in the middle of the day in Egypt that it shone in between the slats so sharply that it appeared to perforate the wood itself.

The high temperature had left me confused and, awakening slowly, I smelt Cairo, my native city, and heard its unmistakable sounds in the distance. As I opened my eyes the brightness of the sun's rays caught the blonde hair of the woman who sat in the chair by the window engrossed in her book and it shone like a golden halo. I thought it was my mother and that I was the sick child in the darkened room but as I called out she raised her head and I saw that it was Gill, my wife.